Contrary Things

Figurae

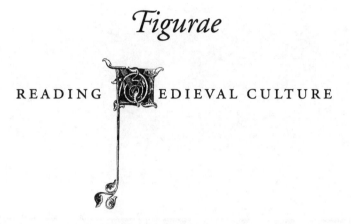

READING MEDIEVAL CULTURE

Contrary Things

Exegesis, Dialectic, and the Poetics of Didacticism

Catherine Brown

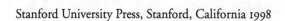

Stanford University Press, Stanford, California 1998

Stanford University Press
Stanford, California
© 1998 by the Board of Trustees of the
Leland Stanford Junior University
Printed in the United States of America
CIP data appear at the end of the book

Frontispiece: Dialectic and her students.
Paris, Bibliothèque Nationale,
MS. Lat. 7900A fol. 132v. Courtesy of the
Bibliothèque Nationale.

*T*o my teachers

Acknowledgments

Learn, teach, love!
—Medieval proverb

Many teachers of many kinds have written this medieval proverb into my heart and thus into this book. My first acknowledgment is owed to my first teachers, Sheila Swenson Brown and Northrop Brown, who taught me to love the taste of word and music. And to other teachers whose active teaching has made thought live for me: R. Howard Bloch, Kevin Brownlee, Allison Goddard Elliott, Charles B. Faulhaber, Francine Masiello, Michael C. J. Putnam, Eugene Vance, Florence Verducci, John K. Walsh.

The Spanish humanist Antonio de Nebrija writes in his *Dictionarium latino—hispanicum* (1492), "The book that is to live has need of a good angel to guard it" (el libro que a de biuir a menester un angel bueno que lo guarde) (fol. iv). This book has had many good angels, who are also teachers in their own right. Among them are my colleagues at the University of Michigan, whose conversation and community were a gift to this book—Santiago Colás, Juli Highfill, William Paulson, Marie-Hélène Huet, José Rabasa, Karla Taylor—as well as readers, friends, and colleagues whose support made this book possible, intellectually and concretely—Ana María López Anderson, Karen Baker, Jason Baluyut, Linde Brocato, Dorothy Duff Brown, James Burke, John Dagenais, Alexandre Dauge-Roth, Katherine Dauge-Roth, Erik Ekman, Melissa Hayes, Amy Hornstein, Kali Israel, April Overstreet, Jeanne Prendergast, Yopie Prins, Jeff Rider, John Strohmeier, Helen Tartar, Elizabeth Wingrove, and an anonymous reader for the press. Thanks to Donka Marcus and Peter Marshall for their advice on Latin translations. Thanks also to the students of the University of California at Berkeley and the University of Michigan, who have taught me what this book teaches in turn.

These teachers' traces are all over this book, and I am deeply grateful to all of them. What strengths are here to be found have been written in the hand of each of these teachers as much as in my own.

Brief sections of this book have appeared elsewhere: portions of Chapter 3 in Brown, "*Muliebriter*" and portions of Chapter 4 in Brown, "Meretricious Letter."

C.B.

Contents

Abbreviations and a Note on Citations and Translations

Primary works are cited by standard divisions, separated with periods (book.chapter.paragraph). After a semicolon follow page numbers (or volume and page numbers) of the translation (designated "tr.") and of the original-language edition used, separated with a slash. Thus, a reference to book 4, chapter 6 of the *Didascalicon* looks like this: *Did.* 4.6; tr. 107/81. For facing-page bilingual editions, or where the translation is my own, only the page number for the original language appears after the semicolon. Here and there I have silently modified passages from the cited published translations. Uncredited translations are my own.

Bible quotations are from the Vulgate; translations are drawn from the Rheims-Douay version.

Abbreviations for frequently cited works are given below, along with publication information on the original and translated editions used. For full information on other originals and translations cited in this study, refer to the bibliography.

Ars   Ovid. *Ars amatoria*. Ed. E. J. Kenney. Oxford: Clarendon, 1961.

Conf.   Augustine of Hippo. *Confessions*. Ed. James J. O'Donnell. 3 vols. Oxford: Clarendon, 1992.

DDC   Augustine of Hippo. *De doctrina christiana*. Ed. Joseph Martin. Corpus Christianorum Series Latina, vol. 32. Turnhout: Brepols, 1962. Translation: *On Christian Doctrine*. Trans. D. W. Robertson, Jr. Indianapolis: Bobbs-Merrill, 1958.

De amore   Andreas Capellanus. *Andreas Capellanus on Love*. Ed. and trans. P. G. Walsh. London: Duckworth, 1982.

Dial.   Augustine of Hippo (attr.). *De dialectica*. Ed. Jan Pinborg. Trans. B. Darrell Jackson. Synthese Historical Library 16. Dordrecht: Reidel, 1975.

Did. Hugh of St. Victor. *Didascalicon.* Ed. Henry Charles Buttimer. Washington, D.C.: Catholic University of America Press, 1939. Translation: *Didascalicon.* Trans. Jerome Taylor. New York: Columbia University Press, 1961.

Exégèse Lubac, Henri de. *Exégèse médiévale: Les quatre sens de l'Écriture.* 2 parts, published in 4 vols. Théologie 42. Paris: Aubier, 1959–64.

Historia Abelard, Peter. *Historia calamitatum.* Ed. J. Monfrin. Paris: Vrin, 1959. Translation: *Historia calamitatum.* In *The Letters of Abelard and Heloise*, trans. Betty Radice, 57–106. Harmondsworth, Eng.: Penguin, 1974.

"Letters" Abelard, Peter, and Heloise. "The Personal Letters Between Abelard and Heloise." Ed. J. T. Muckle. *Mediaeval Studies* 17 (1955): 240–81. Translation: "The Personal Letters." In *The Letters of Abelard and Heloise*, trans. Betty Radice, 109–56. Harmondsworth: Penguin, 1974.

Libro Ruiz, Juan. *Libro de buen amor.* Ed. G. B. Gybbon-Monypenny. Madrid: Clásicos Castalia, 1988. Translation: *Libro de buen amor.* Ed. and trans. Raymond Willis. Princeton, N.J.: Princeton University Press, 1972.

Met. John of Salisbury. *Metalogicon.* Ed. Clement C. J. Webb. Oxford: Clarendon, 1929. Translation: *Metalogicon.* Trans. Daniel D. McGarry. Berkeley: University of California Press, 1955.

Moralia Gregory the Great. *Moralia in Job.* Ed. Marc Adriaen. Corpus Christianorum Series Latina, vols. 143, 143A, 143B. Turnhout: Brepols, 1985.

PL *Patrologia Cursus Completus. Series Latina.* Comp. Jacques Paul Migne. Paris, 1844–1902.

Pol. John of Salisbury. *Policraticus.* Ed. Clement C. J. Webb. 2 vols. Oxford: Clarendon, 1909. Partial translation: *Frivolities of Courtiers and Footprints of Philosophers.* Trans. Joseph B. Pike. Minneapolis: University of Minnesota Press, 1938.

Rem. Ovid. *Remedia amoris.* Ed. E. J. Kenney. Oxford: Clarendon, 1961.

Sic et non Abelard, Peter. *Sic et non.* Ed. Blanche Boyer and Richard McKeon. Chicago: University of Chicago Press, 1976. Partial translation: "Prologue to the *Yes and No.*" Trans. Alastair Minnis. In *Medieval Literary Theory and Criticism, c. 1100–c. 1375: The Commentary Tradition*, ed. Alastair Minnis, A. B. Scott and David Wallace, 87–100. Oxford: Clarendon, 1991.

Imagination sees a lot of various things, and sees them as Like and Unlike, a manifold variety. Reflection, Understanding, relates them and shows how they contradict each other. . . . But Reason, Reason, catches hold of the variety and seeks out the Opposition, the Contradiction, *and drives them together*, ties them together, makes one *the* Other of the other. Then things happen.

—C. L. R. James, *Notes on Dialectics*

Introduction
Reading in Walter's Library

A young man named Walter has just been given a present, one he's needed rather badly for some time. It seems he's in love and in trouble; confused by most everything, he can make his way neither forward nor backward. He's stuck, in short. The present is a book—just the book he needs, it seems, for it comes from a good friend and an experienced lover. So Walter reads, expecting this book to teach him everything he needs to know, as his friend promised it would. As it turns out, the gift both exceeds and falls short of its author's promise. It does in fact contain detailed lessons in seduction, and teaches with some insistence the pleasant doctrine that erotic love between men and women is the highest good. It also, however, teaches just the opposite: erotic love is the root of all evil; women are vile, disgusting, and miserable, and he who courts them is a hell-bound fool. The helpful friend anticipates Walter's surprise at having his educational needs met so thoroughly, and comments in the driest of understatements, if you read this little book carefully, you will see that it teaches you a double lesson (duplex sententia) (*De amore* 3.117; 322). One might imagine Walter scratching his head at this point, and wondering what to make of such contrary things. His friend's laconic answer might not seem much help: read this book carefully, he tells Walter; read it again and again.

Here, caught in repeated readings of a doubled doctrine, we join this puzzled reader. The book is the treatise on love by Andreas Capellanus—*De amore* (c. 1185)—and the studious Walter, its dedicatee, is the fictional placeholder for an extratextual Any Reader—that is, Us. Andreas's book is no anomaly in the Middle Ages. Should Walter have been a truly assiduous (and preternaturally long-lived) reader, he could have filled his library shelves with books much like it—books whose teaching is as self-consciously doubled and divided, as multiple and self-opposed, as the *De amore*'s. He could shelve there the *Roman de la Rose* of Guillaume de Lorris and Jean de Meun, a text at once and in sequence courtly and anticourtly. He could shelve Chaucer there: *Troilus and Criseyde*, with its conflicting loves, and the *Canterbury Tales*, whose earthiness is belied by authorial palinode. Next to these, sheaves of poems, perhaps—debates between body and soul, wine and water, knight and cleric, owl and nightingale; *quaestiones disputatae* in cramped university hands; a book called *Good Love* (*Libro de buen amor*, 1330/1343), which teaches under that equivocal rubric love both carnal and divine.

Since we are imagining Walter a careful and scholarly sort, his library could not be without contradiction's greatest medieval authorities: Ovid, whose *Ars amatoria* and *Remedia amoris* teach how to seduce and how to unseduce after seducing, and Aristotle, with whose logical treatises Walter might try to reason his way through these texts. And finally, he could not be without his Bible, the most enduring provocation to medieval teaching, a text whose contradictions provoked more assiduous reading and writing than any other in the Middle Ages.

To imagine Walter's library, as I have done here, is to make, from a diverse body of texts in various recognized genres, a veritable canon of contradiction. It is to say, these texts belong together, they make sense together, and together they help us understand some of the most striking intellectual particularities of the European Middle Ages. The texts in Walter's library are characterized not just by contrary things but by the *teaching* of contrary things. Their didacticism is not transparent, nor are their contradictions haphazard; rather, both are systematic and self-conscious.

As the massive and cacophonous *Roman de la Rose* draws to conclusion, Jean de Meun's narrator, who has repeatedly assured us that his writing "is all for instruction" (toute est por anseignement) (line 15,173), reveals the epistemological ground of his textual teaching—as well as that of the texts he learned from, and that of the texts that learned from him.

So it goes with contrary things: they are glosses of one another, and the person who wants to define one of them must keep the other in mind, or else, no matter how hard he or she may try, definition will be impossible. For the person who does not have knowledge of both will not be able to know the difference between them, without which no definition one might make can stand.

> (Ainsinc va des contreres choses,
> les unes sunt des autres gloses;
> et qui l'une an veust defenir,
> de l'autre li doit souvenir,
> ou ja, par nule antancion,

n'i metra diffinition;
car qui des .II. n'a connoissance,
ja n'i connoistra differance,
san quoi ne puet venir en place
diffinition que l'an face.)

(lines 21,543–52)

Although for us and for our students, it may be "natural" to see contrary things as obstacles to understanding, it is not always so in the Middle Ages. The opposition of contraries can be a puzzle, even a source of anxiety in the Middle Ages; it is seldom, however, simply an obstacle to understanding. It is instead a hermeneutic irritant, and, as Jean de Meun suggests, one of the very *conditions* for the production of knowledge and understanding.

This book works to understand the recurring connection of teaching with contradiction in some major texts of the European Middle Ages. We will move among several fields of medieval European intellectual production: biblical exegesis, medieval logic, and Ovidian erotodidactics; our path threads between sacred and secular, Latin and vernacular, from one side of the Pyrenees to the other. Reading in Walter's library may well lead us to rethink some of these canonical historiographic polarities; it will certainly teach us to read oppositions in the text of medieval culture.

Chapter 1 studies Christian exegesis, in which biblical contradiction is the textual incarnation of a Truth that is at once and paradoxically singular and multiple. Exegesis will teach us, as it taught its medieval practitioners, to maintain the truth in one biblical proposition and, equally and simultaneously, in its apparent opposite. Under the aegis of dialectic and the Aristotelian rule of noncontradiction, however (Chapters 2 and 3), we are taught to read *either/or*, and to resolve contradiction not through suspension and multiplicity, as in exegesis, but rather through a judgment that favors either one proposition or the other. Chapters 2 and 3 treat the rise of logic to intellectual power in the mid–twelfth century; both show us that logic itself, as practiced then in the schools of Paris, constituted a logical problem not without its own violence. Chapter 2 studies the plays of contradiction in John of Salisbury's *Metalogicon*, an ostensibly moderating critique of the intellectual extremism among Parisian logicians. Chapter 3 reads Peter Abelard, in whose life and writing the forces of contradiction work with maiming and illuminating violence.

The teaching-textuality of two great secular works of the Middle Ages occupies Chapters 4 and 5. This teaching-textuality is formed under the double instruction of the master disciplines of monastic exegesis and dialectic, and under the tutelage of Ovid. Calling simultaneously on the *both-*

and of exegesis and the *either/or* of dialectic, the sophisticated teaching of these two secular texts is both biblical and worldly—impossibly, both at once, always in motion. Chapter 4 studies the *De amore* of Andreas Capellanus, which teaches two opposite propositions and commands that either one or the other must be chosen, yet in practice shows each proposition to be deeply embedded in the other. Chapter 5 turns from the Latin to the vernacular clerical tradition to study one of the lesser-known examples of contradictory teaching, the fourteenth-century *Libro de buen amor* of Juan Ruiz, whose titular "good love" conflates the contrary things of spiritual and carnal love, while reminding readers that the difference between the two is urgently consequential.

In my own readings in Walter's library, I have learned much from the more widely known examples of contradictory textual teaching in the European vernaculars—the *Canterbury Tales, Troilus and Criseyde*, and the *Roman de la Rose*. My own dialogue with and indebtedness to *Rose* and Chaucerian scholarship will be evident throughout.[1] I have chosen, however, to draw my vernacular text from the rich Iberian tradition. While it is central to the current canon of medieval Castilian literature, the *Libro de buen amor* is relatively little known outside its "home" discipline of Iberian studies, a marginalizing situation that this discipline has not yet completely set to rights. The *Libro* is a full and aggressive participant in the great library Ernst Robert Curtius saw in his imagination when he wrote of what he called the Latin Middle Ages. It is part of the contemporary reader's library as well, and participates fully as we construct together our shared and wider fields of medieval literary studies, philosophy, and literary theory. This book is one contribution to the mutual opening of these borders.

Reading Medieval Contradiction

> Since, in such a multitude of words, some statements, even those of the saints, appear not only to differ from one another, but even to be mutually opposed, one should not judge them rashly.
>
> —Peter Abelard, *Sic et non*

> By his contrarie is every thynge declared.
>
> —Chaucer, *Troilus and Criseyde*

Even if medieval readers seem not to have been excessively puzzled by the contrary things in secular texts like the *De amore* or the *Libro de buen amor*, nor provoked by the contradictory structure of Peter Abelard's exegetical workbook *Sic et non*, postmedieval readers certainly have been, and the scholarly library of contrary things contains diverse (even mutually adverse) treatments of contradiction in exegesis, in Chaucer, in the *Rose*, in the *De amore*, in the *Libro de buen amor*. All of us, medieval and postmedieval alike, have, after all, spent at least some time in the school of Aristotle, in which contradiction in an authoritative text is "a sort of scandal" (Jolivet, *Arts de langage*, 194), calling attention to itself in a most uncomfortable fashion. A great medieval student of the Stagirite, Peter Abelard, described this hermeneutic discomfort vividly:

A contradiction has this property . . . namely, that one proposition must be true and the other false. . . . The reader, now as if blaming the words, now confirming them, is thus at first cast into anxiety; then, a solution diligently being found, is liberated completely therefrom.

(Dederat hanc proprietatem contradictionis . . . quod scilicet necesse est alteram esse veram et alteram falsam. . . . Quasi verba illa modo calumnians, modo confirmans in anxietatem prius lectorem ponit ac demum facta diligenter solutione ab omni eum anxietate liberat.) (*Logica ingredientibus*, 445)

This response to contradiction constructs it as a logically and hermeneutically intolerable *either/or* from which, in an equally overdetermined maneuver, the anxious reader seeks release. Such, as we shall see, was the response of some medieval readers to problems of logic, love, and the Bible, and such, too, has been that of many of their twentieth-century expositors. "Apparent contradictions undermine totalizing interpretations," observes John Dagenais, commenting on the *Libro de buen amor*, "and much twentieth-century criticism may be seen as a search for some critical position outside the text . . . from which the contradictions may be viewed as harmonizing to form a coherent and consistent whole" ("Como pella a las dueñas," 1). From such critical positions, we postmedieval readers may try to make sense of the persistent contradictions in our texts, standing back and generalizing from them, making models in which contradiction is no undermining accident but part of a determinative, almost self-explanatory, pattern.

One such model of the Middle Ages represents the period and its people as trapped in continual oscillation between unmediated and opposing extremes. Thus Johan Huizinga described medieval life as "violent and motley," bearing "the mixed smell of blood and of roses. The men of that time always oscillate between the fear of hell and the most naive joy, between cruelty and tenderness, between harsh asceticism and insane attachment to the delights of this world, between hatred and goodness, always running to extremes" (*Waning*, 27). Otis Green, in an essay revealingly entitled "The Medieval Tradition: *Sic et non*," understands medieval culture as a "self-contradicting synthesis" of two irremediably opposed worldviews, one pagan and Roman, the other Christian and Neoplatonic (7). "Attracted both to Greek thought and to the Roman philosophy of power, and only half successful in their adaptations of them to their own situation," he says, "the peoples of Western Europe resemble the Children of Israel in the Wilderness in their long vacillation between Baal and Jehovah" (6). Edgar de Bruyne sees medieval art through an equally oppositional, even dualistic frame: "The aesthetics of the Middle Ages is the result of a conflict of two opposing tendencies: one characterized by simplicity, measure, logic; the other by imagination, exuberance, unrestrained freedom" (quoted in Green, 4). Earnest and jest, model and antimodel, church and carnival, sacred and profane, order and disorder, didacticism and recreation: such are the oppositions, and the zigzag between them is, for many scholars, constitutive of medieval culture.[2]

Another model, best embodied in the work of D. W. Robertson, Jr., constructs medieval culture as based not upon lateral opposition but upon hierarchical symmetry. For Robertson, the two sides of a medieval problem—the two parts of Andreas's treatise, for example—"do not merge to form a new position compounded of their diversity";[3] instead, one proposition—invariably that of Christian "doctrine"—transcends the others, which become ironic, figural, or allegorical preparations for a univocal Truth. Charles Dahlberg glosses Robertson thus: the Middle Ages are characterized by "an underlying coherence of outlook so little questioned as to allow for multiple forms of surface contradiction that confirm rather than confute the principle of coherence."[4]

My aim here is not to present a cultural model of a sweep comparable to that of either of these well-known readings of the Middle Ages. Nor will I engage these models in extended discussion, although a quiet argument with both subtends my own thought, as does a certain solidarity with recent readers, like Michael Camille and Robert Sturges, who have focused less upon opposing and bipolar univocities than upon the in-between.[5] Much is to be gained if we resist the inclination to take these familiar cultural oppositions (vernacular/Latin, secular/sacred, exuberance/measure, blood/roses) as givens, and if we try—insofar as possible—to avoid taking that "position outside the text" *expressly for the historically overdetermined purpose* of resolving or fixing textual activity. Much is to be gained, too, if we read our texts and the weaving of their oppositions intimately, attentive as much to the performative — *how* they teach — as to the constative — *what* they teach. The question, then, is not only "What do these texts teach?" but also "What do they teach about textual teaching?"[6]

Rather than taking the "oppositions" of medieval culture as symptomatic expressions of a medieval *Geist*, we will instead consider them as a problem — as a *quaestio*, in medieval terms — and try to approach the conflicts of our medieval authorities as they approached the conflicts of theirs. As R. W. Southern observed, "The strength of this period lay in its ability to deal with discordant texts, to seize on distinctions of meaning, and to clarify confusions of thought. Contradictions of authorities were the food of thought; where there were no contradictions there was a strong inclination to think that nothing more could be said" (*Medieval Humanism*, 45). Taking contradiction as clerical medieval readers did — that is, as a catalyst for the production of understanding as well as an obstacle to it, we can begin to read medieval contradiction, and read it intimately, as a textual *process* as well as a (logical, epistemological, semantic, ethical) problem.

Taking our medieval partners-in-reading as guides, *Contrary Things* will work through the disciplines in which they had most consistently to deal with contradiction — exegesis and dialectic — and will work with a secular tradition, the Ovidian *ars amatoria*, characterized by explicitly contradictory teaching.

Neither exegesis nor dialectic nor Ovid, taken alone, serves to makes sense of the contradictory teaching of texts like the *De amore* or the *Libro de buen amor*. I take these discourses as teachers in this book, but not as master codes, though it is not without relevance for my argument that all three were constructed as such in the Middle Ages. Scripture, logic, and the Ovidian *ars* all proclaim themselves to be model pedagogical discourses: the Bible, writes St. Paul, is the teaching text par excellence: "But what things soever were written were written for our learning; that, through patience and the comfort of the scriptures, we might have hope" (Quaecumque enim scripta sunt, ad nostram doctrinam scripta sunt; ut per patientiam, et consolationem Scripturarum, spem habeamus) (Romans 15.4). In the early fifth century, Martianus Capella hails dialectic as the only discipline fit to teach before divinity: "It is your right, Dialectic, to speak in the realms of the gods, and to act as teacher in the presence of Jove" (inter templum deum fas est, Dialectica, fari / et Iove conspecto iure docentis agis) (*De nuptiis* 4.327; tr. 107/151). And the narrator of Ovid's metapedagogical *Art of Love* calls himself love's own instructor: "I am Cupid's preceptor" (Ego sum praeceptor Amoris) (*Ars* 1.17). From these three rich sources of teaching theory and practice, and with a pleasure in the mediations of the letter at once intensely sensual and intensely intellectual, medieval clerical writers made textual teaching *poetically*, and we see this poetic Making nowhere better than in those texts that teach through contradiction:[7] a teaching seldom transparent or vehicular, and often far from joyful.

Reading Medieval Teaching

> So now, you do see that in speaking we desire only that we may teach.
>
> Augustine, *De magistro*

In focusing on exegesis, dialectic, and teaching, I am myself being somewhat contrary, for if there is a "black legend" about medieval European literature—and there is; we hear it from students and professional medievalists alike—it is that medieval literature is too Christian, too logic-chopping, and above all too didactic. The urbane sociologist Charles Horton Cooley rather complacently observed, in his manual of student life in the Jazz Age, that "the Dark Ages, it seems, was a time when people read textbooks and thought they were literature" (171). Not modern enough to tell the difference between the textbook and its (apparent) opposite, literature, Cooley's medievals and their fascination with the teaching text are a challenge to postmedieval readers who, in the words of Eugene Vance, are "easily thwarted by the collapse of narrative discourse and the encroachment of anything didactic" (*Mervelous Signals*, 3). Even to construct what happens at the meeting of teaching and narrative in terms of collapse and encroachment is to pitch narrative pleasure and didactic activity as opponents in a pitched battle: Lord Flesh and Lady Lent, perhaps, duking it out on the pages of our editions, as postmedieval readers nod and drowse.

We can only feel "thwarted" at moments like this if we understand the didactic as the opposite of narrative pleasure. Apparent opposites, juxtaposed, will inspire the questioning that leads to something like the truth, Peter Abelard will teach us. Apparent opposites, even when they are defined as mutually exclusive in the most absolute senses available to medieval logic or theology, still have an uncanny way of illuminating each other. The same is true for textual teaching and textual pleasure, conditions intimately interrelated in the Middle Ages, when *narratio* and *enarratio*, story and explanation, are as close in writerly practice as they are in etymology.

I would be the last to deny that medieval texts are often didactic, if by that word we understand that the texts are committed to teaching. But it would be inappropriate—*and anachronistic*—to confine their teaching to the transparent communication of doctrine. To our conceptual poverty, the English word "doctrine" now means only the content of an act of teaching. The Latin *doctrina*, a noun formed on the verb *doceo*, to teach, means first of all the act of teaching or instruction; secondarily, and by figural transfer of meaning, "the knowledge imparted by teaching."[8]

A graduate student of mine recalled in seminar a comment made by a professor of hers some years earlier. The professor said, she wrote, "The Middle Ages are not complicated; the Middle Ages are clear and direct. Obscurity comes later."[9]

The professor was wrong. Obscurity is one of the richest means of teaching that the Middle Ages knew; obscurity and its close cousin, contradiction. Trained intellectually, spiritually, and imaginatively upon one of the densest and most contradictory of teaching texts, the Bible, medieval readers and writers learned that to do *doctrina* is a complex undertaking, requiring as much thought about the nature of teaching in language as it does the absorption of information, Psalm verses, and *auctoritates*.

Year after year, readers come to Robertson's translation of Augustine's *De doctrina christiana* expecting, as I did when I first read it, to be told what to believe: *On Christian Doctrine.* What they get is not so much doctrine as *doctrina*: a teaching text about what is to be taught ("doctrine") and how one is to go about first finding, then teaching it. To construct medieval textual teaching as a transparent communication of "doctrine," as if that were all that texts like Augustine's were or did, lets them speak only half of what they have to say. It is also profoundly anachronistic, assuming as it does that human texts are the vehicles of premade meanings unaltered by their passage through language, a conception quite foreign to medieval Christian semiotic and pedagogical theory.[10]

Remembering that *doctrina* is actively *verbal* as well as nominal in the Middle Ages—a process as well as a product—allows us to see that medieval texts teach as much about teaching as they do about their ostensible subject matter. In fact, we may even be led to conclude that, in many cases, the "doctrine" taught is less the final cause than the pretext of textual teaching. This is why my title offers a *poetics* of medieval didacticism. Teaching in these texts is poetic in the etymological sense: *poiesis* is (a) *making*, and medieval didactic texts constantly and insistently show us this making of *doctrina* in textual and hermeneutic process.[11]

Nowhere is this poetics of process clearer than in texts that teach through opposition. If we simply understand doctrine in its nominal sense as the "content" of a pedagogical act, then the teaching of texts like the Bible, the *De amore*, the *Canterbury Tales*, and the *Libro de buen amor* is almost too abundant and multiple to be coherent. In fact, so excessive is the doctrine of many medieval teaching texts that a student taught to read "doctrine" nominally might be moved to say, with the beleaguered Lover of the *Rose*, "There is so much that's contrary in my lesson that I can learn nothing from it" (En ma leçon a tant contraire / Que je n'en puis neant aprendre) (lines 4,334–35). In the texts in Walter's library, then, "doctrine" is more promise than product. By seeming to block the hermeneutic path with sayings "not only diverse, but also, truly, adverse as well" (non solum ad invicem diversa, verum etiam invicem adversa) (*Sic et non*, Prologue; tr. 87/89) they call readerly attention less to the nominal product than to the verbal, active process of textual teaching.

As represented and performed in medieval texts, then, teaching is an intensely active and intensely self-aware (one might even say self-theorizing) activity. We shall study here texts that teach the fullness of medieval *doctrina*: texts that teach and represent teaching—texts that do one thing and the other in the same textual process.

We thus should study *doctrina* in its medieval Latin complexity—both the active process of teaching and its nominal content. Medieval theoreticians themselves teach us how to do this, for twelfth-century pedagogical theory uses these two senses of *doctrina* to talk about two ways of teaching a subject. Hugh of St. Victor teaches us the difference between them: "treating *of* an art—that is, writing about grammar—and acting *through* an art—that is, writing grammatically—are two different things. Distinguish between them" (duo sunt, agere de arte, et agere per artem. verbi gratia, agere de arte, ut est agere de gramatica, agere per artem, ut est agere gramatice. distingue hec duo) (*Did.* 3.5; my translation/56).

Teaching *de arte* teaches about an art, taking the art as doctrine. It treats its subject constatively as "pure" content, as if the subject taught were a sort of universal manifested only accidentally in texts and authorities. Teaching *ex arte*, on the other hand, is performative: it teaches the art through the process of a particular embodiment of that art. I have tried to talk in this teaching text of mine not only *about* medieval textual teaching but *through* it, remembering that both learning and teaching (those things we may sometimes think of as contraries in our own quotidian academic practice) are, in the medieval vocabulary, matters of reading. John of Salisbury, writing in the mid–twelfth century, tells us so: "The word 'reading' is equivocal. It may refer either to the activity of teaching and being taught, or to the occupation of studying written things by oneself" (Legendi verbum equivocum est, tam ad docentis et discentis exercitium quam ad occupationem per se scrutantis scripturas) (*Met.* 1.24; tr. 65/53).[12]

Terminological Propositions

The teaching process of medieval texts is, as Lacan wrote of Saussure's, "a teaching worthy of the name, that is, that we can come to terms with only on its own terms" (149). In citing and embracing the Lacanian *mot*, I set myself a tall order, for to attempt to come to terms with the past on the past's "own terms" is a delicate proposition on several levels at once. First, it is dangerous if it implies the antihistorical, even arrogant belief that the historian can rid herself of her historicity and "her" terms long enough to look at an object from another period purely on "its" terms. But failing to make this effort is more dangerous still, for to fail to read a text in its difference from the reader is, quite simply, a failure to read, a failure to teach and be taught by the text and its otherness. In the interests of such historical otherness, then, a few words are in order about the terms of this book's propositions: *doctrina*, dialectic, contradiction, contrariety.

"Teaching" in English has the same doubled sense as *doctrina*, but the word and its senses are so familiar to readers of English that they might overlook its conceptual richness and so miss the otherness that I wish to help them imagine. Thus, when I wish to remind readers of the doubled sense of medieval *doctrina*, I will use the Latin word. When I wish for the purpose of argument to separate the meanings of *doctrina*, I will use "nominal doctrine" for the content of an act of teaching and "active doctrine" for the process of teaching.

"Dialectic" I will use in its technical medieval sense as the "science of disputing well" (bene disputandi scientia) (*Dial.* 1; 82)—that is, the discipline of logic, which was, along with grammar and rhetoric, one of the three arts of human language in the medieval trivium. Dialectica, the allegorical goddess of logic who stands watch over countless medieval discussions of her field, is not to be trifled with or contradicted: she holds a snake in one hand, a book of rules and a hook in the other (*De nuptiis*

4.328; tr. 107/152; see frontispiece). As I have written these opening pages, I have heard that snake stir and hiss quietly, for I have been using loosely terms that in Dialectica's presence should be used with care and precision. "Contrary" and "contradiction" are bound together by their manifest "against-ness"—these are clearly things in opposing or contra-position, things against other things, things *spoken* against other things. However, when Aristotle lays out the fundamentals of dialectic in the *Categories* and *On Interpretation*, much depends on the logical distinctions among different types of logical opposition.

So far I have been using "contrary" and "contradiction" as sister words, leaning heuristically upon their shared against-ness as a way into their life in the texts I study here. It is easy to do this in a nontechnical, nonmedieval discursive context. Modern vernacular usage tends to blur the etymological and technical distinction between the terms; many of the published translations of the medieval texts I cite here, for example, use the two terms interchangeably. Helen Solterer has recently pointed out: "The logical distinction between contrary and contradiction is often muddied today. The result is that they are often conflated, understood to signify a single, amorphous type of negation. But in their original Aristotelian formulation . . . the distinction was rigorously maintained" (103).[13] Solterer's warning is salutary: these distinctions are maintained with comparable rigor in the teaching of medieval logic. However, the discursive practice of the teaching texts that we study here is rather another matter, for it more often evades than evinces the symmetries of formal argument. We must, however, define our terms.

What better figure to teach us these logical terms than Dialectic herself? In Martianus Capella's intellectual romance, *The Marriage of Philology and Mercury* (c. 410–39), Dialectica speaks up to explain the intricacies of her craft. Before she can teach us the propositional beauty of the logical square, however, she must define her terms. Following Aristotle, Martianus's Dialectica lays out the varieties of "against-ness":

It remains for me to speak about opposites. Opposites are what are seen to confront each other, as it were, face to face; for instance, contraries. Not all opposites are contraries, but all contraries are opposites. Opposites are opposed either as relatives, as large is opposed to small, or half to double; or as contraries, as foolishness is opposed to wisdom; or as possession to privation, as sight to sightlessness; or as affirmation to negation, as "Cicero discusses" to "Cicero does not discuss."

(restat ut de oppositis dicamus. sunt autem OPPOSITA, quae sibi veluti ex adverso videntur obsistere, ut contraria. nec tamen omnia, quae opponuntur sibi, contraria sunt, sed omnia contraria opposita sunt. opponuntur autem sibi ita, ut aut relativa opponantur, ut magnum parvo et dimidium duplo, aut ut contraria, ut stultitia sapientiae aut ut habitus orbationi, ut cernentia caecitati, aut ut aientia negationi, ut "Cicero disputat," "Cicero non disputat") (*De nuptiis* 4.384; tr. 130/180).[14]

Martianus's Dialectica here presents oppositions as logical minimal pairs, between the members of which various degrees of overlap are possible, from the permeable borders between contraries (gray is both white and black; I may be not-foolish without being wise), the mutual definition of the relative and the privative (we cannot know hunger unless we know satiety, nor blindness unless we know sight), to the absolute silence of contradiction (neither Martianus nor even Dialectica herself can discuss and not discuss at the same time).

Opposition, then, is the genus; the contrary, the relative, the privative, and the contradiction are its species. The teaching practice of the texts we study here partakes of all of these species of opposition, often simultaneously. There will be no shortage of contradictory propositions — "Some earthly pleasure is good" / "No earthly pleasure is good," to continue using Walter's puzzling textbook as our example — but they will be mustered in a discourse that aims to teach very different things and in a very different way from the things taught in Aristotle or in the medieval logical lecture-hall.

Since the practice of textual teaching studied here does not rigorously follow its closest model disciplines, I find myself terminologically hard-pressed. On the one hand, I wish to preserve for heuristic reasons the sense of logical outrageousness and the threat of nonsense communicated by the nontechnical modern use of the word "contradiction." On the other, I feel the need to be terminologically precise, especially in texts that explicitly call upon the logical structures of dialectic. There will thus be some play in my own text between the technical and the common uses of the word "contradiction." When the texts in question explicitly place themselves in the technical world of dialectic, I will follow suit and use the terms "contradiction" and "contrary" in their technical senses. When I wish to stress the apparent logical outrageousness of my texts' *doctrina*, I will use "contradiction" in its looser modern sense. In more general situations, I will follow Martianus's lead and use "opposite," "opposing," and "opposition."

The teaching discourse that we study here partakes both of the irreconcilability of the contradiction and the mutual dependence and interimplication of the other forms of *oppositio*. These are texts that use opposition as a catalyst to create intellectual and moral problems that cannot be resolved by simple decrypting reference to a master code like dialectic or exegesis alone. These are texts that use opposition, and the disciplines that taught it and taught how to use it—that is, exegesis and dialectic—as a catalyst to create a very particular process of *doctrina*. Texts like the *De amore* or the *Libro de buen amor* teach *about* opposition, true; but more importantly, they teach *through* it. Theirs is a discourse that, pedagogically and philosophically speaking, tries to have its cake and eat it, to maintain the inevitable and rigorous symmetries of the contradiction *and* the permeable borders of interdependent opposition. Between these terms—opposition, contradiction, contrariety—and between these disciplines—exegesis, dialectic—lies the space of the textual teaching of *Contrary Things*.

Chapter *I*

Diversa sed non adversa
The Poetics of Exegesis

And it often happens that one and the same passage of Scripture, when
multiply expounded, says many things to us in one.
—Richard of St. Victor, *Benjamin maior*

A single Logos in a multitude of words, the Bible may indeed, as Augustine declared, teach only charity (*DDC* 3.10.15), yet it teaches that single
doctrine in so many ways as to be a lasting provocation to any theory of the
teaching sign. Exegetes of all habits—patristic, monastic, and scholastic—
responded to this divinely ordained provocation with a voluminous body
of texts puzzling over biblical instruction, endlessly unpacking and remaking the single doctrine and multiple teachings embodied in Scripture.

An especially intense hermeneutic provocation is posed by the most
scandalous aspect of scriptural richness, contradiction. Now, Christianity
itself is in a sense built upon oppositions in texts—that is, between its
foundational Testaments, Old and New, and their apparent disagreement
over matters as fundamental as the character of God and the advent of the
Messiah. Asked about the former, the Old replies, jealous (Exodus 20.5);
the New replies, loving (John 3.16); asked if the Messiah has come, the
Old Testament answers *non* and the New, *sic*. Early Christianity articulates
these two textual corpora, Old and New, in a complex supplemental relation based simultaneously on conflict (the New Testament rules out and
over the Old; one must be either Jew or Christian) and on harmony (the
Old Testament prefigures the New; the Pauline Christian is a Jew).[1]

Even within the New Testament itself, writers disagree and teachings
conflict. Peter Abelard (1079–1142), pitches the problem epigrammatically
at the beginning of his workbook of scriptural contradiction entitled *Yes
and No (Sic et non)*. "In such a multitude of words," he says, speaking of
the biblical and the patristic canons, "some statements, even those of the
saints, appear not only to differ from one another, but even to be mutually

opposed" (In tanta verborum multitudine nonnulla etiam sanctorum dicta non solum ab invicem diversa, verum etiam invicem adversa vid(e)ntur) (*Sic et non*, my translation/89). Matthew says not to let your left hand know what your right hand is doing (Matthew 6.3); he also says to let your light shine before men, that they might see your good works (5.15). Which is correct? In what sense can an inspired writer be said to be "wrong"? And why does the Holy Spirit permit Scripture to appear to contradict itself?[2]

Christian literacy in the Middle Ages, then, is reading trained on texts in contraposition, texts locked in a conflicted and mysterious hermeneutic unity. From the necessity of negotiating this unity at every moment of scriptural reading grow theories of disjunctive signification — symbol, allegory, and metaphor among them — and elaborate structures of multi-leveled interpretation, in which a thorough shaking-out of a passage entails readings on as many as seven different figural levels.[3] Exegesis under these modes of meaning-making shuttles back and forth between apparent opposites, between Old and New, outside and inside, manifest and latent, letter and spirit, remaking from these conflicted loci the mysterious whole of Scripture.

Not for nothing does Peter the Chanter (d. 1179) begin his *On the Tropes of Speaking* (*De tropis loquendi*), a treatise collecting and negotiating apparent contradictions in Scripture, with a gloss on 1 Corinthians 13.12: "We see now through a glass in a dark manner" (videmus nunc per speculum in aenigmate).[4] Scriptural textuality — this enigmatic *e pluribus, unum / e uno, plures* — is a spiritual, hermeneutical, and semiotic mystery of the highest order for patristic and medieval commentators. And the mysterious combined text(uality) of Scripture — Old Testament and New, letter and spirit — is, to borrow a phrase of St. Bernard's, a *theoricus sermo*, that is, a discourse both speculative and contemplative.[5] How readers of the Bible theorized (both in their senses and in ours) this relation between univocal nominal doctrine and multiple, even mutually adverse, teachings — between the singular *Verbum* and the *pugnae verborum* (battles of words) (*DDC* 1.6.6) of its scriptural incarnations — is the matter of this chapter. We will here review the ways in which a significant current of patristic and medieval exegesis worked the teaching textuality of the Bible in reading, and reworked it in the writing of commentary. The argumentative net will be cast wide, with testimonies drawn from exegetes as historically and intellectually diverse as Origen and the early Scholastics. I have thought it worth the risk of underplaying the cultural particularities of each commentary's production in order to call attention to their shared understanding of the oppositions in scriptural teaching-textuality. This shared understanding, especially characteristic of but not limited to the monastic tradition of *lectio divina*, takes opposition in Scripture not as an obstacle to meaning but rather as an index of meaning's immanent presence and sacramental multiplicity.[6] Influential hermeneutic "rules" like Origenite allegory and the Augustinian law of charity teach exegetes to read scriptural opposition not primarily through the disambiguating division of *either/or* but rather through the sacramentally multiple *both-and*.

I aim here to read this current of exegesis as Rita Copeland has read medieval commentary on the secular *auctores*—that is, "for what it says about its own discursive action, rather than only for the kinds of readings it produces of other texts" (Copeland, 86). Our subject here will not be exegetical *doctrina* as nominal content, but rather exegetical *doctrina* as an active *process* of signification and of teaching—as a theory and poetics of textual teaching.

"Written for Our Learning"

> But what things soever were written were written for our learning;
> that, through patience and the comfort of the Scriptures, we might
> have hope.
>
> —Romans 15.4

> All Holy Scripture, like rhetorical discourse, aims either to teach or
> to move.
>
> —Peter Abelard, *Commentariam in Romanos*

If, like exegetes ourselves, we sought a story that provoked in the Middle Ages rich thinking on learning, teaching, and signification, we find it best at the beginning: the Fall. Adam and Eve misunderstood God's instructions and succumbed to the Serpent's anti-teaching.[7] Their multiple misreadings cast humanity into sin, mortality, time-bound language—and, as we shall see, labored reading. In the Fall's wake, and from the mercy of God, also comes *doctrina*, for it is in teaching and learning that we are led out of this "region of dissimilitude" (*regio dissimilitudinis*) (*Conf.* 7.10.16) and re-formed into resemblance with the Creator. So says Hugh of St. Victor in his *Didascalicon* (c. 1127):

For the mind, stupefied by bodily sensations and enticed out of itself by sensuous forms, has forgotten what it was, and, because it does not remember that it was anything different, believes that it is nothing except what is seen. But we are restored through *doctrina*, so that we may recognize our nature and learn not to seek outside ourselves what we can find within.

(animus enim, corporeis passionibus consopitus et per sensibiles formas extra semetipsum abductus, oblitus est quid fuerit, et, quia nil aluid fuisse se meminit, nil praeter quod videtur esse credidit. reparamur autem per doctrinam, ut nostram agnoscamus naturam, et ut discamus extra non quaerere quod in nobis possumus invenire.) (*Did.* 1.1; tr. 47/6)

Such "ontologically remedial" *doctrina* (Illich, 11), though generously offered, is not easily received, for the hard human labor following the Fall includes not just Adam's delving and Eve's bloody parturition but also the painstaking study of the divine *doctrina* that was granted humanity as a means of overcoming that transgression. Both *auctor* and *magister*, God makes three sources of *doctrina*, three teaching texts as clear as day and as dark as St. Paul's mirror: Christ, the World, and Scripture. Scripture is of course our main focus here. But before we enter its complexities, it is fitting to consider these other Christian teachers and to get a sense of the metaphorical networks spun among them. This tissue of figuration deserves our attention, for, as we shall see, it is the whole cloth from which the poetics of exegesis is tailored.

In spite (or perhaps because) of the opaque *doctrina* of his parables, which at once teach and screen their nominal doctrine, and mask as much as match meaning to word, Christ the Logos is the only instance in medieval Christianity of a true and truly adequate fit between signifier and signified.[8] Exemplary in pedagogical as well as logological terms,[9] Christ the Instructor (Παιδαγωγός), as Clement of Alexandria calls him in the treatise of the same name, is also the period's most exemplary instance of a perfect fit between word and instruction: *magister* and Logos, word and teacher in one perfectly congruent whole. Thus Augustine's *De magistro* contrasts the radical pedagogical inefficacy of fallen human language with the redeeming *doctrina* of the Christ within, the interior teacher.[10] Peter Damian (d. 1072) declares that he needs no material handbook to teach him eloquence, for Christ is his grammar and in Christ he has both text and teacher of all he needs to know.[11]

Like Christ, God's double works of World and Scripture are both texts and teachers in their turn. Aquinas puts it elegantly:

God, like a good teacher, took care to make two most excellent writings for us, that he might educate us perfectly. "All that is written," the Apostle says, "is written for our learning." These writings are encased in a double book: namely, the book of the Creation and the Book of Scripture.

(Dominus enim tamquam bonus magister fuit sollicitus facere nobis optima scripta, ut nos perfecte erudiret. "Quaecumque," inquit, "scripta sunt, ad nostram doctrinam scripta sunt." Consistunt autem ista scripta in duplici libro: scilicet in libro creaturae et in libro scripturae.) ("Sermones," 194B–95A)

"Scripture explains what the Creation demonstrates" goes the Victorine motto (Scriptura explicat quae creatura probat);[12] the two divinely authored works correspond to each other, then, as text and gloss, both books made by God for our delight and instruction. The Creation, as Alan of Lille says in a well-known passage, is like a book and a picture and a mirror for humanity.[13] Its teaching is double, pointing indexically to its divine *destinateur* even as it mimetically reflects its human *destinataires*. The world's many and diverse creatures mean both multiply and singularly: they point *e pluribus, unum* to their single cause and Creator, and in their noisy conflict, they correspond to the complementary and cacophonous oppositions of fallen life and its languages. Augustine instructs us to read Creation as we would read "an exquisite poem set off as it were with antitheses" (tamquam pulcherrimum carmen etiam ex quibusdam quasi antithetis honesta[tum]):

Just as these contraries opposed to contraries make the beauty of a discourse, so the beauty of the course of this world is built up by a kind of rhetoric, not of words but of things, which employs this opposition of contraries. This is very clearly stated in the book of Ecclesiasticus as follows: "Good is set against evil, and life set against death; so the sinner is set against the godly. And so you are to regard the works of the Most High: two by two, one against the other."

(Sicut ergo ista contraria contrariis opposita sermonis pulchritudinem reddunt, ita quadam non verborum, sed rerum eloquentia contrariorum oppositione saeculi pulchritudo componitur. Apertissime hoc positum est in libro ecclesiastico isto modo: "Contra malum bonum est et contra mortem vita; sic contra pium peccator. Et sic intuere in omnia opera Altissimi, bina bina, unum contra unum.") [14]

Both Scripture and Creation, then, teach pleasantly, "in the manner of rhetorical discourse" (more orationis rhetoricae),[15] delighting and instructing like a good Horatian poem. However—and in this they also resemble Christ—these are anything but transparent texts, an opacity that we may, following Eric Jager, trace back to the Fall. Genesis, in the Bible, also explains—perhaps via a midrashic or mythological narratization—the genesis *of* the Bible, and the subsequent "genesis of hermeneutics."[16] Even as

Adam and Eve's tasting of knowledge led to shame at their nakedness, so too their misinterpretation of God's plain instruction led on the one hand to the educational necessity of Scripture and on the other to Scripture's protective veiling under cover of trope and figure.

Unpacking Doctrine

Adam and Eve ate the apple; now Ezekiel and John—and their followers—must "eat this book."[17] And the eating is no simple operation, for the Bible is a tough nut to crack. Thus Gregory the Great:

Holy Scripture is sometimes food for us, and sometimes drink. It is food in the obscure places, because it is, so to speak, broken when it is explained and absorbed when it is chewed. It is drink in its open places, because it can be absorbed just as it is found.

(Scriptura enim sacra aliquando nobis cibus est, aliquando potus. Cibus est in locis obscurioribus, quia quasi exponendo frangitur et mandendo glutitur. Potus uero est in locis apertioribus quia ita sorbetur sicut inuenitur.) (*Moralia* 1.21.29; 143: 40)

Those places where Scripture must be broken are the places whose teaching we must be taught to read. Whatever is written there is written for our *doctrina*, St. Paul taught, but the manner of scriptural teaching can be opaque to us: "Indeed, all holy Scripture is written for us," says Gregory the Great, "but not all Scripture is comprehensible to us." (Scriptura sacra tota quidem propter nos scripta est, sed non tota intelligitur a nobis).[18] Scriptural doctrine as "content" is clear enough in the disambiguating wake of Augustine's elegantly simple formulation: "But Scripture teaches nothing but charity, nor condemns anything but cupidity" (Non autem precipit scriptura nisi caritatem nec culpat nisi cupiditatem) (*DDC* 3.10.15). But, as Augustine knows well, Scripture-as-writing, and by extension, Scripture-as-reading, is a *process* of teaching as well as teaching's content or result. And what a strange process it is, full of enigmas—barbarisms and bizarre syntax, obscurities, ambiguities, puzzles, and contradictions.

Our exegetes thus know that Scripture teaches, and know well *what* it teaches. Knowing this, they inquire into the manner of scriptural teaching: how does Scripture teach, and why does it teach that way? The question their investigation poses for us, their students, and teachers in our turn, might well be: what does medieval theorizing on the textuality of scriptural teaching have to teach us about teaching (and) textuality in the Middle Ages?

The words for exegesis itself show us a great deal about scriptural textuality: if meaning must be "led out", it must be understood as closed up in text (exegesis, from *ex* + *hegeisthai*, "to lead"); if meaning must be set out or "ex-posed," then it must be locked up or in; if "ex-plicated," then intricately folded; if ironed out through "ex-planation," then rough and uneven.[19] Translating these premodern metaphors into tropes more germane to our own age of spectacle and "information," we might say that, for these readers, Scripture is an encrypted data file that must be, as it were, unzipped; exegesis is the unzipping, the unpacking. Or, alternatively, the Lord in his wisdom put apparently endless clowns in a single Volkswagen. Exegesis unlocks the door and then speculates in awe about what sort of vehicle this might be that can contain such infinite figures.[20]

Thus, confronted with a single *veritas* in a multiplicity of *verba*, with a single teaching in an almost overwhelming abundance of teaching processes, the ordinary human reader cannot proceed safely alone, as the Encyclical of Leo XIII printed at the front of the Rheims-Douay translation of the Vulgate still advises (Leo XIII, xvii). If Scripture teaches people the ways of God, then exegesis teaches them the ways of Scripture, "not only what they understand," says Augustine, "but in addition, those things which are to be observed in understanding" (non solum ea, quae intellegant, sed etiam intellegendo ea, quae obseruent) (*DDC*, Prologue 8).[21] Later in the same text, Augustine picks up the metadidactic thread again: "There are two things necessary to the treatment of the Scriptures: a way of discovering those things which are to be understood, and a way of teaching what we have learned" (Duo sunt res, quibus nititur omnis tractatio scripturarum, modus inueniendi, quae intellegenda sunt, et modus proferendi, quae intellecta sunt) (*DDC* 1.1.1). Thus, in leading out Scripture's teaching, and in teaching us about Scripture's teaching methods, exegesis is almost invariably led to teach about teaching itself, to consider the processes of textual instruction and to draw the student-reader's attention to them.[22]

Contradiction

> These two testaments do not disagree with each other in their words; rather, this quasi-dissonance occurs in order to inflame the zeal of our minds.
>
> —Julian of Toledo, *Antikeimenon*

Biblical contradiction is the most striking—because the most painful—call to such theoretical contemplation. It cannot be ignored, for it extends from the knotty and contrapuntal discursive surface, in which oppositions can be read and enjoyed as ornamental tropes, to the deepest principles of biblical structure: the conflicted and mysterious hermeneutic unity of the Testaments. In between is a seemingly endless list of hermeneutic *cruces*, in which, as Augustine observed, "so obscurely are certain sayings covered with a most dense mist" (ita obscure dicta quaedam densissimam caliginem obducunt) (*DDC* 2.6.7) that the divine meaning is hidden from the human mind.

Why, then, did the Author of the universe entrust *doctrina* to such a dark and conflicted teacher? One set of answers we might call hermeneutic, for they assert that the packed-in textuality of Scripture must be understood as a call to readerly labor. "By following certain traces," says Augustine, the reader "may come upon the hidden sense" of the text (quibusdam uestigiis indagatis ad occultum sensum . . . perueniat) (*DDC*, Prologue 9). Darkest of those traces are the places where the holy text seems to unteach itself.[23] Such patent violations of common sense mark the loci of interpretive labor, where we must read, not naturally, but other-wise — theoretically, even. "No theory is good except on condition that one use it to go beyond," wrote André Gide (2: 238). By Gide's definition, then, the contemplative theory of reading calqued onto the *lectio divina* is a very good theory indeed, for there, "the incoherence of the surface materials is almost essential to the formation of the abstract pattern, for if the surface materials . . . were consistent or spontaneously satisfying . . . , there would be no stimulus to seek something beyond them" (Robertson, *Preface*, 56). Here is Gregory the Great:

Sometimes, too, lest they be taken to the letter, the words and the literal meanings conflict among themselves. . . . But, of course, when the words and their literal meanings are confronted and fail to agree with each other, then they show us that we must look in them for something else, as if they were saying to us: "When you see that our surface is destroyed in this conflict, look in us for that thing which, orderly and coherent with itself, might be discovered intact within us."

(Aliquando etiam ne fortasse intellegi iuxta litteram debeant, ipsa se uerba litterae impugnant. . . . Sed nimirum uerba litterae, dum collata sibi conuenire nequeunt, aliud in se aliquid quod quaeratur ostendunt, ac si quibusdam uocibis dicant: dum nostra nos conspicitis superficie destrui, hoc in nobis quaerite, quod ordinatum sibique congruens apud nos ualeat intus inueniri.) (*Moralia*, Ep. ad Leandrum 3; 143: 5)[24]

These are the places, then, where work must happen, marked by contradictions that, in a fitting paradox, at once reveal and conceal the meaning to be dis/uncovered.[25] Thus, for all its apparent nonsense, contradiction is in fact both symptom and signal of meaning. And the sense that it both designates and protects must be invented (in both rhetorical and common senses) at the spot marked by contradiction's flag and veil; if not, the truth will seem to oppose itself, and we know that such a thing cannot be, since, as Peter the Chanter says, "truth cannot be contrary to truth" (cum verum non sit contrarium vero) (quoted in Evans, *Language and Logic*, 98).

Jean Jolivet puts the ensuing hermeneutical problem elegantly: "If it is true that the fundamental elements of knowledge are found in a text that one *reads*, then a disagreement among texts is a sort of scandal. It seems that truth conflicts with itself, and it is urgent to resolve this tension, and first of all to expose it, so that one can see its terms and meaning" (*Arts de langage*, 194). What we see cannot be; what the text "says" it cannot say; the exegete must act upon the knot before her or him, to untie it and reweave it into a signifying pattern whose meaning is at once completely unpredictable and a foregone conclusion. Exegesis is thus, among other things, a high-stakes reading under pressure, for as we read, we must face—and face down—scriptural aporias. Such places are, in their very knottiness, what Freud would call the navel of the dream—that is, the dark places from which meaning is generated.[26]

Working in the Dark

In this hard labor of teaching and learning lies another explanation of the Bible's difficult teaching-textuality. Augustine, who poses this question in the *De doctrina christiana*, has a ready answer: "to conquer pride by work and to combat disdain in our minds, to which those things which are easily discovered seem frequently to become worthless" (ad edomandam labore superbiam, et intellectum a fastidio reuocandum, cui facile inuestigata plerumque uilescunt) (*DDC* 2.6.7). Maintaining the ethico-hermeneutic focus upon the souls and activities of readers, he adds that scriptural difficulty also has another effect: delight. I contemplate the saints with more pleasure, he says, when I imagine them in the outrageous clothing of an impossible trope (*DDC* 2.6.7).[27] We shall have more to say about this pleasure shortly, but for the moment suffice it to point out how neatly the darkness of scriptural teaching matches two of the most powerful inclinations of the human soul, *intellectus* and *delectatio*.

Such adequation is the base for yet another explanation of scriptural textuality. This is what we might call the *mimetic* reading of Scripture's twists and turns and knots and aporias. We could not begin to understand the unmediated discourse of God, this argument goes. Figures are concessions to a weak and carnal mind that would be blinded by discourse adequate to divinity; to teach humanity, Scripture must, then, *match* humanity, and speak of God only darkly, through dissimilar similitudes.[28] If Scripture is difficult, writes Gregory the Great, this is because *we* are difficult, and it has been made as much in our image and likeness as in God's: "Holy Scripture is placed before the eyes of the mind like a kind of mirror, so that we may in it see our inward face. For therein we may know our uglinesses and our beauties" (Scriptura sacra mentis oculis quasi quoddam speculum opponitur, ut interna nostra facies in ipsa uideatur. Ibi etenim foeda ibi pulchra nostra cognoscimus) (*Moralia* 2.1; 143: 59).[29] Scripture seems dark, then, not because it is so different from human thinking but because it is such a precise imitation of it. Paradoxically, as Gillian Evans has observed, such hermeneutic difficulties become "not stumbling-blocks, but God's aids to a contorted human understanding. Each obscure passage or torturous narrative, each ambiguity or contradiction, meets an obscurity or twist or confusion in human thinking, and is thus more, not less, intelligible to man's clouded sinful mind" (*Language and Logic*, 2–3). Mimetic Scripture thus fits both mind and world, and by doing so, assures a mysteriously adequate match between word, audience, and teaching. A fit as perfectly matched to the human condition as that of the incarnate Christ, "who saw fit to make himself congruous with such infirmity as ours" (nostrae infirmitati congruere dignaretur) (*DDC* 1.9.11), becoming for humanity both flesh and book.

The Language of Exegesis

According to Umberto Eco, incarnational textuality, with its "puzzling identification of the sender (the divine Logos), the signifying message (words, Logoi), the content (the divine message, Logos), and the referent (Christ, the Logos)" generated meanings too multiple for medieval readers to bear:

> Thus, both Testaments spoke at the same time of their sender, their content, and their referent, and their meaning was a nebula of all possible archetypes. The scriptures were in the position of saying everything. Everything, though, was rather too much for interpreters interested in truth.
>
> The symbolical nature of sacred scripture has therefore to be tamed. Potentially, the scriptures had every possible meaning; so the reading of them had to be governed by a code. (Eco, *Aesthetics*, 145)

Eco's own language deserves some exegetical unpacking, structured as it is by figuration. Domestication and containment shape what Eco sees here, and he constructs scriptural textuality as a wild thing from "out there" in need of taming before the medieval exegete could bring it "in here." This view would lead us to imagine exegesis not so much as a house, as exegetes were wont to do,[30] but as a fortress, designed to keep out the polysemic otherness of Scripture, to protect the faithful from it. Such, in fact, says Lee Patterson, is the purpose of Augustine's master code of charity, the blueprint on which this edifice is built. In the *De doctrina christiana*, Augustine began on the premise that Scripture teaches nothing but charity; this being so, the reader's task is to labor toward the edification of charity. In cases of difficult interpretation, Augustine declares, "a rule such as this will serve, that what is read should be subjected to diligent scrutiny until an interpretation contributing to the reign of charity is produced" (seruabitur . . . regula huiusmodi, ut tam diu uersetur diligenti consideratione quod legitur, donec ad regnum caritatis interpretatio perducatur) (*DDC* 3.15.23).

Patterson sees this Augustinian precept as a "preemptive hermeneutic" that aims "to *inoculate* the reader against the sweetness of the letter" (151; emphasis added). It certainly seems to be exactly that when the "exegetical" critics of the mid–twentieth century take Augustine's formulation as a master code not for the production but for the *regulation* of meaning, applying it mechanically (and, in spite of Augustine himself, literal-mindedly) to medieval texts.[31] Such is not, however, the case in exegetical practice itself, where the "charitable" meaning of a scriptural text is *both* a foregone conclusion *and* infinitely variable in its incarnations.

There is no denying the ascetic suspicion of the letter that subtends much exegetical writing,[32] and Eco is right to say that the troping codes of exegesis systematize biblical signification, if only by giving exegetes a metalanguage with which to talk about it. However, as we have seen, the multiplicity of scriptural textuality is for a long line of readers both Other and Us, a source of pleasure as much as of anxiety, a discourse that in its singularity is the embodiment of God but at the same time made to human measure in its multiplicity.[33]

From this point of view, then, the "identification of the sender, the signifying message, the content, and the referent" that provoked Eco is simply the logological working-out of a *mysterium*. And in the language of exegesis, this working out is concrete and corporeal, even erotic. Origen, for example, saw Christ as twice incarnate: once in human and once in textual body: "The Word," he wrote, "has continually been becoming flesh in the Scriptures in order that he might tabernacle with us" (quoted in Dungey, 8). Beatus of Liébana (c. 785) goes a step further:

> What is this letter that you read in the Gospels or in the other Holy Scriptures, but the body of Christ, the flesh of Christ, which is eaten by Christians? . . . Truly, the body of Christ and his blood are the discourse of the Scriptures, holy *doctrina*; and when we read it, we chew the flesh of Christ, and drink his blood.
>
> (Quid est haec littera quam in Evangelio legis vel in caeteris Scripturis sanctis, nisi corpus Christi, nisi caro Christi, quae ab omnibus christianis comeditur? . . . vere corpus Christi, et sanguis eius, sermo Scripturarum est, doctrina divina est. Et cum legimus eam, carnem Christi manducamus, et sanguinem eius bibimus.) (*Apologeticum* 1.66, 1.97; 772–74, 808) [34]

Later medieval devotion takes the identification of holy body and sacred corpus as far as it will go, making Christ's flesh not simply discourse but text(uality) itself: Christ on the cross is troped as parchment on a frame; his wounds the punctuation, his blood the script. Not simply textual content, that is, but the very material process of text-and-meaning-making.[35] Thinking the biblical corpus through the *corpus Christi* may well be the sacramentalizing condition under which the Bible's heterogeneous, oppositional, and even contradictory richness might be analyzed as well as savored.

That unpacking this multiplicity is as much a source of aesthetic, even erotic delight as it is of ascetic self-control is especially clear in the language exegetes use when they contemplate the mysterious textuality—Us and yet not-Us, providentially Same yet ineluctably Other—of Scripture. Summoning their words in representation of Scripture, monastic exegetes write about the experience of exegetical reading with a poetic extravagance that a surrealist would envy, reproducing in their own commentaries the poetics of the target text. The Bible opens before them like a peacock's tail, with as many colors as meanings, as many meanings as colors.[36] The two testaments are two fish in a basket, the wings of an eagle, the breasts of the Church. Scripture, writes Gregory the Great, "is, as it were, like some great river, smooth and deep, in which the lamb might walk and the elephant swim" (quasi quidam quippe est fluvius, ut ita dixerim, planus et altus, in quo et agnus ambulet et elephas natet) (*Moralia*, Ep. ad Leandrum 4; 143: 6).[37] These metaphors are as wild and as sensually immediate as the most vivid passages of the Song of Songs, from which many of them draw their inspiration. Gilbert of Stanford takes the two testaments as the lips of a lover; to read them is to participate in the divinest of kisses.[38] Gregory the

Great compares the biblical corpus, with its innumerable meanings, to the richly ornamented body of that poem's Spouse:

As, from a single lump of gold, some make necklaces, some rings, some bracelets, and all for adornment, so from one understanding of Holy Scripture, the expositors, through innumerable meanings, compose as it were various ornaments, which all serve to adorn the beauty of the celestial Spouse.

(Sicut enim ex uno auro alii murenulas, alii annulos, alii dextralia ad ornamentum faciunt, ita ex una sacrae Scripturae intelligentia expositores quique per innumeros intellectus quasi varia ornamenta componunt, quae tamen omnia ad decorem coelestis sponsae proficiunt.) [39]

This trope is especially tasty. Reading meaning through corporeal ornamentation, it shows us that, for all monastic reading's reliance on the apparently stable hermeneutic oppositions (inside/outside, meaning/ornament, spirit/body, *spiritus/littera*), the poetics driving exegesis collapses them — as we shall see, not *either/or* but *both-and*.

Both this rhapsodic prose and the biblical style it at once describes and performs are in fact sites of a very particular and intense literary pleasure: the one associated with infinite, infinitely variable interpretation.[40] A Northern French canon whom we know only by his first initial, "B.," provides us with a stunning example of this monastic *plaisir du texte.* "We take refuge in the Church," he writes, "and are fattened on Scripture" (ad ecclesiam confugimus, et scriptura sancta saginamur).[41] Then the metaphors come tumbling out, some borrowed from Gregory, and a very striking one, apparently of "B.'s" own coin: "Holy Scripture is food and drink, a perforated gemstone, a lake in which the elephant swims and the lamb walks. To be brief, the letter (or literal sense) is a whore accommodated to any senses whatever" (Scriptura enim sancta cibus est et potus, gemma perforata, pelagus in quo elephas natat et agnus pedat et ambulat et, ut compendiose dicamus, littera meretrix est ad quoslibet sensus accomodata) (fols. 84v–85r).

This prose has surely not been inoculated against the pleasures of the letter. Though certainly titillating, "B.'s" language is unusual only in that it performs an already deeply, if implicitly, eroticized kind of reading through metaphors drawn from an equally eroticized field. "B." repeats, pushing even further: "Holy Scripture is a whore accommodated to any senses whatever. For even as the whore exposes herself to many, or rather to almost all, so in the letter there are multiple senses: the historical, the allegorical, the tropological" (Scriptura sancta meretrix est ad quoslibet sensus accomodata. Sicut enim meretrix multis, immo quam plurimis, sese exponit, ita in littera multiplex est sensus: est enim sensus historialis, allegoricus, tropologicus) (fol. 85r).

"A language will develop when important new things are to be said," writes Beryl Smalley; she concludes, "this alone will explain the exuberance of the queer language of the spiritual senses" (*Study*, 246). I am not sure that the queerly exuberant expositors of Scripture sow these tropes in order to say some important new thing; what they are saying, in fact, is the oldest of old hats—Scripture is rich; Scripture is full of teaching; we like Scripture. One can speak here more aptly, perhaps, of a *poetics* than of a language; and a poetics will develop, I would say, when there is something sweet in words that can be tasted on the tongue of the mind. Scripture, says the appropriately named Peter the Eater, is God's dining room, "in which he makes his people drunk, in order to make them sober" (in qua sic suos inebriat, ut sobrios reddat) (*Historia scholastica*, in *PL* 198: 1053).

The Poetics of Exegesis: Both Yes *and* No

> Interpretation is a feast, not a fast. It imposes an obligatory excess.
>
> —Geoffrey Hartman, "The Interpreter"

> That *doctrina* might be multiple, the truth remaining the same.
>
> —Hugh of St. Victor, *De Arca Noe Morali*

Medieval and patristic commentators sit down with enthusiasm at the table of the Book. Both the textual food that they eat and the writings in which they manifest their ruminations are characterized by a glorious— they would say mysterious—poetics of excess.[42] On this table the bread, like the five loaves Christ used to feed the multitude,[43] is miraculously never exhausted, for, as Eriugena says epigrammatically, "the interpretation of Holy Scripture is infinite" (sacrae scripturae interpretatio infinita est).[44] Many mouths fed from five loaves; one river, much water. One and the same passage of Scripture, writes Richard of St. Victor, says many things in one, always already both one and many.[45]

This mysterious and sacramental multiplicity, then, is the proper home —in the monastic tradition of *lectio divina*—for the scriptural phenomenon that we have been calling contradiction, along with its misty sisters, obscurity and ambiguity. In fact, exegetes are quick to remind us, there can be no contradiction at all in Scripture. However noisy the apparent clash of meanings, we may rest assured that, since truth may not be contrary to truth, statements appearing adverse are only in fact diverse, and what seems to be logical incoherence, a harmonious and congruent showing of divine generosity.[46] Says Hugh of St. Victor: "The divine deeper meaning can never be absurd, never false. Although in the sense, as has been said, many contrary things are found, the deeper meaning admits no conflict, is always harmonious, always true" (Sententia divina numquam absurda, numquam falsa esse potest, sed cum in sensu, ut dictum est, multa inveniantur contraria, sententia nullam admittit repugnantiam, semper congrua est, semper vera) (*Did.* 6.11; tr. 149–50/128).[47]

Eco's and Patterson's critiques of the systematizing impulse of exegesis would lead one to call this denial of conflict an egregious ecclesiastical takeover of the production of meaning, an eternal imposition of the Same over disjunction and difference. Such is the argument of Jesse Gellrich in *The Idea of the Book in the Middle Ages*, which constructs exegetical culture as a nearly totalitarian government of univocity, authority, and order under the rule of Augustinian charity: "The writing that composed the Book of culture is preoccupied with foreground; questioning, contradiction, and uncertainty cannot disturb the authority of traditional meanings. That the New Law of Charity organized a discipline — if not an entire intellectual tradition — for well over a millennium testifies to the strength of this principle" (137).

Gellrich does, however, call our attention to the fact that many exegetes offer contrary readings of the same scriptural image. Augustine, for example, is quite clear that the thing evoked in a scriptural figuration may signify in contrary ways, being used in one place in a good sense (*in bono*) and in another in an evil sense (*in malo*) (*DDC* 3.25.36). Augustine does not shy away from the twinned inversion of this phenomenon, either; namely, that there may be images, like the strong wine of Psalm 74.9, whose "good" or "bad" flavor is undecidable. Since, Augustine concludes, "one thing may have significations which are not contrary but diverse" (res eadem non in contraria, sed tantum in diversa significatione ponitur) (3.25.36), then, so long as one's interpretive will is not contrary to the faith, the field is open for all sorts of richly varied readings. Such, for example, are those produced by Pierre Bersuire (d. 1362), whose *Repertorium morale* generates multiple and contrary readings of the same scriptural images. For the ram of Genesis 22.13, Gellrich notes, Bersuire offers three readings that construe it positively (*in bono*) and one that reads it negatively (*in malo*). Comments Gellrich: "Opposites produce meaning just as readily as similarities in Bersuire's entry; for the transformation rests on the larger assumption that contradictions do not exist" (133).

For Gellrich, the rule that Scripture cannot contradict itself acts, technically, as a mystifying ideology; that is, exegesis pretends that contradiction does not exist while taking advantage of its activity as producer of linguistic meaning. If, for the sake of historical (and theoretical) understanding, we adopt the exegetical point of view—that Truth is extra- and supra-linguistic—then apparent contradiction appears one of the paths to truth rather than an obstacle blocking the way. Contradiction is thus not a subversive, Other element in Scripture but rather a manifestation of its richness, mystery, and multiplicity. Thus, the "miracle" of the supralinguistic Logos in which opposites become one, the last first and the first last, speaks in displaced directness in the wonderful profundity of a Scripture that says at once one thing only and more things than the human mind can comprehend: "that *doctrina* might be multiple," says Hugh of St. Victor, "the truth remaining the same" (ut doctrina multiplex fiat, manente eadem veritate).[48]

Gellrich compares these structures of mysterious and sacramental (non)contradiction to those of Lévi-Straussian mythological thinking, and would seem to castigate the exegetes for their repression of doubt (130). I use the term "repression" advisedly here, for if we are going to find a twentieth-century parallel to exegetical processes, the most illuminating correspondence will come not from Lévi-Strauss but from Freud; not the language of myth but the language of dreams.

The way in which dreams treat the category of contraries and contradictories is highly remarkable. It is simply disregarded. "No" seems not to exist so far as dreams are concerned. They show a particular preference for combining contraries into a unity or for representing them as one and the same thing. Dreams feel themselves at liberty, moreover, to represent any element by its wishful contrary; so there is no way of deciding at first glance whether any element that admits of a contrary is present in the dream-thoughts as a positive or as a negative. (Freud, *Interpretation*, 353)[49]

Both dream-language and scriptural *sermo* are *mises-en-discours* of an extra-linguistic (even supralinguistic) *res* that admits no contradiction. They are constituted by a semiotic liberty that permits the most florid nonsense and outrageous superficial contradictions imaginable, in which any image can mean x, not-x, and anti-x, *in bono* and *in malo*, at once or in sequence. "We have already become acquainted with the interpretive rule according to which every element in a dream can, for the purposes of interpretation, stand for its opposite just as easily as for itself. We can never tell before-hand whether it stands for the one or for the other; only the context can decide" (Freud, *Interpretation*, 508). Instead of an *either/or* semiotics of difference and minimal pairs (bit/bat, *siccus/succus*) medieval exegesis runs under the aegis of *both-and*, where an image can be both dry and juicy, and equally true in both constructions.[50]

This is not to suggest that we read Scripture as dream or read exegesis as *Traumdeutung*. It is to say: here are two constructions of the production and communication of meaning, imagined in uncannily similar terms across wide gulfs of culture and history. It is, I might hope, to defamiliarize exegesis enough that we can look at it as text and textual process and speak of its poetics. These poetics, I think, are what Smalley was unwittingly getting at when, with an almost audible sniff, she wrote that in medieval Bible study, "one finds, as did Alice, a country governed by queer laws which the inhabitants oddly regard as rational" (*Study*, 5). One of those "queer laws" is this rule of scriptural noncontradiction, which produces signification processes comparable in their almost unimaginable luxuriance and mysterious cohesiveness to the discourse of dreams. Writes Hugh of St. Victor:

Sometimes there is a single deeper meaning for a single expression; sometimes there are several deeper meanings for a single expression; sometimes there is a single deeper meaning for several expressions; sometimes there are several deeper meanings for several expressions.

(aliquando unius enuntiationis una est sententia, aliquando unius enuntiationis plures sunt sententiae, aliquando plurimum enuntiationum una est sententia, aliquando plurimum enuntiationum plures sunt sententiae.) (*Did.* 6.11; tr. 150/128)[51]

This is the active teaching-textuality—the *doctrina*—that, as we have seen, exegesis at once describes in Scripture and performs therefrom. The more interpretations, in this view, the merrier—so long as they are made in double allegiance to the faith and to the text. For monastic exegetes and their fellow travelers, then, scriptural contradiction and obscurity do anything but block the transmission of meaning; in fact, they are the very conditions for its continued and continual production.

For example, William of Conches, one of many exegetically trained readers bridging into secular commentary, acknowledges that his reading of the Orpheus legend differs mightily from that of Fulgentius, but concludes that, so long as each interpretation does not contradict *itself*, there should be no dismay at the disagreement among interpreters but rather rejoicing.[52] Augustine rejoices, too:

We see that the obscurity of the divine Word actually has the advantage of engendering more than one interpretation of the truth and of bringing these interpretations into the bright light of general knowledge, as different readers understand a passage differently.

(Quamvis itaque divini sermonis obscuritas etiam ad hoc sit utilis, quod plures sententias veritatis parit et in lucem notitiae producit, dum alius eum sic, alius sic intellegit.) (*De civitate Dei* 11.19; 3: 497)

Darkly knotted scriptural textuality, then, does not simply *accommodate* many meanings but rather sets up the conditions under which Truth is served in their endless production. Contradiction and, more generally, obscurity ensure such production of meaning as generations of readers construe the target text according to their differing skills, wills, understandings, and desires, and come away the better for it. Humbler and more diligent, of course, for we remember that interpretive work conquers pride (*DDC* 2.6.7), but also richer. Thus Augustine again: "It is put down obscurely, so that it might generate many meanings, and men might come away from it the richer" (Obscurius positum est, ut multos intellectus generet, et ditiores discedant homines).[53]

Scriptural meaning is at once immanent—the Holy Spirit, we are told, anticipated all possible meanings[54]—and constructed, both found and made. *Invented*, that is to say, for what Rita Copeland has found for secular commentary holds true for exegesis as well. Commentary is an act of invention, both in the latter term's classical, rhetorical sense and in its modern, "creative" one. In exegesis, obscurity and its recalcitrant sister contradiction are the conditions, nay, the very *guarantees*, for such invention.[55] For example, the twelfth-century mathematical exegete Thibaut of Langres makes it very clear that meaning-making is a labor of both will and invention.[56] It begins, he says, in the exegete's desire to "sacramentize" a number, that is, to *make it mean*:

When you want to sacramentize a number, you should unfold the aforesaid ways of sacramentizing, and turn them over in your mind, because in such frequent consideration, *you may perhaps find what you are looking for, lying hidden.*

(Quotiens igitur aliquem volueris numerum sacramentare, debes predictos sacramentandi modos explicare, explicitosque revolvere, quia crebra fortassis revolutione, *quod queris, invenies inter eos latere.*) (Lange, 106; emphasis added)

What you wish, and seek, you shall find: what better way of explaining exegetical invention's simultaneous dis/uncovery and construction of meaning. *Pace* Patterson, the Augustinian rule of charity does not inoculate against this *dulcedo inventionis* (sweetness of invention) [57] so much as ensure its displacement to and, ultimately, efflorescence upon the surface of exegetical discourse itself (*caritas*, after all, subsumes and transmutes allied sensations of *delectatio* and even *concupiscentia*).

The danger, of course, is that exegetical discourse may also simply cloak these less holy desires. We should not, then, let delight at the luxuriant poetics of exegesis blind us to the current of anxiety that runs there with equal insistence. Eco, Patterson, and Gellrich all felt that current but misread its source. If scriptural multiplicity and contradiction pose a problem in exegesis, they do so not in themselves but in their ethico-hermeneutic effect. Writers worry that talking openly about contradiction in Scripture will sow doubts among the untrained.[58] Worse still, among the trained, such abundant interpretation could easily turn out to be not so much inventive as *arbitrary*, taking that last term in its etymological sense as an imposition of will and an indulgence in pride in one's own powers of invention.[59] Medieval exegetes felt this danger too, and warned against it. Thus Peter the Eater:

There are others who destroy: those who disappear into their own thoughts, who paint the images of their minds on the pages of Holy Scripture, who accommodate the reluctant letter to their own inventions, and blow the nose of Scripture's meaning until it bleeds.

(Sunt alii qui destruunt: hi sunt, qui evanuerunt in cogitationibus suis; qui imagines cordis sui in paginis sacrae Scripturae depingunt, qui litteram renitentem suis adinventionibus accommodant, et intellectum Scripturae usque ad sanguinem emungunt.)[60]

Overinterpretation is as much a danger as refusal to interpret at all; the stakes are high, and *lectio divina*, for all its chaste pleasures, and in spite of the circumcision of its lips (*Conf.* 11.2.3), is certainly not without its dangers. Characteristically, though—and here we return to the poetics of exegesis—these warnings against proud and arbitrary overreading are often couched in the very "carnal" language that they reprehend. We are warned, for example, against pressing dry the Bible's breasts, against blowing Scripture's nose until it bleeds.[61]

However, with the proper restraints of faith and humility, there is little to fear in such arbitrated invention of meaning. Hugh of St. Victor, for example, writes warmly of those who, "in accordance with that knowledge of the truth upon which, interiorly, they are solidly based, know how to bend all Scriptural passages whatever into fitting interpretations" (secundum illam veritatis agnitionem, qua intus firmati sunt, quaslibet scripturas ad congruas interpretationes flectere noverunt) (*Did.* 6.4; tr. 143–44/121). The flexible slipperiness of such scriptural reading is made clearest, as usual, in a tasty trope, this one by the Benedictine Wolbero of Cologne (d. 1167), who remakes the apparent conflict between the Testaments into a living tangle of meanings: "The two Testaments are said to be eels, because they can be twisted round in many ways in exposition, wrapped up in many meanings, while sounding nothing contrary to faith" (Duo testamenta murenulae dicuntur, quia in diversos modos expositionum flecti possunt, multis involuta sententiis, tantum ut nihil fidei contrarium sonent).[62]

Thus, the contemplative practices of *lectio divina* set up conditions wherein, for the most part, the hermeneutic response to contradictory teaching is not a choice of either one thing or the other but rather a reading of both.[63] In the monastic tradition, the dynamic of reading set off by contradiction is characterized not by *either/or* but rather by *both-and*. Reasons the Cistercian Isaac of Stella (fl. 1155–69):

> Truly, Scripture is multiform, for even though the wisdom of God is most simple, and even though it is uniformly one, nevertheless it is found to be multiple in multiple ways. . . . Whence it is often possible that readers who disagree or perceive diverse things in the same passage of Scripture, by means of the Holy Spirit are able to agree or reach consensus as long as it is firmly decided not to depart from the faith in truth, from the edification of charity and the subversion of cupidity, things on which Holy Scripture keeps a watchful eye. . . . For truth is not to be asserted against charity, nor is charity to be held against truth.

> (Vere multiformis est, cum sit tamen simplicissima Dei sapientia, et cum sit uniformiter una, multipliciter tamen multiplex invenitur. . . . Unde possibile factu saepe est, in eadem Scriptura dissentientes, vel diversa sentientes, Spiritui sancto posse optime convenire, vel consentire, dum a fide veritatis, et aedificatione charitatis, ac subversione cupiditatis, quibus omnis oculus Scripturae sanctae invigilat, constiterit non dissentire. . . . Neque enim veritas asserenda est contra charitatem: aut charitas tenenda est contra veritatem.) (*Sermo* 16, in *PL* 194: 1741A, 1741C)

There is another rule of noncontradiction, though, one less forgiving and considerably less flexible than the Augustinian law of charity: I mean the Aristotelian law of noncontradiction, one of the first principles of logic, as Augustine's is for exegesis. Though Matthew may say that we should both hide and not hide our good works (Matthew 6.3, 5.5), Aristotle cannot both dispute and not dispute at the same time.

As Aristotelian logic was institutionalized in the twelfth century, another breed of readers, not monks now but professional teachers, thought

—and *taught*—through textual conflict. Though dialectic intertwines with exegesis in the schools of the central Middle Ages, and though contradiction is *a priori* impossible in both disciplines, the two fields are fundamentally different in register, aims, and procedures.

Exegesis, for all its attention to the scriptural *littera*, is ultimately concerned with words only insofar as they point to things. Since those things are by disciplinary fiat harmonious with the divine will, then verbal contradiction is an index for the multiplicity of things, all of which redound to the praise of a singular Truth. We can thus read for both one thing and the other, so long as we operate with charity and faith. For exegesis, under the *both-and* of the law of charity, contradictory textual teaching provides the conditions for luxuriant growth of meaning, "that *doctrina* might be multiple, the truth remaining the same" (ut doctrina multiplex fiat, manente eadem veritate).[64]

For dialectic, as for exegesis, contradiction is a provocation to thought and discourse. Tools developed in dialectic for resolving contradiction are, not surprisingly, powerful additions to the arms of the hermeneut, but they are built upon an *either/or* reasoning pattern deeply at odds with— one might say contrary to—the multiple *both-and* of monastic exegetical noncontradiction. However, since dialectic serves not things but words, as a discipline it lacks the onto-hermeneutical guarantees of exegesis. Thus earthbound dialectic is trapped in a world where multiplicity is inevitably contradiction, a contradiction painful rather than miraculous. Still the condition for learning and teaching, contradiction for dialectic is also— and troublingly—an obstacle to them. We turn now to these growing pains, moving as we do so from monastic quiet to the contentious clamor of the urban schools.

Chapter 2

Contradiction in the City
John of Salisbury and the Practice of Dialectic

*This is Dialectic, to whom indeed the discrimination of all truth and all falsehood
is so subject, that she, the chief of all* doctrina, *possesses the dominion and
command of all philosophies.*

—Peter Abelard, *Dialectica*

*I think that masters are made many when they perceive both diverse
and adverse things among themselves.*

—Augustine, *Retractationes*

The first half of the twelfth century was a noisy time in the schools of
Western Europe, and for many observers, it was hard to hear singular
Truth for the yakkity clamor of multiple teachings. "The saying of the
comic poet that 'There are as many opinions as heads,' has almost come
to hold true," wrote John of Salisbury at midcentury about the schools of
Paris (ut uerbo comici utar, fere quot homines, tot sententie) (*Met.* 2.18; tr.
116/96). A generation later, Bishop Stephen of Tournai (d. 1203) thundered
that in Paris, there were "as many . . . errors as doctors, as many scandals
as classrooms, and as many blasphemies as squares" (tot . . . errores quot
doctores, tot scandala quot auditoria, tot blasphemie quot platee).[1]

From the quiet of St. Victor, Master Hugh had recently declared scriptural textuality to be governed by the divine mandate "that *doctrina* might
be multiple, the truth remaining the same" (ut doctrina multiplex fiat,
manente eadem veritate) (*PL* 176: 678D), but in the nearby classrooms
and public squares, doctrinal multiplicity was no rich and tranquil gift.
Deafened contemplatives often attributed this noisy and divisive multi-
plication of doctrine to the increasing professionalization of the trivium
disciplines of the word. Particularly noisome on this account is dialectic,
the "science of disputing well" (bene disputandi scientia).[2] Says Hugh Primas (c. 1093–c. 1160), who taught at Orléans and at Paris, and so, one
imagines, knows whereof he speaks:

In the schools of disputation they're discordant and diverse, aberrant and dispersed. What this man denies, this one affirms; this man's conquered, this one conquers: the Doctor contradicts it all.

> (Set in scolis disputa[n]tum
> sunt discordes et diversi,
> aberrantes et dispersi;
> quod hic negat, ille dicit;
> hic est victus, ille vicit
> doctor totum contradicit.)
> (Hugh Primas, poem 18, lines 58–63)

It is not surprising that this imagined master of dialectic "contradicts it all," for such is his discipline's stock in trade: dialectic teaches how to manage contradiction, how to argue with, out of, and into contradiction. A twelfth-century compiler described these activities thus: "as Aristotle says, dialectic is a disputation that makes a conclusion of contradiction from probabilities" (dialectica disputatio est, ut ait Aristoteles, collectiva contradictionis ex probabilibus).[3] Without dialectic, wrote Martianus Capella, "nothing follows, and likewise, nothing stands in opposition" (nil sequitur nilque repugnat item) (*De nuptiis* 4.327; tr. 106/150). As arguments cannot move forward without dialectic, dialectical arguments cannot move forward without contradiction.

Dialectic and the Road of Reason

We know medieval dialectic as that body of logical teachings and practices inherited in the West from Aristotle through Boethius.[4] Medieval definitions of the discipline repeatedly tell us three important things about it. One, it is a disambiguating discourse that helps its users negotiate opposition: it is, as a conventional medieval definition says, "capable in discerning true things from false" (vera a falsis discernendi potens).[5] Two, dialectic, while itself neither Wisdom nor Truth, is a means whereby wisdom and truths may be discovered. John of Salisbury tells us that, ideally, dialectic "serves as an interpreter of both words and meanings" (uocum et intellectuum interpres est) (*Met.* 2.3; tr. 78/64). A go-between, dialectic shuttles among and fixes the relations between word and meaning, truth and falsehood, humanity and wisdom. It is, in Alan of Lille's instrumental metaphors, like "a road, a gate, a key" that "points to, unlocks, opens the secrets of Sophia" (tamquam via, ianua, clavis, / ostendit, reserat, aperit secreta sophie).[6] Three, dialectic opens up the processes of reading and teaching, giving practitioners the means by which to think about the very processes of thought. Peter Abelard defends dialectic in ringing praise drawn from Augustine himself (*De ordine* 2.13.38), praise that makes dialectic not just a canon of nominal doctrines but the very model of active *doctrina*—how we teach and how we learn:

> The aforesaid doctor . . . dared to commend dialectic. He seems to profess that it alone is knowledge, since he says that dialectic alone can make human beings knowledgeable: "It is the discipline of disciplines," he says. "Dialectic teaches how to teach, and it teaches how to learn. In dialectic, reason itself demonstrates and reveals what it is, what it wants. Dialectic knows how to know. It alone not only wants to make people knowledgeable, but also has the power to do so."
>
> (Predictus doctor . . . dialecticam commendare ausus est, ut eam solam scientiam esse profiteri videatur, cum eam solam posse facere scientes dicat: "Disciplinam," inquit, "disciplinarum, quam dialecticam vocant. Hec docet docere, hec docet discere. In hac seipsa ratio demonstrat atque aperit que sit, quid velit; scit scire; sola scientes facere non solum vult, sed etiam potest.") (*Theologia "Scholarium"* 2.19; 415) [7]

For Augustine, as for his medieval students, dialectic is thus the very model of the master epistemo-pedagogic discourse. Boethius, in his commentary on Porphyry, imagines dialectic's origin in one of these very moments of metadisciplinary opening up. Dialectic was born, he says, when the opposition of contrary things led disputation to a dead end:

> When the ancients . . . produced false and mutually contrary conclusions in disputation, and it seemed impossible that both contrary conclusions regarding the same issue should be true (as reasoning, dissenting against itself, concluded), and it was ambiguous which of the contrary reasonings should be believed, it was decided that they should first of all consider the true and whole nature of disputation itself.
>
> (Cum igitur ueteres . . . falsa quaedam et sibimet contraria in disputatione colligerent atque id fieri impossibile uideretur, ut de eadem re contraria conclusione facta utraque essent uera que sibi dissentiens ratiocinatio conclusisset, cuique ratiocinationi credi opporteret, esset ambiguum, uisum est prius disputationis ipsius ueram atque integram considerare naturam.) (*In Isagogen Porphyrii* 1.2; 139)

For Boethius's anxious ancients, the way out of ambiguity lay in self-reflective and theoretical thought about the conditions of argument itself. From such thought arose the axiomatic conditions of argument: the law of contraries, which states that, given two contrary propositions ("Every pleasure is good" / "No pleasure is good"), if one is true, the other is false, but not vice versa; and the law of contradictories, which states that, given two contradictory propositions ("Every pleasure is good" / "Not every pleasure is good"), if one is true, the other is false, and vice versa.[8] With foundational first principles, and theoretical metadiscourse, then, a discipline was born. Boethius continues:

The nature of disputation being known, then it could be known whether what had been found by disputation had been truly understood. Hence, therefore, skill was established in the discipline of logic, which provides paths to understanding and mutually distinguishing among the manners of argument and kinds of reasoning, so that it can be known which reasoning is sometimes false and sometimes true, which is always false, and which never false.

(Qua cognita tum illud quoque quod per disputationem inueniretur, an uere comprehensum esset, posset intellegi. Hinc igitur profecta est logicae peritia disciplinae que disputandi modos atque ipsas ratiocinationes internoscendi uias parat, ut quae ratiocinatio nunc quidem falsa, nunc autem uera sit, quae uero semper falsa, quae numquam falsa, possit agnosci.) (ibid.)

From its very genesis, then, dialectic trades in opposition; all the more so when the discipline itself becomes a trade, as it did with the Sophists and, more to our point here, in the contentious schools of twelfth-century France.[9] This is the period of great intellectual conflicts over the articulation of word and thing, conflicts spawning those apparent philosophical opposites "Realism" and "Nominalism." This is a period, too, marked by spectacular quarrels between masters who teach and write not only for themselves but *against* each other. We are fortunate to have abundant contemporary witnesses to this conflicted secular world of teaching and reading.[10] In the next two chapters, we will consider these witnesses as readers and teachers—teachers of reading, too, and readers of teaching. These chapters study the oppositional teaching of dialectic from the accounts of two participants in and readers of contradiction in the city: John of Salisbury and his teacher Peter Abelard. Again, as in Chapter 1, we will be studying dialectic not for the fine points of its nominal doctrine, nor for what it helps us see about other texts, but rather for what it says about its discursive and epistemological action, especially with regard to its problematic relation with opposition.

Like exegesis, dialectic is born from opposition, born to work opposition in the service of truth. Like exegesis, too, dialectic entails, both in medieval theory and in medieval practice, a meta-meditation on the conditions of interpretation and textual teaching. Such similarities become pronounced as, over the course of the eleventh and twelfth centuries, dialectic, theology, and exegesis intertwine and cross-fertilize. Exegetes and theologians turn dialectical arguments loose on difficult scriptural problems, and dialecticians use scriptural examples to teach the intricacies of argument.[11]

Such disciplinary crossing and coincidence was far from smooth, of course, as the veritable flood of antidialectical writings from the cathedrals and the monasteries amply demonstrates.[12] Dialectic's claim to distinguish truth from falsehood, for one, is indeed problematic. Unlike that other disambiguating master discourse, the *aedificatio caritatis* of Augustinian exegesis, dialectic is theologically neutral and empty of content. Thus, whatever truth is distinguished in dialectic's operations seems often to stand just beyond the discipline's reach. Proof of the dialecticians' claim that the discipline teaches the difference between truth and falsehood is ever deferred, and dialectic's teaching ambiguates as often as it disambiguates. In exegesis, as we have seen, such discursive difficulties are not obstacles to but rather catalysts for textual teaching and the discovery of Truth. Secular dialectic's relation to such difficulties is rather more problematic, not least because, unlike exegesis, it ultimately has no access to onto-theological *res*. It remains word-bound, tangled, as the implacable Peter Damian said, "in the consequences of the exterior of words" (exteriorum verborum . . . consequentias) (*PL* 145: 603D).

This chapter examines the knots into which the teaching of dialectic entangled itself in the first half of the twelfth century, as described and performed in the *Metalogicon* (1159) of John of Salisbury. John knew the Parisian intellectual scene intimately, having studied with the greatest masters of the time (among them Peter Abelard, William of Conches, Thierry of Chartres, and Peter Helias);[13] he writes the *Metalogicon* as a moderate and moderating critique of the excesses of contemporary dialectical teaching and reading. If moderation is absent, John says, everything falls into contraries (*Met.* 2.8); his textual practice bears this out. He embodies excess in the logical incoherences with which he represents his opponents and into which he casts their teaching. These incoherences partake of both meanings of medieval *doctrina*—they are both nominal (*what* was taught) and active (*how* it was taught). Again and again, John makes opposing things proliferate, representing (and, as we shall see, *performing*) the impasse on which, he says, trivium studies were stuck in his day. He figures these impediments to truth in the shuttling movement between opposite extremes, and in their oxymoronic fusion. What is most interesting—and troubling, given the status of dialectic as master discourse—is that neither dialectic, which John praises as a disambiguator, nor John's own ostensibly disambiguating text will ever be far from an anchorless *either/or* teaching discourse around the true and the false.

The consequences of truth-seeking dialectic's entanglement in opposition on the one hand and in words on the other are significant. We shall see this pattern again and again in the literature of and around medieval logic, but also in fields as far removed from Aristotle and the syllogism as secular fiction and the arts of love. If, as the discipline's promoters so often remind us, dialectic is the master discourse not only for teaching and learning but also for knowledge itself, then the features that we see in representations of dialectical pedagogy can serve, *on medieval terms*, as models to help us better understand medieval clerical teaching-texts.

Contradiction in the City

> Cast down, O Lord, and divide their tongues: for I have seen
> iniquity and contradiction in the city.
>
> —Psalms 54.10

The *Metalogicon*'s preface makes clear that John imagines the world into and against which he directs his text as one riven with conflict and noisy with opposition. He wants the *Metalogicon* to be a moderate response to the calumnies of an opponent; he aims, he says, to defend logic from those who say it should not be studied, and he expects opposition in return for his efforts (*Met.*, Prologue; tr. 5/3). This expectation is reasonable, John says, for all behavior in his discursive world is subject to the skewed hermeneutic of the court, in which the truths of human actions are falsely read as their opposites:

In our day . . . the habit of obedience is branded as servility, and the absence of guilt is deemed an admission of impotence. A person who is quiet is accused of ignorance, one who is fluent is classed with the garrulous. A man whose manner is serious is suspected of dark designs, one of less gravity is charged with levity and incompetence. Anyone who makes an effort to be modest in word and action is adjudged to be a sycophant, who is courting popularity.

(Nunc autem . . . obsequendi mos nota abiectionis inuritur; innocentia impotentie esse uidetur professio. Taciturnus criminatur indoctus; facundus accedit ad garrulos. Vir grauis sedere dicitur in insidiis, minus grauis a leuitate culpatur ineptus. Qui modestiam sequitur sermonis et operis, censetur factiosus.) (*Met.*, Prologue; tr. 3–4/1)

The *Metalogicon*'s world upside down is one of systematic and oppositional disruptions of the relations between word and thing, word and action; its mistress, two-faced Fortune. Thus John's younger contemporary Walter Map: "if we apply to the court Boethius's true definition of fortune, we find it also correct in saying that the court is constant in its inconstancy" (si quod Boecius de fortuna veraciter asserit de curia dixerimus, recte quidem et hoc, ut sola sit mobilitate stabilis) (*De nugis* 1.1; 3–4).

Constant inconstancy: opposites paired and set in motion on Fortune's wheel. In another of his works from the late 1150s, John takes Fortune not as a pretext for spinning antinomies but as their very origin. In a striking turn of image, John imagines Fortune's activity as a disruption of signification, perception, and teaching. She is mistress of a countertrivium: her grammar pins false names on things, and her dialectic *substitutes* false for true instead of distinguishing them. Her teaching is so much the opposite of proper that John finds a striking word for it, one that will carry the weight of his critique of contemporary teaching. If Dialectic taught Boethius's testy ancients to reason their way out of impasse, this goddess does just the opposite:

The wheel of Fortune, like an empty illusion, *unteaches* the weak, whom she could have taught: she shows false appearances and makes small things seem large and, contrariwise, large things small; she puts adverse faces on things, and gives false names on a whim; she pretends false things are something and true things nothing, so as to block the path of reason.

> (Praestigio rota Fortunae conformis inani
>   *dedocet* infirmos, quos docuisse potest:
> ostentat falsas species, et parva videri
>   magna, vel e contra grandia parva facit;
> adversas rebus facies inducit, et illis
>   ponit ad arbitrium nomina falsa suum;
> res falsas aliquid, et res veras nihil esse
>   fingit, ut obcludat sic rationis iter.)
> (*Entheticus*, lines 255–62; emphasis added, my translation)

Fortune's antidialectic is no road to wisdom, then, but roadblock; her polarizing *de-doctrina* disrupts relations between *verba* and *res* and blocks reason's path, which path, John explains, proceeds from perception to naming of things and thence to the construction of propositions and their dialectical interpretation in terms of truth and falsehood (*Met.* 4.11–19). In an ordered world, John says, reason and its instrument, dialectic, mediate between word and understanding, adequating one to the other, and both to the capabilities of the audience. Disturbance of this adequation has the gravest of consequences in John's view. It drives cities to ruin, he says, and breaks down mediating human relations like linguistic and economic exchange (*Met.* 1.1). "Behold, all things were made new," he says of the intellectual changes he witnessed, sarcastically quoting the Apocalypse. "Grammar was made over; logic was remodelled; rhetoric was despised" (Ecce noua fiebant omnia; innouabatur gramatica, immutabatur dialectica, contemnebatur rethorica) (*Met.* 1.4; tr. 16/12). The twelfth-century "Renaissance," in this view from the Parisian trenches, is certainly a world of great intellectual excitement, but also a world defined and structured by error, excess, and contrary things.

"Without moderation, everything falls into contraries" (si autem moderatio desit, omnia hec in contrarium cedunt) (*Met.* 2.8; my translation/ 74). When moderation does not contemper human reading and teaching, then they fall precipitously into contraries, and opposition—along with its master discipline, dialectic—becomes an obstacle on the road of understanding. John of Salisbury tries to remove those obstacles, to correct and re-adequate dialectical teaching and reading in an intellectual world characterized by excess and contradiction.[14]

"The underlying theme of John's critique of twelfth-century education," writes Katherine Keats-Rohan, "will be a castigation and rejection of all forms of excess, or nimiety. . . . Nimiety subsumes that part of excess which is guilty of expending an excessive parvitude, or too little, of its attention on that which is important" ("John of Salisbury and Education," 4–5). Pedagogical and doctrinal errors born of excess indeed order the *Metalogicon*, but the resulting topography of error is not simply bipolar. "Too much" and "too little" are indeed opposites, but in John's practice they are not poles apart. While John is perfectly capable of using the logical laws of the contrary and the contradictory as stable anchors for his critique of contemporary philosophical extremism (*Met.* 4.33–34; tr. 253–57/201–4; *Pol.* 2.29; tr. 150/1: 168), he is not disturbed to find incoherences proliferating, "since I am aware that the effects of contraries are generally the same" (cum sciam contrariorum plerumque esse eundem effectum) (*Pol.* 2.29; tr. 151/1: 168). The identical effect of contraries in practice at once partakes of error's movement between opposites and arrests it in in-difference. This paradoxical stasis-in-movement is apparent both in the activities of John's unteachers and in that of his texts that represent and critique them.

Teaching

The intellectual history of the twelfth century has something of the excessive about it that piques the curiosity.

—Bruno Roy and Hugues Shooner,
"Querelles de maîtres au XIIe siècle"

John identifies his principal opponent in the *Metalogicon* as one Cornificius, adding that, for reasons of professional and Christian respect, he is hiding the man's real name under a pseudonym.[15] Specific information about the doctrines of Cornificius and his followers emerges haltingly in the *Metalogicon*; not until chapter 6 does John present a refutation of Cornifician doctrine, and even that explanation does not cover all the errors against which the *Metalogicon* inveighs. Until that point—and, characteristically, throughout the text—John seems more interested in active than in nominal doctrine: the "how" of teaching takes precedence over the "what." The *Metalogicon*, that is to say, conducts much of its attack on Cornifician doctrine through stories of Cornifician teaching.

The oppositional patterning of John's own text is immediately clear, for Cornificius, John's agent of contradiction, is nothing of the kind in his own pedagogical practice. Quite the contrary, in fact:

He himself learned from his own teachers what he is today passing on to his pupils. He is ladling out the very same kind of instruction that he himself received. He will make his disciples his equals in philosophy. What more could they wish? Will they not thus, in accordance with the saying, be perfect? Do we not read in the Gospel: "Every disciple who becomes like his master is perfect"?

(Nam et ipse accepit a doctoribus quod nunc discipulis tradit, eosque sic instituit, sicut et ipse institutus est. Discipulos ergo in philosophia sibi faciet coequales. Quid multa? Nonne sic perfecti erunt, iuxta illud Euangelii: Discipulus omnis perfectus est, si sit sicut magister eius?) (*Met.* 1.3; tr. 14/10)

John here represents Cornifician pedagogy as exaggerated continuity from teacher to student.[16] This mass production of little Cornificians, according to John, has the paradoxical aim of reducing the master's inexperience by broadcasting it: "barring no means in his effort to console himself for his own want of knowledge, he has contrived to improve his reputation by making many others ignoramuses like himself" (conquirens undique imperitie sue solatia, sibi proficere sperat ad gloriam, si multos similes sui, id est, si eos uiderit imperitos) (*Met.* 1.1; tr. 9/5). Cornificius simply repeats the teachings of his masters and makes his students over in his own image.

At this point, Cornificius seems an emblem for pedagogical and intellectual continuity in its immoderate extreme. His students, however, will reveal the extreme instability of such imitation:

Everyone enshrined his own and his master's inventions. Yet even this situation could not abide. Students were soon swept along in the current, and, like their fellows in error, came to spurn what they had learned from their teachers, and to form new sects of their own.

(Suis enim aut magistri sui quisque incumbebat inuentis. Nec hoc tamen diu licitum, cum ipsi auditores in breui coerrantium impetu urgerentur, ut et ipsi, spretis his que a doctoribus suis audierant, cuderent et conderent nouas sectas.) (*Met.* 1.3; tr. 15/11)

The immoderate intellectual stasis of Cornificius's autoreproduction has produced its own opposites: rupture with the singular teacher, formation of multiple and conflicting sects.

The paired opposites of repetition and rupture underlie and inform John's discussions of pedagogical and hermeneutic error in the *Metalogicon*; he will often swing from one to the other without seeming concerned or even aware that doing so reduces the referential coherence of his account. Take, for example, his portrait of the "pure philosophers" in *Metalogicon* 2.7. Like Cornificius, an old man with a boy's powers of understanding (*Met.* 1.5; tr. 22/17), these aging scholars "remain preoccupied with the concerns of boyhood" (fiunt itaque in puerilibus Achademici senes) (*Met.* 2.7; tr. 88/72), devoting their entire lives to logic and logic alone. Their exclusive pursuit of logic is as extreme as Cornificius's, and it has similarly extreme results. "Either unfamiliar with or contemptuous of the views of the ancient authorities," these eternal children "relieve their embarrassment by proposing new errors" (nescientes quid loquantur aut de quibus asserant, errores condunt nouos, et antiquorum aut nesciunt aut dedignantur sententias imitari) (tr. 89/73). In his very next sentence, however, John changes tack and attributes to these know-nothing rebels the opposite vice of overinformed conservatism: "They make compilations of what everybody has ever thought on the subject. Lacking judgement, they copy and quote all that has ever been said or written, even by the most obscure" (Compilant omnium opiniones, et ea que etiam a uilissimis dicta uel scripta sunt, ab inopia iudicii scribunt et referunt) (tr. 89/73). The *either/or* extremism of this procedure is clear in *Met.* 1.24: "To study everything that everyone, no matter how insignificant, has ever said, is either to be excessively humble and cautious, or overly vain and ostentatious" (siquidem persequi quid quis unquam uel contemptissimorum hominum dixerit, aut nimie miserie, aut inanis iactantie est) (tr. 70/56–57). The opposing attributes of rubber-stamp replication and violent rupture exist side by side and simultaneously in the same subjects, an incoherence figured in their preferred philosophical genre, the sentence collection, which, in spite of its constant movement from opinion to opposition, goes precisely nowhere (*Met.* 2.7; tr. 89/73).

Contemporary intellectual life as represented in the *Metalogicon* thus shuttles between the opposing extremes of total rupture and repetitive continuity, often and impossibly incarnating both in the same subjects. One way to arrest this shuttling would be to anchor the opposing teaching-acts in their context and compare their respective referential truth-values. However good its Aristotelian precedent, such an effort would be in vain in the *Metalogicon*, for John's consistent preference for teaching process over content taught—for active over nominal *doctrina*—does not give would-be interpreters the information necessary for such a resolution.

The case of the brilliant but excessively questioning teacher Alberic of Rheims is instructive here. Both Alberic and his opposite, the wily Robert of Melun, who was ever ready with multiple answers to every question, are criticized by John for taking too much delight in their own inventions (2.10; tr. 96/79). Alberic's extremism, to John's mind, leads the logician directly into self-contradiction: "One of them (Alberic) departed for Bologna, where he 'unlearned' what he had formerly taught; and subsequently, on returning, 'untaught' it. Whether he then taught it better, let them judge who heard his lectures both before his departure and after his return" (Unus eorum, profectus Bononiam, dedidicit quod docuerat; siquidem et reuersus dedocuit. An melius, iudicent qui eum ante et postea audierunt) (tr. 97/79). Only one who had heard the lectures could tell the difference between them, John says; we cannot distinguish between these paired scenes of teaching, then, for John tells us nothing about them.[17] Presented like this, as contradictory pedagogical performances empty of doctrinal content, Alberic's reversal can be read only as an indicator of excess. Teaching and unteaching, like repetition and rupture, may be opposites, but in the *Metalogicon*'s practice, they come inevitably and repeatedly down to the same thing. We shall see the same (con)fusion of opposites in John's representations of the hermeneutic errors of his opponents.

Reading

The oppositional extremes of "Cornifician" *(de)doctrina*, which we have already seen displayed in teaching methods, also appear in ways of reading. Cornificius, it seems, learned to read under a hypostatized and over-literal application of Pauline hermeneutics to the liberal arts. "What he now teaches," John says, suppressing once again exactly what the nominal content of that *doctrina* was, "Cornificius learned at a time when there was no 'letter' in liberal studies, and everyone sought the 'spirit,' which, so they tell us, lies hidden in the letter" (ista Cornificius didicit . . . quando in liberalibus disciplinis littera nichil erat et ubique spiritus querebatur, qui (ut aiunt) latet in littera) (*Met.* 1.3; tr. 14/10). This Cornificius would undoubtedly agree with the philosopher in John's *Policraticus* who teaches that "the written word is useless and you must not worry about what it has to say," warning his student to "avoid it as dangerous, for the letter killeth" (littera inutilis est, nec curandum est quid loquatur. Si instas, moneberis fugere quoniam perniciosa est et occidit) (*Pol.* 7.12; tr. 258/2: 138).

However, those same teachers who taught Cornificius to reject the letter did precisely the opposite in their own interpretive practice. While the letter of the target text was "useless," the theoretical letter of commentary—its metalanguage—was master of all:

At that time this was considered the proper way to teach everything. . . . Speech in which the words "consistent" and "inconsistent," "argument" and "reason" did not resound, with negative particles multiplied and transposed through assertions of existence and non-existence, was entirely unacceptable. So true was this that one had to bring along a counter whenever he went to a disputation, if he was to keep apprized of the force of affirmation or negation.

(In hunc modum docere omnia, studium illius etatis erat. . . . Inconueniens prorsus erat oratio, in qua hec uerba, "conueniens" et "inconueniens," "argumentum" et "ratio" non perstrepebant, multiplicatis particulis negatiuis, et traiectis per "esse" et "non esse," ita ut calculo opus esset, quotiens fuerat disputandum; alioquin uis affirmationis et negationis erat incognita.) (*Met.* 1.3; tr. 14–15/10–11)

Thus to privilege letter over sense makes it nearly impossible to sift out meaning from the accumulated contradictions of disputation. Using counters to record the argumentative give and take does not so much enable disambiguation as reveal its impossibility. Keeping tally of *sics* and *nons* that may or may not cancel each other out leads the hapless student-scribe into that aporetic place from which Boethius's imaginary disputants invented dialectic as a means of escape.

For generally a double negative is equivalent to affirmation, whereas the force of a negation is increased if it is repeated an uneven number of times. At the same time, a negation repeated over and over usually loses its effect, and becomes equivalent to a contradiction, as we find stated in the rules.

(Nam plerumque uim affirmationis habet geminata negatio; itemque uis negatoria ab impari numero conualescit; siquidem negatio iterata plerumque seipsam perimit, et contradictioni, sicut regulariter proditum est, coequatur.) (*Met.* 1.3; tr. 15/11)

These are unteachers, then, not only because what they teach and how they teach it leads ultimately to contradiction, but also because their teaching upsets the balance between letter and meaning, reader and read, that we have seen to be so important, yet so delicate, in that other hermeneutical discipline, exegesis. John's unteachers ignore the letter of their target text, while fetishizing the letter of their own. John thus imagines the logical "renaissance" as a monstrous flowering, not of the language arts but of their metalanguage. Such metalinguistic nominalism makes the existence of a thing entirely conditional upon language:

Not even an argument was admitted unless it was prefaced by its name. . . . They would probably teach that a poet cannot write poetry unless he at the same time names the verse he is using; and that the carpenter cannot make a bench unless he is simultaneously forming on his lips the word "bench" or "wooden seat."

(Nec argumentum fieri licitum, nisi premisso nomine argumenti. . . . Docebunt hi forte quod poeta uersifice nichil dicet, nisi connominet uersum, quod faber lignarius scannum facere nequeat, nisi scannum aut lignum uoluat in ore.) (*Met.* 1.3; tr. 16/12)

According to John's account, both speech acts and physical acts are thus absorbed into metalanguage, the only practice being the practice of theory. These are the philosophers who, in the *Policraticus*, think wisdom is a matter of words, not *res*.[18]

As John was studying in Paris, the schools at Chartres and Saint Victor were beginning to use an oppositional distinction between theory and practice to systematize textual interpretation and the arts in general. Both Hugh of Saint Victor's restructuring of human knowledge and Thierry of Chartres's construction of the *accessus ad artem* depend upon this distinction. "Treating of an art—that is, writing about grammar—and acting through an art—that is, writing grammatically—are two different things," says Hugh; "distinguish between them" (Duo sunt, agere de arte et agere per artem; verbi gratia, agere de arte, ut est agere de gramatica, agere per artem, ut est agere gramatice. Distingue hec duo) (*Did.* 3.5; my translation/56).[19]

Rather than separating discourse *de arte* and *per artem*, the hermeneutic of the *Metalogicon*'s erring masters conflates them, disrupting the proper relation of reader and text. By failing to balance the competing demands of letter and sense, John says, these masters would reduce the foundational opposition of medieval hermeneutics to confusion and incoherence. This, I think, is what John means when he concludes that, for these logicians, "to act with reference to an art and according to the art were the same" (ex arte et de arte agere idem erat) (*Met.* 1.3; tr. 16/12). The metalinguistic absorption of *de/ex arte* distinction effects an impossible fusion of opposites. As a consequence, the interpretive act is no smooth negotiation between practice and theory, *littera* and *sensus*, but rather an interminable shuttling between extreme emphasis on one to extreme emphasis on the other. It privileges, as Cornificius was taught, the sense over the letter, or, as he practiced, the letter over the sense.

We have seen the latter error manifest itself in a theoretical metalanguage so overgrown that interpreters must call on counters to extract what is said from how it is said. Other teachers, similarly stressing the letter, end up at the opposite extreme: not abundant letter and impossible sense now, but a single letter filled with more *sensus* than it can hold. While their companions in error generate free-standing (and incomprehensible) discourse *de arte*, these scholars err *ex arte*, reading too much into their source:

First, they load "insupportable burdens" on the shoulders of their students. Second, they pay no attention to proper order in teaching, and diligently take care lest "all things be suitably arranged, each in its own place." Thus they, so to speak, read the whole art into its title. . . . Finally, they go against the mind of the author, and comb, as it were, in the opposite direction.

(Primum quod onera importabilia teneris auditorum humeris imponunt. Deinde quod, docendi ordine pretermisso, diligentissime cauent ne "singula queque locum teneant sortita decenter"; finem enim artis, ut sic dixerim, legunt in titulo. . . . Postremo quod, quasi ab aduerso pectentes, ueniunt contra mentem auctoris.) (*Met.* 2.19; tr. 117–18/97)

We have seen that such overreading, while admittedly dangerous in exegesis, is, however, not only redeemable but practically obligatory in that discipline. John agrees:

I would perhaps concede that the Holy Scriptures, whose every title is filled with holy signs, should be read with such solemnity for the reason that the treasure of the Holy Ghost by whose hand they have been written cannot entirely be plumbed.

(Diuinae paginae libros, quorum singuli apices diuinis pleni sunt sacramentis, tanta grauitate legendos forte concesserim, eo quod thesaurus Spiritus sancti, cuius digito scripti sunt, omnino nequeat exhauriri.) (*Pol.* 7.12; tr. 264/2: 144)

However, he denies such holy overreading to the teacher of secular letters:

In liberal studies where *not things but words merely have meaning*, he who is not content with the first meaning of the letter seems to me to lose himself, or to be desirous of leading his auditors away from an understanding of truth.

(In liberalibus disciplinis, ubi *non res sed dumtaxat uerba significant*, quibus primo sensu litterae contentus non est, aberrare uidetur michi ab intelligentia ueritatis . . . se uelle suos abducere auditores.) (*Pol.* 7.12; tr. 264/2: 144–45; emphasis added)

To teach in such a way is to fall into contraries:

Those who read everything into this little book [i.e., Aristotle's *Categories*] and refuse to allow it to rest content with its own brevity, evidently "unteach" rather than instruct. Such teachers, who would sooner ignore than admit the truth, cram into their commentary on this book every possible sort of discussion.

(Sed plane magis dedocent quam erudiunt qui in hoc libello legunt uniuersa et eum breuitate sua contentum esse non sinunt. Quicquid alicubi dici potest, hic congerunt quibus grauior esse uidetur confessio quam ignorantia ueri.) (*Met.* 3.3; tr. 164/134)

Indulgence in overreading thus not only is pedagogically counterproductive but also produces the very counter of teaching itself—unteaching.

A Middle Term

> The fruit of the lecture on the authors is proportionate both to the capacity of the students and to the industrious diligence of the teacher.
>
> —John of Salisbury, *Metalogicon*

Our discussion so far has focused almost exclusively on John of Salisbury's ways of understanding and representing pedagogical and hermeneutical error. Since the *Metalogicon* aims not only to represent error but also to reeducate the erring, we must now consider the solutions that John proposes for the incoherent oppositions that he has described—and performed. Like the well-trained reader that he is, John is equipped to deal with the conflict of oppositions, as he perhaps learned from William of Champeaux, who taught, says John, that "when inherent agreement is doubted, it is necessary to search for some middle term whereby extremes may be copulated" (cum enim de inherentia dubitatur, necessarium est aliquod inquiri medium, cuius interuentu copulentur extrema) (*Met.* 3.9; tr. 187/152). One might argue that there is no need to copulate extremes in the *Metalogicon*, since they seem quite ready to do so of their own accord. But an orderly mating, like the one celebrated between Mercury and Philology in Martianus Capella's philosophical romance, would put a stop to the continual shuttling between one extreme and the other, or to their oxymoronic fusion, removing an obstacle from John's path of reason.

The most orderly of the *Metalogicon*'s teachers is certainly Bernard of Chartres, whose moderation John offers as a corrective to the extremism of his contemporaries. The unstable oppositions characterizing the Cornifician relation to teachers (repetition/rupture) and to reading (letter/sense, *de arte/ex arte*) are here harmoniously resolved in the mediating figure of Bernard, John's model of moderate innovation in pedagogy and hermeneutics:[20]

Bernard of Chartres used to compare us to dwarves perched on the shoulders of giants. He pointed out that we see more and farther than our predecessors, not because we have keener vision or greater height, but because we are lifted up and borne aloft by their gigantic stature.

(Dicebat Bernardus Carnotensis nos esse quasi nanos gigantium humeris insidentes, ut possimus plura eis et remotiora uidere, non utique proprii uisus acumine aut eminentia corporis, sed quia in altum subuehimur et extollimur magnitudine gigantea.) (*Met.* 3.4; tr. 167/136)[21]

Bernard imagines intellectual modernity as neither violent rupture nor specular repetition; for him, the opposites of giant and dwarf are a sort of mutually supplementing compound—text and gloss, perhaps. Bernard's teaching, as John presents it, leads students to become *both* giant *and* dwarf, first incorporating the ancient texts, and then remaking that incorporated authority into a new composition of their own. Pedagogical time is a smooth continuity; time and teaching are understood through each other, in fact, in a mutual metaphor of moderate innovation. As "each succeeding day thus became the disciple of its predecessor" (precedentis discipulus sequens dies) (*Met.* 1.24; tr. 68/55), the student became a disciple of the ancients, linked to the unbroken chain of writers from Rome forward: "he who had imitated his predecessors would come to be deserving of imitation by his successors" (qui maiores imitabatur, fieret posteris imitandus) (tr. 69/59).

John's ideal pedagogical hermeneutic is formed on this very model. The exemplary teachers here are first Quintilian and then, among the moderns, Bernard. Proper reading, for John, should "shake out" its texts, sorting the "feathers which (crow fashion), they have borrowed from the several branches of learning" (auctores excutiat, et . . . eos plumis spoliet, quas (ad modum cornicule) ex uariis disciplinis . . . suis operibus indiderunt) (*Met.* 1.24; tr. 66/54). Such *ex arte* reading is itself a sort of master discipline; read this way, a single text "would seem to image all the arts" (omnium artium quodammodo videretur imago) (tr. 67/54). This stress on pedagogy *ex arte* would connect Bernard to the metonymic overreaders we have just been examining but for one significant difference: Bernard's teaching is adequated to the context in which it is deployed—by the syntax, as it were, of the pedagogical discourse that he shares with his students:

He would explain grammatical figures, rhetorical embellishment, and sophistical quibbling, as well as the relation of given passages to other studies. He would do so, however, without trying to teach everything at one time. On the contrary, he would dispense his instruction to his hearers gradually, in a manner commensurate with their powers of assimilation.

(Figuras gramatice, colores rethoricos, cavillationes sophismatum, et qua parte sui proposite lectionis articulus respiciebat ad alias disciplinas, proponebat in medio; ita tamen ut non in singulis universa doceret, sed pro capacitate audientium dispensaret eis in tempore doctrine mensuram.) (*Met.* 1.24; tr. 67/55)

Bernard's teaching method, then, mediates and adequates. It stands between the extremes that, John says, will inevitably make everything fall into contraries (*Met.* 2.8). Bernard is the only one of the *Metalogicon's* teachers who can do this. Even John, for all his ambitions to make a moderate correction of pedagogical and hermeneutic error, finds himself not quite equal to the effort of reteaching the unteachers.

Modal Truth

> To contemper words with things and things with the times and to
> censure widely intruding fallacies is not a matter of a few days nor an
> easy task.
>
> —John of Salisbury, *Policraticus*

John's critique of pedagogico-hermeneutic error has focused on the oppositions that engulf all things when dialectical, pedagogical, and hermeneutic acts are inadequately grounded in their contexts. Without such moderating context, "everything falls into contraries" (*Met.* 2.8; 74), and John's
dialectic is hard put to extricate itself from contradiction enough to do its
proper job of mediation and discrimination between truth and falsehood.
How exactly is such discrimination to be made? Given John's oft-repeated
preference for probable logic, which shies away from demonstration of in-
controvertible truth, this question is a pressing one.[22]

John certainly knows that reference is the ultimate test of a statement's
truth; logic, then, considers not only the statement itself but the discourse
in which it is deployed and the thing to which it refers (*Met.* 4.33; tr.
254/201). The truth-effect of opinions, terms, and propositions depends
upon their mode of signification and interpretation:

The truth or falsity of both opinions and things accordingly depends on, and
is judged by, our mode of perception (namely, the way in which our opinions
perceive, or in which things are perceived); while the truth or falsity of speech
depends on, and is judged by its mode of signifying.

(Ergo a modo percipiendi (scilicet quo percipiuntur aut percipiunt) conuincitur
ueritas aut falsitas tam opinionum quam rerum; sermonum uero a modo signifi-
candi.) (*Met.* 4.37; tr. 262/208)

In view of this, some philosophers have held, with probability, that the truth
because of which an opinion or speech is called true, is, as it were, an inter-
relationship of things that are examined extrinsic to reason. If reason is solidly
based on these realities in its investigations, it does not flounder in error.

(Unde nonnullis philosophorum probabiliter placuit ueritatem, unde opinio uera
dicitur aut sermo uerus, quasi medium quendam habitum esse rerum que exami-
nantur extrinsecus ad rationem.) (*Met.* 4.33; tr. 254/201)

Here, probable truth itself is seen as a sort of middle term between *res* and
ratio. It is modal, dependent on the manner of signification, perception,
and examination.[23]

This emphasis on mode in the dialectical judgment of truth and false-hood is consistent with the *Metalogicon*'s persistent interest in active over nominal doctrine, yet at critical points the two are in fact at odds. In the first chapter of *Metalogicon* 3, John declares that the letter of the text should not be "tortured on the rack, like a helpless prisoner, until it renders what it never received" (non more captiuorum acerbe torquenda, donec restituat quod non accepit) (tr. 148/121). In contrast to such letter-torturing overreading, John says, adequate teaching and reading are rooted in a context, whether woven by the *littera* or produced by reference to a *res* outside it:

A trustworthy and a prudent reader will respect as inviolable the evident literal meaning of what is written, until he obtains a fuller and surer grasp of the truth by further reading or by divine revelation. . . . A good teacher dispenses his instruction in a way that is suited to the time and adapted to his students.

(Quicquid autem littere facies indicat, lector fidelis et prudens interim ueneretur ut sacrosanctum, donec ei alia docente aut Domino reuelante ueritas plenius et familiarius innotescat. . . . Siquidem recte docentis officium pro ratione temporis et persone quod cuique nouerit expedire dispensat.) (*Met.* 3.1; tr. 148/122)

As if to remind us of the alternative, John sandwiches between these two idealized moments of *lectio* a negative example of contemporary un-teaching—completely decontextualized and immoderately, aporetically uninterpretable: "As it is, what one claims to teach with faithfulness and utility, another claims to unteach with equal faithfulness and utility" (Quod enim unus fideliter et utiliter docet, alter eque fideliter et utiliter dedocet) (*Met.* 3.1; tr. 148/122). As he did before with the auto-unteaching of Alberic of Rheims, John casts his opponents into contradiction and makes his readers unable to evaluate the truth content of these empty and perfectly contradictory pedagogical acts. Relying on intention, as John elsewhere suggests as a means of resolving contrary scriptural teachings,[24] is of no help, for these masters teach with equally faithful intentions; effectiveness is no measure either, for they teach with equal utility. As Alberic untaught himself, these teachers unteach each other, and the reader, deprived of the context that knowledge of their material would provide, can go no further. We cannot evaluate their truth; we are blocked—we stand at the crossroads of a true Aristotelian *aporia*, an "instance of two contrary and equally reasonable opinions" (Lalande, s.v. *aporia*).

The dedoctrinal impasse that results here is of course John's ironic, perhaps even sophistical, doing: what better way to represent erroneous methods than, through their performance, to show how truth cannot be recovered from them? However, there are places in the text where John himself stumbles over the same obstacle. Such difficulties are apparent even as John attempts to anchor his critique of error in an adequate definition of truth. First, he roots the word in its etymology; then, as he does throughout the *Metalogicon*, he further defines the term by contrast with its contraries, *falsitas* and *vanitas* (*Met.* 4.34; tr. 257/203). The next sentences, while meant to defend the fine points of his opposition, slide vertiginously, first into propositional logic and then into ontology:

By the law of contraries, what is true is opposed both to what is empty and to what is false, since the last two are the same. In my estimation, the fact that something that exists is opposed to something that is non-existent does not jeopardize this principle. Such evidently happens in propositions that are opposed in a contradictory manner. For Aristotle teaches that one must always be, while the other must, of necessity, not be.

(Ergo uerum uano falsoque, quoniam idem sunt, lege contrarietatis opponitur. Nec moueor si res existens rei non existenti opponatur; cum hoc palam sit in enuntiabilibus que contradictorie opponuntur. Nam Aristotiles docet alterum eorum esse semper, et alterum ex necessitate non esse.) (*Met.* 4.34; tr. 257/204)

John's gloss of the *lex contrarietatis* takes the discussion in an altogether unexpected direction. First he turns the statement into a question: "Cannot the existence of one thing denote the non-existence of another?" Then he adds an example from life: "A ruddy sky may bespeak calm and undisturbed weather, as well as a tempest, in accordance with the saying: 'A blushing sky at dawn forebodes a storm, / But at set of sun promises smooth sailing'" (Nonne res existens rei non existentis est signum, ut rubor future serenitatis aut tempestatis? Siquidem "mane rubens celum notat imbres, sero serenum") (ibid.).

John thus proves that the existence of one thing (a red sky at night) does indeed signify the nonexistence of another (a storm), but the example proves much more than that. The sign that should get us out of the ontological pickle has gotten us smack into another, semiotic one, for the red sky signifies, at different times of day, the opposite states of tempest and calm. Without knowing at which time this sign occurs, we are left with two simultaneous and opposing meanings; the signification is at once perfectly adequate and perfectly ambiguous. Between the extremes of bad and good weather lies the third term of the ambiguous natural sign. The solid oppositions of truth and falsehood, good and bad weather coincide in uneasy, even incoherent, multiplicity.[25]

Collectiva Contradictionis

MASTER: Dialectic is the discipline of rational inquiry, definition,
and discourse; it is capable of discerning true things from
false.

STUDENT: Why is it called dialectic?

MASTER: It is called dialectic, because in it we dispute about words.

—Alcuin, *De dialectica*

As when one sifteth with a sieve, the dust will remain, so will the
perplexity of a man in his thought.

—Ecclesiastes 27.5

The ambiguity of John's red-sky sign might make us think for a moment of the ambiguity and multiplicity of Scripture, but the relation between the book of the world and John's book of logic is nowhere near as harmonious, nor as adequate, as that between the Creation and Scripture. John is, after all, looking to define truth, in however limited a way. The abrupt misting into ambiguity of that definition, built as it is upon the Aristotelian *lex contrarietatis*, in which we reason not *both-and* but *either/or*, reduces John's argument to something perilously close to incoherence. Even as he reduced the arguments of his opponents, making them walking contradictions, impossibly oxymoronic fusions of opposing positions, so too his own argument at the most crucial of moments. This shuttling coimplication of opposites throughout the *Metalogicon* is furthered by the fact that the moderate middle term, for all John's praise of it, is in fact hard to come by in his textual practice, where it is often smothered in a congeries of opposing arguments, inaccessible for reasons of personal incapacity, veiled in ambiguity, or outright contradicted.[26]

The moderate unteacher of dialectical error thus stands on uneasy ground, for his own dialectical gestures of correction perform the dialectical movement he describes. This performance becomes explicit as John concludes, in *Metalogicon* 2.17, a review of the multiple, letter-torturing solutions to the problem of universals. Multiplicity of *doctrina* here is no divine gift, as Hugh of St. Victor said it was for Scripture. These masters and their teachings are not only diverse but adverse as well:

The saying of the comic poet that "There are as many opinions as heads," has almost come to hold true. Rarely, if ever, do we find a teacher who is content to follow in the footsteps of his master. Each, to make a name for himself, coins his own special error. Wherewith, while promising to correct his master, he sets himself up as a target for correction and condemnation by his own disciples as well as posterity.

(Vt uerbo comici utar, fere quot homines, tot sententie. Nam de magistris aut nullus aut rarus est qui doctoris sui uelit inherere uestigiis. Ut sibi faciat nomen, quisque proprium cudit errorem; sicque fit, ut, dum se doctorem corrigere promittit, seipsum corrigendum aut reprehendendum tam discipulis quam posteris prebeat.) (*Met.* 2.18; tr. 116–17/96)

Here masters from Abelard to Gilbert of Poitiers and Bernard of Chartres (who taught or influenced John) are all packed into the same boat as Cornificius and his followers, who "came to spurn what they learned from their teachers, and to form new sects of their own" (spretis his que a doctoribus suis audierant, cuderent et conderent nouas sectas) (*Met.* 1.3; tr. 15/11). John, too, rides in this ship of fools, as he immediately makes clear: "I recognize that the same rule threatens to apply to me. By disagreeing with others and committing my dissent to writing, I am, in fact, laying myself open to be criticized by many" (Ego ipse michi legem hanc non ambigo imminere, ut, dum ab aliis dissentio et dissensum scripto profiteor, me obicio reprehensionibus plurimorum) (*Met.* 2.18; tr. 117/96). Like his own teachers, who "themselves became temporarily insane while combating insanity," John has at crucial points "floundered in error while trying to combat it" (insipientes itaque facti sunt, dum insipientie resistebant, et erronei diutius habiti, dum obuiare nitebantur errori) (*Met.* 1.5; tr. 22/17).

John's English translator John Dickinson noticed this about the writer's works: "The point is that (John) draws no clear line. Every important idea is deeply tinged with what we conceive to be its opposite." Dickinson's explanation for this mutual "tingeing" of opposites is simple: "Early thought, Maitland has said, is confused thought. . . . The significance of the *Policraticus* for students of the political ideas of after times consists precisely in the fact that it discloses the more or less confused mass of contradictory ideas in which they were originally embedded."[27] Such teleological tale-telling does little to help us understand the intellectual texture of John's writing and that of other intellectuals of the central Middle Ages. John's repeated falls into contrariety are not due to anything so simple as dullness or a primitive mind. They are rather textual and argumentative manifestations of the ways in which John and writers like him constructed the activity of their master discourse, dialectic, particularly in regard to its relation to contradiction.

In exegesis, contradiction preexists the hermeneutic movement—it is always already in Scripture, a source of interpretive pleasure, a concession to our multiple and multiply fallen understanding, a source of sacramentally plural meaning, multiple yet ever singular at the same time. Exegetes work Scripture under the guarantee that its ultimate referent is an extra- (even supra-) linguistic *res* which admits no contradiction, and that the *doctrina* found in Scripture is multiply and mysteriously adequated to the understanding of each human reader. Dialectic, however, works contradiction with less onto-theological security, for properly dialectical contradictions are produced in and by the dialectical process. Fundamentally, dialectic's contradictions are of its own making, as John of Salisbury observes: "Dialectic resolves questions relative to itself. Thus it supplies answers to such questions as: 'Is affirmation also enunciation?' and 'Can two contradictory propositions be simultaneously true?'" (Propositas enim de se expedit questiones . . . quale est: An affirmare sit enuntiare, et: An simul extare possit contradictio) (*Met.* 2.11; tr. 100/83).[28]

While John attacks the pursuit of dialectic by itself and for itself, he also makes clear that such pursuit is a logical, if extreme, response to the discipline's own self-referential nature. Quoting Augustine's famous definition (*De ordine* 2.13.38), John adds that this self-reference grows from the discipline's very origin:

After the work of completing grammar and organizing it had been accomplished, reason was led to investigate and scrutinize the very power whereby it had begotten this art. . . . Was it not fitting, then, that before reason should proceed to the construction of additional arts and sciences, it should first distinguish, observe, and classify its own processes and instruments, and thus bring to light that discipline of disciplines called dialectic?

(Cum perfecta esset dispositaque gramatica, admonita est ratio querere atque attendere hanc ipsam uim que peperit artem. . . . Quando ergo transiret ad alia fabricanda, nisi ipsa sua prius quasi quedam machinamenta et instrumenta distringeret, notaret, digereret, proderetque ipsam disciplinam disciplinarum, quam dialecticam uocat?) (*Met.* 4.25; tr. 241–42/192)

John's logicians further replicate this solipsism in their own research, in which dialectic "remains forever engrossed in itself, walking 'round about and forever surveying itself, ransacking its own depths and secrets" (in se rotetur, se circumeat, sua rimetur archana) (*Met.* 2.9; tr. 94/76). Dialectic is thus a double discipline, whose object of study is at once a canon of texts and "doctrines" and reason(ing) itself. It is thus not just nominal but active doctrine; not just a body of knowledge but the very process of knowledge itself. It does not teach—or offer access to—*things*. Rather, it

teaches the activities of the mind—teaching, thinking, knowing. It teaches
not the contents of Reason's head, so to speak, but the theory of Reason:
Reason's way of seeing, Reason's process. Dialectic is thus as much about
itself as it is "a road, a gate, a key" to anything else.

Dialectic being conceived as the road to understanding and wisdom,
oppositions can work toward this end when mustered into dialectical arguments. This is not as often the case as John of Salisbury would have
it be, even in his own moderate and moderating arguments. Things go
right dialectically, John says, only when dialectic is adequated to its purpose, its audience, and the syntax of argument—to borrow John's phrase,
when language users "contemper words with things and things with the
times" (uerba rebus, res temporibus contemperare) (*Pol.* 7.12; my transla-
tion/2: 140).

Now, such adequation always already and by definition obtains between Scripture and its human students; it is the condition upon which
the disambiguating multiplicity of the *aedificatio caritatis* rests. In dialectic, however, such adequation is hard to come by because, unlike exegesis,
dialectic trades in words, not things, and the two cannot be contempered
by dialectic alone. Says John in the *Policraticus*:

I would perhaps concede that the Holy Scriptures, whose every title is filled with
holy signs, should be read with such solemnity for the reason that the treasure
of the Holy Ghost, by whose hand they have been written, cannot entirely be
plumbed. For although on the face of it the written word lends itself to one meaning only, manifold mysteries lie hidden within, and from the same source allegory
often edifies faith and character in various ways.

(Diuinae paginae libros, quorum singuli apices diuinis pleni sunt sacramentis,
tanta grauitate legendos forte concesserim, eo quod thesaurus Spiritus sancti,
cuius digito scripti sunt, omnino nequeat exhauriri. Licet enim ad unum tantum-
modo sensum accomodata sit superficies litterae, multiplicitas misteriorum in-
trinsecus latet et ab eadem re saepe allegoria fidem, tropologia mores uariis modis
edificet.) (*Pol.* 7.12; tr. 264/2: 144)

"But," he continues,

in liberal studies where not things but words merely have meaning, he who is not
content with the first meaning of the letter seems to me to lose himself, or to be
desirous of leading his auditors away from an understanding of truth.

(In liberalibus disciplinis, ubi non res sed dumtaxat uerba significant, quisquis
primo sensu litterae contentus non est, aberrare uidetur michi aut ab intelligentia
ueritatis . . . se uelle suos abducere auditores.) (*Pol.* 7.12; tr. 264/2: 144)

Dialectic, that master art that knows "the way to the principles of all methods" (ad omnium methodorum principia viam) (Peter of Spain, *Summulae logicales*, fol. 2v), deals not with Word and Truth but with words and truths. The treatise on dialectic that the Middle Ages attributed to Augustine says as much, and does not hesitate bluntly and inelegantly to state the obvious—and the obvious difficulty.[29] Dialectic, it says, "is the science of arguing well. We always dispute with words" (Dialectica est bene disputandi scientia. Disputamus autem utique verbis) (*Dial.* 1; 82). Words, it says, have force (*vis*) to affect and move an audience; this force, however, is hard to harness. Toward the end of the treatise, having demonstrated how dialectic harnesses the *vis verborum*, the writer pauses, gathering his own argumentative strength to deal with the very discursive difficulties to which, in the *De doctrina*, the *aedificatio caritatis* is an exegetical response. He is about to discuss ambiguity and incoherence. "Because the business of dialectic is to discern the truth, let us look now at the hindrances which may arise because of the force of words" (Itaque nunc propter veritatem diiudicandam, quod dialectica profitetur, ex hac verborum vi . . . quae impedimenta nascantur, videamus) (*Dial.* 8; 102–3).

We have seen in Chapter 1 how biblical exegesis works and is worked by the *vis verborum*, how it works and is worked by scriptural ambiguity, obscurity, and contradiction. In exegesis, as we have seen, such discursive difficulties are not obstacles to but rather catalysts for textual teaching and the discovery of Truth. Secular dialectic's relation to such "impediments" is rather more problematic, as the author of the *De dialectica* acknowledges, quoting the jibe made in Cicero's (lost) *Hortensius*. It is an accusation that both he and dialectic itself will have a hard time completely disproving:

They say that they listen for ambiguous words in order to explain them clearly; and yet they say that every word is ambiguous. How will they explain ambiguities by ambiguities? This is like bringing an unlighted lamp into the darkness.

(Ambigua se audere aiunt explicare dilucide. Idem omne verbum ambiguum esse dicunt. Quomodo igitur ambigua ambiguis explicabunt? Nam hoc est in tenebras extinctum lumen inferre.) (*Dial.* 9; 106–8)

"Wittily and skillfully said" (facete quidem atque callide dictum), the author comments dryly (*Dial.* 9; 108). He will argue, contrariwise, that yes, all words are ambiguous, but only when taken in isolation. We dispute not with single words but with utterances—that is, with words in *context*: "No one explains ambiguous words by ambiguous words; and although every word is ambiguous, no one will explain the ambiguity of words except by means of words, but words already combined which are not ambiguous" (Nemo igitur ambigua verba verbis ambiguis explicabit. Et tamen cum omne verbum ambiguum sit, nemo verborum ambiguitatem nisi verbis sed iam coniunctis quae ambigua non erunt explicabit) (*Dial.* 9; 108). This is skillfully done, but it does not get the author—or dialectic—off the hook. For however much dialectic might point to extralinguistic "truth" or "falsehood," it is still and ever emphatically word-bound, as the *De dialectica*'s own vertiginously verbal defense makes clear. A revealing formulation is that of the eternally huffy Peter Damian (he who needed no grammar books, since he had Christ), for whom dialectic was attuned "not to the force nor to the material of things, but to the manner and order of discourse and to the consequences of words" (non ad virtutem, vel materiam rerum, sed ad modum et ordinem disserendi, et consequentiam verborum) (*PL* 145: 604B).[30]

Dialectic's oppositions can thus be the very path to truth—the instruments of disambiguation—or impediments upon it. The *De dialectica* offers a most striking image of this difficult road as it explains the obstacles born of the *vis verborum*: it is, the treatise says,

as when someone who is walking on a road comes upon a junction with two, three, or even more forks of the road, but can see none of them on account of the thickness of a fog. Thus at first he is kept from proceeding by obscurity. When the fog begins to lift, something can be seen, but it is uncertain whether there is any road. . . . This is obscurity similar to ambiguity. When the sky clears enough for good visibility, the direction of all the roads is apparent, but which is to be taken is still in doubt, not because of any obscurity but solely because of ambiguity.

(Veluti si quis ingrediens iter excipiatur aliquo bivio vel trivio vel etiam ut ita dicam multivio loco, ibique densitate nebulae nihil viarum quod est eluceat. Ergo a pergendo prius obscuritate terretur; at ubi aliquantum rarescere nebulae coeperint, videtur aliquid, quod utrum via sit . . . incertum est. Hoc est obscurum ambiguo simile. Dilucescente autem caelo quantum oculis satis sit iam omnium viarum deductio clara est, sed qua sit pergendum non obscuritate sed ambiguitate dubitatur.) (*Dial.* 8; 104)

Dialectic stands at this crossroads. Working the *words* "true" and "false," dialectic is free to occupy itself in a constant and impossible shuttling between opposing or even contradictory propositions. Such sophistry is the butt of innumerable jokes in clerical texts of the central Middle Ages, but the wit points, as wit always does, to serious concerns. Eustache Deschamps (d. 1406) elaborates such concerns in his translation of the twelfth-century comedy *Geta*:

For logic serves this function, and by its arguments makes something which is not seem to be and makes one thing resemble its opposite.

> (Car logique sert de ceste oeuvre,
> e fait par arguments sembler
> ce qui n'est pas et ressembler
> une chose a l'autre opposite.)[31]

We have seen this kind of polar transformation before, in the critique of perverse worldly discourse with which we began discussion of John of Salisbury (pp. 41–42). Here, however, the agent of incoherence is not the relatively easy target of court or Fortune but rather Dialectica herself. Deschamps's dialectic is no producer of truth. Its arguments produce not *res* but simulacra, and its operations convert everything they touch into its opposite. Its arguments produce not truth, then, but *fiction*, and rather than clarifying distinctions and mediating between opposites, it makes them impossible to tell apart, makes the ontological and epistemological boundaries between them ambiguous.

The interminable movement of dialectical teaching is most appropriately figured in that well-known logical puzzle, the Liar's Paradox:

Surely the foundation of dialectic is that any statement is either true or false—they call this an axiom. What, then, is true or false here?: If you say that you lie, and speak the truth in saying so, then you lie, speaking truth.

(Nempe fundamentum dialectice est, quicquid enuncietur—id autem appellant axioma, est quasi effatum—aut verum esse aut falsum. Quid igitur, haec vera an falsa sunt? Si te mentiri dicis, idque verum dicis mentiris, verum dicis.)[32]

The discipline which by definition has the power to distinguish truth from falsehood here is of no help. It has, rather, produced a very headache of a problem: a text that, while demanding an *either/or* interpretation (I lie; I do not lie: one, and only one, must be true), seems to fuse the two propositions into a single, impossibly oxymoronic text: I am a liar; I am telling the truth. For all its promoters' praise of dialectic as the royal road of reason, wisdom, and understanding, the discipline's own path goes often round and round itself in circles, abutting often in epistemological *culs de sac* of the very ambiguity, obscurity, and contradiction that it seeks to dissolve. Thus entrapped, says John, "dialectic is in a way maimed and practically helpless" (manca est et inutilis fere) (*Met.* 2.9; tr. 93–94/76). We shall hear more of this unmanned dialectic in our next chapter.

Chapter 3

"Negation Is Stronger"
The Question of Abelard

Humanity, therefore, is something named accidentally rather than
substantially. . . . O insanity! The dialectician proposes: every man is man in his
humanity. The heretic adds: but humanity is nothing. The devil concludes:
therefore every man is nothing. If man is man in his humanity, and every man and
humanity are nothing, then every man does not exist. Monstrous!

—Walter of St. Victor, *Contra quatuor labyrinthos Franciae*

The eponymous hero of Vitalis of Blois's Latin comedy *Geta* (mid–twelfth
century) thinks himself on the road to success with his school-bred skill.
Like his mistress Dialectica, Geta can make what *is* seem not to be; he
can make a case or an ass of Socrates. "I have here some marvelous sophisms," he boasts; "indeed, I know how to prove that a man is an ass" (sed
precium pene miranda sophismata porto, / iamque probare scio quod sit
asellus homo) (*Geta*, lines 163–64). But this same maiming dialectic will
be quite literally the cause of Geta's undoing. Having seen his own double
in the form of the disguised Jove, Geta knows something is wrong. There
cannot be two of him, of course; either he is or he is not Geta. His dialectic does not help him resolve this question at all. In fact, it leads him not
out of *aporia* but further and deeper into it:

Therefore I am, therefore I am nothing. Damn this dialectic that thus completely
undoes me. Now I know: knowledge hurts. When Geta learned logic, then he
ceased to be: what makes bulls of other men makes nothing of me. Thus painful sophisms are applied to me; as it did to so many others, logic takes away my
being. Woe to all logicians, if this be so!

> (Sic sum, sic nil sum. Pereat dialectica per quam
>   sic perii penitus. Nunc scio: scire nocet.
> Cum didicit Geta logicam, tunc desiit esse,
>   queque boues alios me facit esse nichil.
> Sic in me grauius experta sophismata! mutans

> tantum alios michimet abstulit esse meum.
> Ve logicis, si sic est, omnibus!)
>
> (lines 401–7)

The troublesome marriage to sophistry of Geta's disambiguating discipline
has undone both him and truth.

Twelfth-century readers more acerbic and theologically minded than
Vitalis opposed themselves to dialectic, not just for the trouble it made
at the misty crossroads (*Dial.* 8), but also for the deformations it could
exert upon theological truth. What dialectic could do to the human person, after all, it could also do to the persons of the Trinity. A generation
after Hugh, another member of his community, Walter of St. Victor, wrote
a vitriolic condemnation of intellectual currents in France, a work whose
contrariness is apparent even in its title, *Against the Four Labyrinths of
France* (*Contra quatuor labyrinthos Franciae*) (c. 1177–78):

> Marvel, all of you, at this art not dialectical but most surely diabolical. Ergo one
> is not one, the same is not the same, himself is not himself, Christ is not Christ,
> the same person is not the same person, the Son of God is not the Son of God.
>
> (Obstupescite omnes, non dialecticam sed plane diabolicam artem. Ergo unus
> non est unus, idem non est idem, ipse non est ipse, Christus non est Christus,
> eadem persona non est eadem persona, Filius Dei non est Filius Dei.) (2.4; 232)

One of Walter's four "labyrinths" is Peter Abelard (1079–1142), a troublesome teacher, exegete, and dialectician, master of John of Salisbury
(*Met.* 2.10; tr. 95/78) and, perhaps, of Vitalis himself (Bertini).[1] Peter Abelard is well known even today for an act of division and an act of com-
bination—for an *either/or* and a *both-and*—that is, his castration at the
order of his lover Heloise's uncle Fulbert, and his spectacular (and to some
eyes scandalous) intermingling of dialectic and theology. We are fortunate to have a rich set of biographical texts surrounding the life of this
major figure of twelfth-century intellectual life.[2] This chapter continues
the study of dialectical representations of teaching and reading that began
in Chapter 2 with a case study of the teaching and reading of Peter Abelard. Abelard's representation and performance of these two activities are
painfully structured on dialectical models of opposition, on *quaestio* and
disputatio. Contemporary representations of Abelard—his own included
—present him as a problem—as a *quaestio* with no easy resolution.

Boethius reminds us that the *quaestio* consists in contradiction.[3] We
should thus return to Boethius's definition of contradiction for a moment:

Contradiction is the opposition of affirmation and negation. When one person affirms what another denies, this very conflict among propositions is called contradiction. . . . And let this be contradiction, affirmation and negation opposed. When affirmation is opposed to negation, it is a contradiction.

(Est enim contradictio affirmationis et negationis oppositio. Cum enim quis affirmat quod alius negat, ipsa utrarumque propositionum pugna contradictio nominatur. . . . Et sit hoc contradictio, affirmatio et negatio opposita. Cum enim affirmatio negationi opponitur, contradictio est.) (*In librum de interpretatione Aristotelis*, in *PL* 64: 318A)

Regarded through the dialectical lens that Abelard and many of his contemporary readers looked through, Abelard's "identity" becomes deeply questionable.[4] Abelard is worked by contrary things, even as John of Salisbury's erring dialecticians were. Maimed by his insistent use of *either/or* reasoning and affirmation through negation, Abelard as biographical subject will become as one of John's walking contradictions, an apparently incoherent fusion of *either/or* and *both-and*: both monk and not-monk when he must be one or the other; both lover and lover-in-Christ when he would rather be only one; both man and, anatomically, not-man by Fulbert's negating razor-swipe. These subject positions are defined in the Abelardian dossier as mutually exclusive, yet he occupies all of them, often simultaneously, much to his own and his contemporaries' consternation. The unresolved tension between a biographical affirmation (Abelard is a monk; Abelard is a teacher; Abelard is a man) and its corresponding contrary negation (not-monk, not-teacher, not-man) makes Peter Abelard himself a *quaestio*: he is, as Bernard of Clairvaux wrote, "a man dissimilar to himself, a Herod within, a John without; completely ambiguous" (homo sibi dissimilis est, intus Herodes, foris Joannes; totus ambiguus) (*Epistolae*, Ep. 193; 44–45). This apparent irresolution produces a longing for closure that Abelard will teach us to call interpretive anxiety.

The labor of oppositional instruction was difficult for John of Salisbury and, as we have seen, even dangerous for the coherence of his normative, moderating *Metalogicon*. Precisely these dangers painfully make and unmake Abelard's career, but, at least in one register, Abelard proves himself able to work opposition as his English student could not. "Maimed" by the clash of opposites in his life story, Abelard will harness if not completely master them in the exegetical method of his *Sic et non*, which makes opposition not an obstacle to understanding but its fundamental condition.

Abelard Teaching

My name will grow; I am called Master Geta. The shadow of my
name will terrify the multitudes.

—Vitalis of Blois, *Geta*

Abelard has left us an intellectual and biographical self-representation in
the consolatory letter to a friend now usually known as the *Historia calamitatum*, and a corpus of letters exchanged with his student, lover, wife,
and colleague, Heloise.[5] From its very beginning, the *Historia calamitatum* defines its protagonist through opposition and negation. This eldest
son of Breton nobility first asserts himself by negating his birthright, re-
nouncing chivalry, and making over his inheritance to his brothers.[6] His
choice between Mars and Minerva, however, is not as absolute as it here
seems. Between arms and letters, here opposed so strikingly, there is in
fact a middle term, as Abelard's metaphors make clear:

I preferred the weapons of dialectic to all the other teachings of philosophy, and
armed with these I chose the conflicts of disputation instead of the trophies of war.
I began to travel about in several provinces disputing, like a true peripatetic philosopher, wherever I had heard that there was a keen interest in the art of dialectic.

(Quoniam dialecticarum rationum armaturam omnibus philosophie documentis
pretuli, his armis alia commutavi et tropheis bellorum conflictus pretuli disputationum. Proinde diversas disputando perambulans provincias, ubicunque hujus
artis vigere studium audieram, peripateticorum emulator factus sum.) (*Historia*,
tr. 58/63–64)

Abelard has successfully accomplished his first act of self-definition, combining the commonplace opposites of cleric and knight in philosophical
knight-errantry. In practice, however, this model identity will have biographical and literary consequences that will be difficult to master.

The transfer of martial antagonism into the "conflicts of disputation"
continues to inform Abelard's self-presentation throughout the troubled
relations with academic and ecclesiastical authority that structure the *Historia*. It is good dialectical practice to define a thing through knowledge
of and opposition to its contraries. We have seen John of Salisbury do this
in the *Metalogicon* (4.34; see Chapter 2, p. 55, above); Peter Abelard will
do the same in his self-construction as reader and teacher.

The first teacher named in the *Historia* is the same William of Champeaux who taught John of Salisbury about the middle term (*Met.* 3.9) and

who was in Abelard's day head of the Cathedral School in Paris.[7] This is how Abelard records the beginning of his studies with William:

At last I came to Paris, where dialectic had long been particularly flourishing, and joined William of Champeaux, who at that time was the supreme master of the subject, both in reputation and in fact. I stayed in his school for a time, but though he welcomed me at first he soon took a violent dislike to me because I set out to refute some of his arguments and frequently reasoned against him. On several occasions I proved myself his superior in debate.

(Perveni tandem Parisius, ubi jam maxime disciplina hec florere consueverat, ad Guillhelmum scilicet Campellensem preceptorem meum in hoc tunc magisterio re et fama precipuum; cum quo aliquantulum moratus, primo ei aceptus, postmodum gravissimus extiti, cum nonnullas scilicet ejus sententias refellere conarer et ratiocinari contra eum sepius aggrederer et nonnumquam superior in disputanto viderer.) (*Historia*, tr. 58/64)

In this brief narrative (a single sentence in the Latin), we have the model of Abelardian self-definition in its most condensed form. In the first clause, William is indisputably the master (*preceptorem meum*), Abelard his disciple; in the second, Abelard transforms from a welcome to an unwelcome student; in the third, Abelard becomes master by unmastering William. Finally, Abelard undoes his master completely. The preening narrative of the *Historia calamitatum* insists upon this point, stressing the act of unteaching with synonyms:

In the course of our philosophic disputes I produced a sequence of clear logical arguments to make him *amend, or rather abandon*, his previous attitude to universals. . . . William had *modified or rather been forced to give up* his original position.

(Inter cetera disputationum nostrarum conamina antiquam ejus de universalibus sententiam patentissimis argumentorum rationibus ipsum *commutare, immo destruere*, compuli. . . . Hanc ille *correxerit immo coactus dimiserit* sententiam.) (*Historia*, tr. 60/65–66; emphasis added)

We shall return below to the doctrines under dispute; what interests us here is that Abelard conquers his master by forcing him to revise his teachings. Abelard has taught William the opposite of what William taught before; he has compelled William to unteach himself, much as the trip to Bologna did to Alberic of Rheims (*Met.* 2.10; see Chapter 2, p. 46, above).

The story is not over yet, however: it is not complete until Abelard, having opposed and undone his teacher in disputation, not only takes on his former peers as his disciples but also takes over his former master's place. Humiliated, William leaves Paris. His replacement, a man who should technically be Abelard's teacher, in turn relinquishes *his* place to become a student again. By extension, then, Abelard teaches now not only his former fellow students but his master as well (*Historia*, tr. 60/66).

The *Metalogicon*, it will be remembered, represents contemporary intellectual "progress" in the shuttling movement between the extremes of rupture and repetition. Abelard's advancement from upstart student to acknowledged master is built upon the same structure of rupture and repetition, for he has broken with his master in order to stand in his master's place. Beneath the break with William lies the desire to teach William's curriculum to William's students—to *become* William, one might venture to add.[8] So strong is this desire that it drives Abelard from Paris to Laon, where he redoes William's theological studies with Anselm of Laon before he undoes this teacher in his turn.

Abelard's story of his studies with Anselm follows the same pattern as that of his studies with William; it begins, in fact, in almost exactly the same way: "I therefore approached this old man" (Accessi igitur ad hunc senem) (*Historia*, tr. 62/68). Here, however, instead of adding some words of praise in his relative clause (as he did for William), Abelard moves immediately into a pointed critique of the teaching of his new master, "who owed his reputation more to long practice than to intelligence or memory" (cui magis longevus usus quam ingenium vel memoria nomen comparaverat) (*Historia*, tr. 68/62). Abelard's studies with Anselm end, once again, in his self-assertion by negation: as he defeated William in dialectic, he will conquer Anselm in exegesis. Though Abelard is moving from one discipline to another, he takes the oppositional model of self-definition with him.

Abelard's peers, knowing that his previous experience has been principally in dialectic, challenge him to improvise a reading of an obscure passage from Ezekiel, with only the text and a commentary for guidance (*Historia*, tr. 63/68–69). In taking the podium to explicate Scripture, Abelard is, for the moment, a teacherless master. His gloss recognizes no teacher but the text; his method implicitly repudiates that of his master Anselm, patient assembler of authorities, worker in the vineyard of the *glossa ordinaria*.[9] Teacherless teacher of an all but naked text, Abelard constructs his very teacherness through negation, by juxtaposition of opposites, defining himself as much by what he is *not* as by what he *is*. To his peers' suggestion that he take more time to prepare his commentary, Abelard retorts that "it was not my custom to benefit by practice, but I relied on my own intelligence" (non esse mee consuetudinis per usum proficere sed per ingenium) (*Historia*, tr. 63/69).[10] Abelard thus presents himself as Anselm's opposite—the representative of *ingenium* as opposed to mere *usus*. His self-definition as master depends upon opposing Anselm in this way, that is, upon being Anselm's opposite and upon countering Anselm's exegetical and pedagogical practices. Simultaneously, however, he asserts the conquered master's positions even as he negates them, outdoing Anselm in the master's own material. So effective is this repetitive rupture that Anselm must formally break off the relation in order to forestall further identification with his former student (*Historia*, tr. 64/70).

Abelard's conquest of Anselm marks, in the *Historia* at least, the younger man's accession to the position of *magister*, a position asserted through negating (unteaching and outteaching) his masters. In the *Historia*, Abelard makes himself master by conquering his teachers and presents as signs of his pedagogical prowess his followers' devotion and his rivals' envy. However, this oppositional model of pedagogical power comes perilously close to another way of imagining intellectual activity: John of Salisbury's paradigm of error, unteaching.

The time has come, then, to return to John and his picture of twelfth-century French education. The *Historia*'s self-construction shows that this "error," in Abelard's case, is less a matter of nominal doctrine than of pedagogical ethos. Like John of Salisbury's fresh-baked experts who "prematurely seated themselves in the master's chair" (magisterii presumpserant fastum) (*Met.* 1.4; tr. 17/13), Abelard, "young as I was and estimating my capacities too highly for my years" (supra vires etatis de ingenio meo presumens) (*Historia*, tr. 59/64), cuts around established authority and sets up schools of his own at Melun, Corbeil, and the Mont Sainte Geneviève. He defines himself over and against his masters through paired and contradictory acts negating his masters and affirming them, only to see the same attacks repeated against himself. In this oscillation of teaching and unteaching, he too participates in Saresberian error, for

rarely, if ever, do we find a teacher who is content to follow in the footsteps of his master. Each, to make a name for himself, coins his own special error. Wherewith, while promising to correct his master, he sets himself up as a target for correction and condemnation by his own disciples as well as posterity.

(De magistris aut nullus aut rarus est qui doctoris sui uelit inherere uestigiis. Ut sibi faciat nomen, quisque proprium cudit errorem; sicque fit, ut, dum se doctorem corrigere promittit, seipsum corrigendum aut reprehendendum tam discipulis quam posteris prebeat.) (*Met.* 2.18; tr. 116–17/96)

Abelard, as we have seen, presents himself as a philosophical knight-errant in the early episodes of the *Historia*. He uses his wanderings as a sign of his pedagogical prowess; they are quite literally "his own special error" (*Met.* 2.18; tr. 116–17/96). Now that he is settled down in Paris, apparently in full possession of conquered pedagogical authority, one wonders what will become of the oppositional paradigm that structures his narrative.

The Instruction of Heloise

> Now Love, who's captured many worthy men, unlearns me, to catch me better. In learning I have unlearned; I have unlearned in learning.
>
> —Henri d'Andeli, *Lai d'Aristote*

After defeating Anselm, Abelard conquers Paris. He is at the height of his powers, both intellectual and academic. While he has not completely silenced his enemies, he certainly has come to dominate intellectual life in the city. The time has come for a test of his teaching. This test comes in a dialectic more erotic than Aristotelian, and one in which the apparent opposites of affirmation and negation, master and student, are harder to maintain, less stable, and less easy to distinguish than they are in the lecture hall. Besotted with pride, Abelard begins to plot a seduction that would reinscribe in an erotic register his earlier conquests in the schools. He has made a name for himself as a teacher of dialectic and of Scripture; he will now make his name as a *praeceptor amoris*, and he undertakes the task with appropriately Ovidian detachment. He chooses his student, Heloise, for her skill in letters, promising for the arts of language; he chooses her for her attractive face, promising for the *ars amatoria*: "I considered all the usual attractions for a lover and decided that she was the one to bring to my bed, confident that I should have an easy success" (Hanc igitur, omnibus circunspectis que amantes allicere solent, commodiorem censui in amorem mihi copulare, et me id facillime credidi posse) (*Historia*, tr. 71/66).

A medieval schoolmaster is entitled to use violence in teaching,[11] and Abelard reports his surprised delight when the girl's uncle Fulbert grants him this authority over his new pupil (*Historia*, tr. 67/72). He intended, he says, to divert such violence from the pedagogical to the erotic, and expected no problems in the transfer. The developing relation with Heloise, however, forcibly redefines this expectation. The couple's course of study does indeed include violence, but it differs profoundly and subversively from the teacher's masterful punishment:

With our books open before us, more words of love than of our reading passed between us, and more kissing than teaching. Hands strayed oftener to bosoms than to the pages; love drew our eyes to look on each other more than reading kept them on our texts. To avert suspicion love—not anger—sometimes administered blows, prompted by tender feeling, not irritation, and they were sweeter than any balm could be.

(Apertis itaque libris, plura de amore quam de lectione verba se ingerebant, plura erant oscula quam sententie; sepius ad sinus quam ad libros reducebantur manus, crebrius oculos amor in se reflectebat quam lectio in scriptura dirigebat. Quoque minus suspicionis haberemus, verbera quandoque dabat amor, non furor, gratia, non ira, que omnium unguentorum suavitatem transcenderent.) (*Historia*, tr. 67/72–73) [12]

This exchange undermines Abelard's absolute pedagogical authority on several levels. First, this is a *mutual* undertaking, as the plurals running throughout the passage indicate. Second, as the passive constructions suggest, *amor* and *gratia*, and not Peter Abelard, are in charge here, and the violence they inspire is administered not toward a higher end but for its own sake—its sweetness. [13]

For a moment, then, the *Historia*'s preoccupation with demonstrations of mastery and conquest, assertion and negation, fades as master and student, lover and beloved become interchangeable positions not particularly marked for gender:

In short, our desires left no stage of love-making untried, and if love could devise something new, we welcomed it. We entered on each joy the more eagerly for our previous inexperience, and were the less easily sated.

(Nullus a Cupidis intermissus est gradus amoris, et si quid insolitum amor excogitare potuit, est additum; et quo minus ista fueramus experti gaudia, ardentius illis insistebamus, et minus in fastidium vertebantur.) (*Historia*, tr. 67–68/73)

This period forms a very brief pause in the careers of both Abelard and Heloise. The rest of the *Historia calamitatum* and the ensuing correspondence between the lovers will show us these two subjects engaged in high-stakes disputation with each other—over, among other things, their respective and mutually determining subject positions. [14] With Heloise's unambiguous pregnancy, the erotic dialectic between the two lovers turns quite quickly into a disputation far more gender-marked and exclusive in its reasoning. In the erotic interlude, both Heloise and Abelard were master and student, lover and beloved; when they try to decide whether or not to marry, their conflict turns precisely around the impossibility of such multiple identification. "What harmony can there be between pupils and nursemaids, desks and cradles, books or tablets and distaffs, pen or stylus and spindles?" (Que enim conventio scolarium ad pedissequas, scriptoriorum ad cunabula, librorum sive tabularium ad colos, stilorum sive calamorum ad fusos?) (*Historia*, tr. 71/76), demands Heloise, and she summons a whole line of authorities who answer: None. One cannot be at the same time both philosopher and husband—not by law, in Heloise's argument, but by the very nature of the categories. It is as if "philosopher" were defined as "not-husband," as if the categories were mutually exclusive. To be both, Heloise's argument implies, would be a violation of the law of non-contradiction, and thus an impossibility and a humiliation for a logician of Abelard's standing.[15]

In some ways, then, in contradicting Abelard, Heloise has in fact reinforced his mastery: she makes him philosopher, in effect, by expelling him from the category "husband." Her discourse demonstrates the success of Abelard's teaching by showing her as a disciple able to use in practice the rhetoric, dialectic, and knowledge of the Authorities learned in the schoolroom. The surprisingly *non sequitur* conclusion of her discourse (since marriage is condemned by the Fathers and an obstacle to Philosophy, let me be your mistress instead of your wife) seems designed to show off Abelard's logical superiority, at least according to clerical standards.[16] However, this is a victory bought at the expense of a paradox, for, if Abelard asserts his mastery over Heloise by representing her argument as incoherent, does he not also impeach his own teaching? In order to assert himself over Heloise intellectually, he must negate the effectiveness of his own instruction.

Each one of these opposing interpretations—one stressing Abelard's rhetorical and pedagogical mastery, the other his nonmastery—inevitably leads to the other. Abelard teaches Heloise about dialectic; Heloise teaches Abelard about marriage and the origin of philosophy.[17] Abelard proves his success as a teacher in Heloise's abundant erudition; her apparent illogic proves his failure. He gives her the word and thus lets her momentarily dominate his text; the words he gives her, however, are often his own. This confusion is echoed in the lecture's oscillation between direct and indirect discourse: it begins and ends as reported speech, its verbs in the third person, but it slips into the first in the middle. Does this speaking "I" in-

dicate that these are Heloise's very words reported by Abelard's pen? Or
are they Abelard's words in Heloise's (fictional) mouth? It is, then, hard
to tell who is asserting him/herself, who is master here, hard to tell who is
teaching whom. The blurring of borders between master and student repeats the eroticized pedagogy of their *studium amoris*, in which, as Henri
d'Andeli's *Lai d'Aristote* pointedly teaches, logic and grammar are of little
importance.[18] In fact, suggests the *Lai*, Love masters the master by unteaching him:

Now Love, who's captured many worthy men, unlearns me, to catch me better.
In learning I have unlearned; I have unlearned in learning.

(Or me desaprent por mielz prendre
Amors, qui maint preudome a pris.
En aprenant ai desapris,
desapris ai en aprenant.)

(lines 338–43)

After such reindoctrination, the philosopher-lover's authority is never
again the same, as Abelard's own career will painfully illustrate.

Abelard Untaught

But what do they want for themselves, these vain men, these
sacrilegious teachers of dogma—these men who, while they lay traps
for others with their questions, do not expect that they themselves
might fall into them?

—Peter Damian, *De divina omnipotentia*

As Abelard used to say, negation is stronger.

—John of Salisbury, *Metalogicon*

It is thus not surprising to find that the study of love has affected Abelard's
teaching, not only in the house of Fulbert but in the cloister of Notre
Dame as well. It seems that Heloise was right—a married philosopher is a
contradiction in terms:

Now the more I was taken up with these pleasures, the less time I could give to
my school. It was utterly boring for me to have to go to the school, and equally
wearisome to remain there and spend my days on study when my nights were
sleepless with love-making.

(Et quo me amplius hec voluptas occupaverat, minus philosophie vaccare poteram
et scolis operam dare. Tediosum mihi vehementer erat ad scolas procedere vel in

eis morari; pariter et laboriosum, cum nocturnas amori vigilias et diurnas studio conservarem.) (*Historia*, tr. 68/73)

Now himself a recognized master, Abelard has fallen into the pedagogical error with which he mocked Anselm of Laon, "who owed his reputation more to long practice than to intelligence or memory" (*Historia*, tr. 62/68): "As my interest and concentration flagged, my lectures lacked all inspiration and were merely repetitive" (Quem etiam ita negligentem et tepidum lectio tunc habebat, ut jam nichil ex ingenio sed ex usu cuncta proferrem) (*Historia*, tr. 68/73).[19] Abelard's fall away from *ingenium* into habit, which he defined as *ingenium*'s opposite, makes him less of a teacher than he once was. In fact, since he now lacks that wit by which he oppositionally defined the teacher, he can hardly be called a teacher at all. This intellectual emagistration has, of course, a figural resemblance to his physical emasculation, the story of which the *Historia* is preparing to relate. The similarity of the two events, however, goes much deeper, for, just as now Abelard cannot by his own definition easily be called a teacher, so after his castration will he only improperly be called a man.

Having considered the classificational problems posed by and for both the concupiscent and the castrated Abelard, we can now return to the specifics of the young scholar's conquest of William of Champeaux. Abelard engaged his master in one of the thorniest problems of twelfth- and thirteenth-century philosophy: the question of universals.[20] William, says Abelard,

had maintained that in the common existence of universals, the whole species was essentially the same in each of its individuals, and among these there was no essential difference, but only variety due to a multiplicity of accidents. Now he modified his view to say that it was the same not in essence but through non-difference.

(Erat autem in ea sententia de communitate universalium, ut eamdem essentialiter rem totam simul singulis suis inesse adstrueret individuis, quorum quidem nulla esset in essentia diversitas sed sola multitudine accidentium varietas. Sic autem istam tunc suam correxit sententiam, ut deinceps rem eamdem non essentialiter sed indifferenter diceret.) (*Historia*, tr. 60/65–66)[21]

Abelard's violent rejection of William's argument is in part determined by the structuring tension set up in the *Historia* between the individual and the crowd. Throughout, Abelard insists on his difference, his singularity; he defines himself by negation with singular placeholders (William, Anselm) or with singular terms (*usus/ingenium*). For this *superbia*, pride in singularity, and its sister vice *luxuria*, the healing punishment, according to the *Historia*, is castration.[22] In removing the primary signifiers of male-ness, Abelard's punishment paradoxically *inscribes* on his body the differ-ence of which he was so proud. Now he can no longer be called a man; his singularity is a monstrous spectacle, his removal from manhood truly an *ab-hominatio*:[23]

I thought how my rivals would exult over my fitting punishment . . . and how fast the news of this singular disgrace would spread over the whole world. . . . How could I show my face in public, to be pointed at by every finger, derided by every tongue, a monstrous spectacle to all I met? I was also appalled to remember that according to the cruel letter of the Law, a eunuch is such an abomination to the Lord that men made eunuchs by amputation or mutilation of their testicles are forbidden to enter a church as if they were stinking and unclean.

(Occurrebat animo . . . quanta laude mei emuli tam manifestam equitatem effer-rent; . . . quanta dilatatione hec singularis infamia universum mundum esset oc-cupatura. . . . Qua fronte in publicum prodirem, omnium digitis demonstrandus, omnium linguis corrodendus, omnibus monstruosum spectaculum futurus. Nec me etiam parum confundebat, quod secundum occidentem legis litteram tanta sit apud Deum eunuchorum abhominatio, ut homines amputates vel attritis tes-ticulis eunuchizati intrare ecclesiam tamquam olentes et immundi prohibeantur.) (*Historia*, tr. 76/80)

William had argued that the universal is essentially present in all mem-bers of the species and that variation among individuals is due merely to accident, which in no way lessens their participation in the general term. By this reasoning, then, "man" is present equally in all men, however varied their appearance. Abelard forced William to discard this argument for one that gives more place to individual variation: members participate in the species not by their identity but by their *nondifference* one from another.

Abelard's fate (or his narrative) has thus led him to the same problem on which he undid William: gender, genus, and the individual.[24] After his castration, how is Abelard a man? If he is *essentially* male, then his dif-ference from other men is merely accidental, and the word "man" can be properly applied to him. If, on the other hand, he is only a man insofar as he is *nondifferent* from other men, how much of a man is he now? In other words, is his castration an accidental variation from the universal "man"? Or is it a determining difference that expels him from that category as it casts him from the Temple?

Abelard Unmanned

> A man holding a discussion with another submits the proposition:
> "What I am, you are not." The other, because it is true in part, or
> because the speaker is deceitful and he is simple, agrees. Then the
> first adds, "I am a man." When this too is agreed upon, he
> concludes, saying, "Therefore you are not a man."
>
> —Augustine, *De doctrina christiana*

We have seen Abelard repeatedly vanquished by the consequences of his
conquest of intellectual authority. The story of Abelard and his teachers, however, is not yet complete; to finish it, we must look outside the
Historia calamitatum, for its main character is nowhere mentioned there.
Judging from his own words and those of his contemporaries, Roscelin of
Compeigne (d. 1120 or 1125) was Abelard's first great teacher.[25] Abelard,
however, ventures no comments on his teaching, neither on his material
(compare Abelard's remarks on William of Champeaux) nor on his style
(compare his critique of Anselm). In fact, Abelard has nothing to say about
Roscelin at all in the *Historia*. However, he *did* have bones to pick with
his old master, and engaged in a public feud with him over, among other
things, the nature of the Trinity.[26]

Roscelin replied to Abelard's allegations in a long and venomous letter.
J. Reiners, its editor, does not date the text, but since it does not mention
the Council of Soissons, it was probably written before 1121. Much of the
letter is devoted to closely argued refutations of Abelard's teachings and
defenses of Roscelin's own. However, near the close, Roscelin gets down
to business and shifts his attention from Abelard's teaching to his person.
The rest of the text is a viciously *ad hominem* (or, as Roscelin might say,
ad eunuchum) attack on Abelard's way of life, his relations with his monks
and with the nuns of the Paraclete (Heloise in particular), and, of course,
his castration. Roscelin's is a fascinating text for our inquiry because it
presents so neatly and so violently many of the issues with which we have
been concerned: teaching, reading, the erotic; affirmation and negation.
It connects, in an extremely provocative way, notions of sexuality, gender,
teaching, and naming. It traps "Peter Abelard" in an *either/or* reasoning
that undoes him quite.

Roscelin begins by specifically invoking Abelard's failure to live up to
his responsibilities as a student; he devotes the body of the letter to turning Abelard's refutations of Roscelin's teaching against him, refuting and

impugning in turn Abelard's teaching. In his carefully orchestrated conclusion, Roscelin returns to the personal, attacking Abelard's behavior as a teacher. The first target is, as one might expect, the affair with Heloise: "Indeed, not sparing the virgin committed to you, whom you should have conserved as she was and taught as a student, moved by an unbridled spirit of lust, you taught her not to dispute, but to fornicate" (Tu vero . . . commissae tibi virgini non parcens, quam conservare ut commissam, docere ut discipulam debueras, effreno luxuriae spiritu agitatus non argumentari, sed eam fornicari docuisti) (78). Abelard's account of the *studium amoris* made mastery a fluid category, not fixed essentially to any particular subject. Roscelin, however, assigns Abelard all the mastery and responsibility. According to his teacher, Abelard violates professional ethics in both his treatment of his pupil and his treatment of the material studied—he teaches what should not be taught to one to whom he should not teach it.

Roscelin then turns to Abelard's more recent specializations—his double identity as monk and teacher—and further develops this double accusation, slicing the construct "Abelard" apart on the razor of the *either/or*. He glosses Jerome's declaration, "The monk's office is not teaching but lamenting" (Monachus autem non doctoris habet, sed plangentis officium) (*Contra Vigilantium*, in *PL* 23: 351B), using this citation from one of Abelard's favorite authors to catch him in yet another violation of duty: "you do not stop teaching what should not be taught, when, even if it were to be taught, you should not teach it" (non docenda docere non desinis, cum etiam docenda docere non debueras) (79). What Abelard teaches is not proper, and what *can* be taught, he, a monk, cannot properly teach.

Therefore, because, having taken the habit, you usurped the profession of teacher by teaching lies, you certainly ceased being a monk, for St. Jerome, himself a monk, defining a monk, said: "the monk's office is not teaching, but lamenting."

(Quia igitur suscepto habitu doctoris officium mendacia docendo usurpasti, utique monachus esse cessasti, quia beatus Hieronymus monachum, monachus ipse, diffiniens: "Monachus," inquit, "non doctoris, sed plangentis habet officium.") (80)

Because he teaches what should not be taught, Abelard can no longer properly be called a teacher, and because he teaches at all, he cannot be called a monk. How, then, is he to be named?

But the abandonment of the clerical habit proves that you are not a cleric. But you are certainly not a layman, as your tonsure demonstrates. If, therefore, you are neither cleric, nor layman, nor monk, I cannot think of what name I should call you.

(Sed neque clericum te esse habitus clerici convincit abiectio. Sed multo minus laicus es, quod coronae tuae satis probat ostensio. Si igitur neque clericus neque laicus neque monachus es, quo nomine te censeam, reperire non valeo.) (80)

With this dilemma of naming Peter Abelard, we return to the problem of universals raised by the conquest of William of Champeaux. Roscelin concludes that, though Abelard may resemble a monk in his accidents (his habit and tonsure), he is *essentialiter* not a monk at all. What, then, *is* he?

Roscelin's radical solution to the nominational problem posed by Abelard is explicitly grammatical and dialectical; it expels Abelard from the category in which his accidents might lead one to place him:[27]

But perhaps you will lie and say that you can be called Peter as you once were. I am certain that if a noun of masculine gender falls away from its genus, it will refuse to signify the customary thing. Nouns customarily lose proper signification when it happens that the things they signify recede from their perfection. For a building without wall or roof will be called not house but imperfect house. *Therefore, having lost that part which makes a man, you are to be called not Peter but Peter imperfect.*

(Sed forte Petrum te appellari posse ex consuetudine mentieris. Certus sum autem, quod masculini generis nomen, si a suo genere deciderit, rem solitam significare recusabit. . . . Solent enim nomina propriam significationem amittere, cum eorum significata contigerit a sua perfectione recedere. Neque enim ablato tecto vel pariete domus, sed imperfecta domus vocabitur. *Sublata igitur parte quae hominem facit non Petrus, sed imperfectus Petrus appellandus es.*) (80; emphasis added) [28]

Roscelin's addressee (it is not clear to me at this point exactly how I should name him) can be called neither by his proper name Petrus nor by the noun *homo*; Roscelin has made Abelard an ontological, grammatical, and dialectical anomaly.[29] In so doing, he forces Abelard into the consequences of his own logic. The transformation of this great teacher of philosophy, theology, and grammar into a mere solecism reduces *ad absurdum* the problems into which Abelard's narrative and pedagogical wanderings (his *error!*) have led him.

In this light, Abelard's condemnation at the Council of Soissons (1121), as he relates it in the *Historia calamitatum*, makes new sense as a necessary product of Abelard's self-definition by negation. Abelard's peripatetic mastery has made enemies of his former masters, and they exact revenge before ecclesiastical council, mutilating Abelard once again by forcing him to burn his book on the Trinity.[30] The charges that they bring against him cast the personal grudge in theological terms: they accuse him of supplanting ecclesiastical authority and cutting apart the Trinity in his teaching. The council turns Abelard's accomplishments as a teacher against him one by one. His conquest of Anselm was "proven" by his fellow students' enthusiastic copying of his glosses on Ezekiel (*Historia*, tr. 65/70); now he is accused of unauthorized circulation of texts (*Historia*, tr. 82/87). Abelard proved himself as a teacher by unmaking his masters, and he made his name as an exegete by commenting on Scripture with no teacher but text and commentary; now he is accused of presuming to ascend "without a teacher to the teaching of Scripture" (sine magistro ad magisterium divine lectionis) (*Historia*; my translation/82).

Abelard's circumvention of the usual routes of meditated education in the end works to silence him: at Soissons, his book is burned; at Sens in 1140, he is "unteachered," condemned to silence. His victories over Anselm and William ring ironically hollow when their repetitions unteach and unman him. His *ingenium* loses its edge during the affair with Heloise, and at the hands of his first great teacher, his professional and personal identities are reduced to nonsense.

Geta, in Vitalis of Blois's comedy of the same name, has studied so much dialectic in Paris that he considers himself a Master of the Universe, only to find himself unmanned on a thorny tangle of sophistical syllogisms. "Dialectic has made me insane; I who was once only a fool" (reddidit insanum de me dialectica stulto) (line 419), Geta concludes. In doing so, he sounds much like Abelard himself, who at the end of his life confesses to Heloise, "Logic has made me hateful to the world" (Odiosum me mundo reddidit logica).[31]

The Question of Abelard

> A fool, I diligently raise an objection to logicians inasmuch as I am subject to two contraries.
>
> —Walter of Châtillon, Poem 21

> I refuse to be such a philosopher as to reject St. Paul, or such an Aristotle to be shut out from Christ.
>
> —Peter Abelard, "Confessio Fidei ad Heloissam"

In the *Historia calamitatum*, Abelard constructs his identity as master in a fundamentally negative and exclusive movement. Calling on the *either/or* reasoning patterns of dialectic and its habit of definition through opposition, he makes his name in more ways than one. He defines himself as a true teacher against Anselm of Laon through *ingenium*, without which, he implies, one is no master at all. By definition, it would seem, the place of true mastery can only be occupied by one man at a time; thus, Abelard's ability to take the place of his teacher, too, makes him master. We have seen him caught in this exclusive definition when Heloise taught him that one cannot be both philosopher and husband, when Roscelin reminded him that one cannot be both monk and teacher.

The man who made his name through dialectical conquest is now himself a troubling logical puzzle, a *quaestio* aporetically caught between an affirmation and its more powerful negation. Abelard has made his name with dialectic's *vis verborum*; now he—and we his readers—come up against that crossroads that Augustine used as image for ambiguity. As his eloquent opponent Bernard of Clairvaux neatly put it, Peter Abelard is "a monk without a rule, a prelate without responsibility. He is neither in order nor of an order. A man dissimilar to himself, a Herod within, a John without; completely ambiguous" (sine regula monachus, sine sollicitudine praelatus, nec ordinem tenet, nec tenetur ab ordine. Homo sibi dissimilis est, intus Herodes, foris Ioannes, totus ambiguus, nihil habens de monacho praeter nomen et habitum) (*Epistolae*, Ep. 193; 44–45).[32] Abelard is ambiguous because his identity is caught between biographical propositions defined so exclusively as to make them contradictories—Abelard is a man, Abelard is not a man; Abelard is a monk, Abelard is a teacher; Abelard is a married man, Abelard is a philosopher—and being contradictory, they cannot, as John of Salisbury remembered and Abelard himself taught, at the same time be true. Since the terms of Abelard's professional self-definition allow no comfortable middle term, no conjunction of opposites like the one he forged between arms and letters at the beginning of his career, or like the momentary erotic confusion effected with Heloise, his life story repeatedly and inevitably returns him and his readers to Augustine's ambiguous crossroads, untaught, unmanned, and unnamed. Is Abelard minus his *ingenium* still a master? Is Abelard minus the *pars quae hominem facit* still a man? Is there a neuter form of the proper name *Petrus*, and, if there were, would it fit this creature?[33]

The *Historia calamitatum* does not resolve these questions as it strains toward closure in an uneasy atmosphere of frustration; in fact, the text does not conclude so much as simply stop. The final pages of the *Historia* repeatedly lament the lack of resolution in what Abelard calls the life of a man inefficient at all he undertakes (*Historia*, tr. 96/99). At the moment of writing, Abelard is abbot of the wild Breton monastery of St. Gildas de Rhuys, persecuted by his monks, tormented by anxiety and by "battles and fears both within and without" (tam foris quam intus pugne pariter et timores) (*Historia*, my translation/105).[34]

Such anxiety is of course rooted in calamitous autobiographical events, but it is also and equally a response to a problem raised by their textual performance. Writing on contradiction in one of his dialectical treatises, Abelard remarks that a logical problem of this sort "first causes the reader inevitable anxiety and then, a solution at last having diligently been found, frees him completely therefrom" (in anxietatem inevitabilem prius lectorem ponit ac demum facta diligenter solutione ab omni eum anxietate liberat) (*Logica ingredientibus*, 445).[35] This is the anxiety that rules the *Historia calamitatum*, and from which it is never fully freed. The *Historia* and related letters present Abelard's identity dialectically, as a *quaestio* with no easy answer, and the unresolved tension between a biographical affirmation (Abelard is a teacher, Abelard is a monk, Abelard is a man) and its corresponding negation produces a longing for closure that one could call hermeneutic anxiety. This is the anxiety that provokes Heloise, in her first letter, to request another text from Abelard (*Letters*, tr. 110/69); it is likewise one of the motivations behind the compilation of their correspondence into the form preserved in the manuscripts.[36]

The *Historia*'s one successful resolution of such conflict takes place in the affair with Heloise's eroticization of dialectic, which redefined and confused the poles of a relation that promised (in Abelard's expectation at least) to be as neatly oppositional as any other in his experience. That resolution is, however, short-lived. It is also, and for our purposes more interestingly, ideologically intolerable for Abelard: he will later, in his second letter to Heloise, rewrite it so as to suppress its pleasure completely (*Letters*, tr. 146–48/88–89). A brief look at one final unresolved *quaestio* raised in the *Historia* will, however, indicate a means of resolving such biographical *quaestiones*.

After the condemnation at Soissons, Abelard retreats to the monastery of St. Denis near Paris, where he promptly makes more enemies:

It happened that one day in my reading I came across a statement of Bede . . . which asserted that Dionysus the Areopagite was bishop of Corinth, not of Athens. This seemed the direct contrary of their [the monks'] claim that their patron Denis is to be identified with the famous Areopagite whose history shows him to have been bishop of Athens.

(Fortuitu namque mihi quadam die legenti occurrit quedam Bede sententia qua
. . . asserit Dyonisium Ariopagitam Corinthiorum potiusquam Atheniensium
fuisse episcopum. Quod valde eis contrarium videbatur, qui suum Dyonisium
esse illum Ariopagitam jactitant, quem ipsum Atheniensem episcopum gesta ejus
fuisse profitentur.) (*Historia*, tr. 85/89–90)

The ensuing conflict is again a *quaestio* strung between apparently irrec-
oncilable oppositions—of patrons (Dionysus of Corinth and Dionysus of
Athens); of authorities (the Venerable Bede and the ninth-century abbot
Hilduin); of disputants (Abelard and the community of St. Denis). As
the *Historia* tells it, Abelard's only move toward resolving the conflict, beside appealing to ecclesiastical and political authorities, is to offer a faintly
flippant explanation to his angry brothers: "I said that I had not denied
(that the Areopagite was the patron), nor did it matter whether he was
the Areopagite or came from somewhere else, seeing that he had won so
bright a crown in the eyes of God" (Ego autem respondi nec me hoc dene-
gasse nec multum curandum esse utrum ipse Ariopagita an aliunde fuerit,
dummodo tantam apud Deum adeptus sit coronam) (*Historia*, tr. 86/90).
When this strategy fails, he appears before the abbot, is condemned, flees
to the country, and starts his own foundation, which in time attracts flocks
of eager students.

The *Historia*'s version of the St. Denis controversy, as this brief sketch
shows, has a familiar narrative structure: Abelard attacks a paternal superior, is persecuted by jealous rivals, escapes, and founds a new estab-
lishment. So powerful, in fact, is this narrative paradigm of assertion and
negation that the text elides details of what seems to be Abelard's historical
attempt to resolve the conflict. A letter written by Abelard to Abbot Adam
of St. Denis, however, provides more information. There, Abelard brings
to bear on the intellectual *quaestio* powers that he seems unable or unwilling to apply to biographical problems in the *Historia*. After summoning
his authorities (Eusebius and Jerome on one side and Bede on the other),
he returns the monks' patron to them and offers three possible solutions
in conclusion:

I think, therefore, that all controversy on this point can be resolved. In brief, my
suggestions for a solution are as follows: we must concede that Bede was deceived,
that he was presenting the opinion of other persons, or that there were two bishops of Corinth.

(Atque ita arbitror omnem controversiam absolvi posse. Omnium igitur, quae ad
solutionem proposuimus, haec summa est, ut vel Bedam deceptum fuisse con-

cedamus; vel eum aliorum nobis opinionem praesentasse: vel duos Corinthiorum episcopos exstitisse.) (*PL* 178: 344D)

By showing Abelard turning his dialectical powers upon a *quaestio* in order to mediate a solution, this letter does indeed resolve some of the problems raised by the *Historia*'s version of the episode. If this is a resolution, however, it must be so only in a limited sense, for, as we know from the *Historia*, the letter did not successfully extricate Abelard from his biographical problem (only Adam's death and the intercession of Count Thibaut of Champagne would do that). Full solution of the intellectual question is likewise lacking, deferred to the extratext. As the problems in the *Historia* are only resolved outside it, so, here, the "correct" explanation for the controversy remains for the reader to decide: Was Bede wrong? Was he reporting someone else's opinion? Were there two bishops of Corinth named Denis, one of whom moved to Athens?

Assiduous Interrogation

To question wisely is to teach.

—Alcuin, *De rhetorica et virtutibus*

If we have learned anything from John of Salisbury and Peter Abelard and the medieval texts around them, it is that the Aristotelian structures of opposition do not produce for dialectical readers and teachers the same effects of epistemological, pedagogical, hermeneutic, and even ontological security that scriptural contradiction (and its impossibility) offered exegetes in the contemplative tradition. Opposites are not held in the mysterious suspension of *both-and* in Abelard's and John's narratives as they are in a contemplative reading of Scripture. Here, when teachers are or teach both one thing and its opposite, the text tightens up around them — John of Salisbury's ostensibly moderate and mediating *Metalogicon* is itself drawn into performing as well as representing contradiction; Peter Abelard both is and cannot be either/both one thing or/and the other. The dialectical world, then, is one in which multiplicity is inevitably contradiction, a contradiction less easy to work, resolve, and manage in practice than the dialecticians, in their moments of metadisciplinary pride, would have us believe. Once opposites are set in motion against each other, their behavior is hard to control, and the resulting movement is fraught with perils, not the least of which are ambiguity and contradiction. Abelard himself, however, suggests a way in which this movement may be directed toward an epistemologically powerful result. I am thinking here, of course, of the *Sic et non*, an exegetical workbook that is at once aggressively contradictory and directed toward resolution of contradiction.

Abelard worked for some twenty years on the *Sic et non*, apparently putting it through at least five revisions, right up to his death in 1142. The *Sic et non* is perhaps the most exhaustive—and certainly the best-known—collection of contrary things left us by the Middle Ages; it offers us contradiction, teaches us to read it, then leaves us on our own to invent interpretation(s) from it.

Judging from the work's title alone, it might seem that the *Sic et non*, like the *Historia*, is built upon an endless cycle of negation and affirmation. The body of the text, after the prologue, consists entirely of conflicting biblical and patristic citations, arranged in *quaestiones* (such as, for example, "That marriage is a good; *et contra*")[37] juxtaposed without the buffering mediation of authorial commentary and resolution.[38] Judging from the title and structure alone, one might expect the *Sic et non* to violate the teaching method advocated by Abelard's pupil John of Salisbury:

> A trustworthy and a prudent lecturer will respect as inviolable the evident literal meaning of what is written, until he obtains a fuller and surer grasp of the truth by further reading or by divine revelation. As it is, what one claims to teach with faithfulness and utility, another claims to unteach with equal faithfulness and utility.
>
> (Quicquid autem littere facies indicat, lector fidelis et prudens interim ueneretur ut sacrosanctum, donec ei alia docente aut Domino reuelante ueritas plenius et familiarius innotescat. Quod enim unus fideliter et utiliter docet, alter eque fideliter et utiliter dedocet.) (*Met.* 3.1; tr. 148/122)

We have seen that John's unteachers of dialectic displayed their error in an incoherent coincidence of unthinking conservatism and rupture with tradition. These scholars, John says, "relieve their embarrassment by proposing new errors. . . . Lacking judgement, they copy and quote all that has ever been said or written, even by the most obscure" (nescientes quid loquantur aut de quibus asserant, errores condunt nouos. . . . Compilant omnium opiniones, et ea que etiam a uilissimis dicta uel scripta sunt, ab inopia iudicii scribunt et referunt) (*Met.* 2.7; tr. 89/73). John incarnates such philosophical folly in a paratactic collection of opinions and oppositions very like, perhaps, the *Sic et non* itself. Such "oppositions," John concludes, are rightly named, "for they are opposed to better studies, and constitute impediments to progress" (recte autem dicuntur oppositiones, quia melioribus studiis opponuntur; obstant enim profectui) (*Met.* 2.7; tr. 89/73).

The 158 unanswered *quaestiones* of the *Sic et non* thus threaten to strand the reader at the blocked crossroads that Augustine spoke of in the *De dialectica*, to pick fights with Scripture, as he commanded us not to do in the *De doctrina christiana* (1.6.6), or to chase our own tails like the self-absorbed logicians of the *Metalogicon* (2.10). Theologically speaking, the dangers of such a strategy are clear: the *Sic et non* could attack scriptural and patristic authority by setting that authority against itself. The *Sic et non* could set itself up as generator of alternative Scripture, an interminable series of interpretations as multiple and conflicting as the authoritative texts themselves. It could seduce readers into the kind of arbitrary overinterpretation that Bede called blowing the nose of Scripture, or worse still, it could seduce them into doubt.[39]

Fully aware of these risks, Abelard prefaces the work with a theoretical discussion that aims to limit and justify them. We would not be mistaken here to think of Augustine's introduction to reading another contradictory text—the Bible—in the *De doctrina christiana*. Abelard begins by laying out the problem in the most simple and precise of terms: "Since, in such a multitude of words, some statements, even those of the saints, appear not only to differ from one another, but even to be mutually opposed, one should not judge them rashly" (*Sic et non*, my translation/89).

The first sentence of the book makes the problem of conflicting authorities a result of canonical multiplicity. While the multiple nature of holy writing is, as we have seen, a common enough element in any exegete's ideological *florilegium*, the linguistic emphasis here is typically Abelardian. So, too, is the undercurrent of anxiety, which continues in the almost mournful enumeration of the obstacles between *sacra pagina* and mortal reader:

So it is little wonder that if we lack that Spirit, by whose agency these writings were written and dictated, and communicated directly by it to the writers, we may fail to understand their actual writings. The greatest barrier to our understanding is the unusual style and the fact that very often the same words have different meanings, when one and the same word has been used to express now one meaning, now another. For each person has an abundant supply of words, just as of thoughts.

(Quid itaque mirum si absente nobis spiritu ipso, per quem ea et scripta sunt et dictata atque ipso quoque scriptoribus intimata, ipsorum nobis desit intelligentia? Ad quam nos maxime pervenire impedit inusitatis locutionis modus ac plerumque earundem vocum significatio diversa, cum modo in hac modo in illa significatione vox eadem sit posita. Quippe quemadmodum in sensu suo ita et in verbis suis unusquisque abundat.) (*Sic et non*, tr. 87/89)

Like the book it introduces, this passage is organized around painful opposites: the abundance of words, meanings, and individual subjectivities; the loss of the knowledge that would facilitate their interpretation.

The preface thus pitches hermeneutic anxiety at an unbearable level for a clerical reader, who, if well trained in exegesis, will seek to assuage that anxiety through the pleasurable release of interpretation. As the book's structure will demand an anxious effort at reconciliation, its preface offers structures to protect the intellectual activity thus provoked—a theoretical framework wherein the repeated pairing of opposites, of affirmation and negation, that makes up the rest of the book will be hermeneutically manageable and theologically safe.[40]

This Abelard does in a recasting of Augustine's rules for reading in the *De doctrina christiana*, a revision notable for its attention to the circumstances of both the scriptural and the interpretive acts. By attending to the contexts of an act of writing—the literary context (the author's style), the rhetorical (his addressee and mode of speech), the historical (diachronic changes in human customs; transmission history and scribal variation), and the psychological (authorial intention)—Abelard says, the reader will find a way out of the *aporias* into which both Scripture and the *Sic et non* will insistently place him. Ideally, this rigorously contextualized method of reading will complete the task John of Salisbury found so difficult: "to contemper words with things and things with the times" (uerba rebus, res temporibus contemperare) (*Pol.* 7.12; my translation/2: 140).

The final step in Abelard's circumscription of his book's impending contradictions further anchors the interpretative act. When these contextualized rules for reading do not work, Abelard says, the reader should turn to the hierarchical structure of authority itself—much as he himself did in his attempt to resolve the St. Denis controversy: "But if the dispute is so obvious that it cannot be resolved by having recourse to reasoning, then authorities must be compared, and that authority retained which has more value as evidence and greater weight" (Quod si forte adeo manifesta sit controversia, ut nulla potest absolvi ratione, conferendae sint auctoritates, et quae potioris est testimonii et maioris confirmationis potissimum retinenda) (*Sic et non*, tr. 94/96).

Once the preface has thus anchored the hermeneutic act, its anxious

tone relaxes, and Abelard turns his attention to the justification of his
strategy. In so doing, he offers a defense of pedagogical contrary things,
the first we have so far encountered. This is a teaching process that mirrors the dissonant teaching-textuality of Scripture itself, whose obscurities,
ambiguities, and apparent contradictions are arranged, Augustine said,
that men might go away from reading the richer (*Enarrationes in Psalmos*
126.ii, in *PL* 37: 1675):

This having been said by way of preliminary, it is my purpose, according to my
original intention, to gather together the sayings of the holy Fathers which have
occurred to me as being surrounded by some degree of uncertainty because of
their seeming incompatibility. These may encourage inexperienced readers to engage in that most important exercise, enquiry into truth, and as a result of that
enquiry give an edge to their critical faculty.

(His autem praelibatis, placet ut instituimus, diversa sanctorum patrum dicta
colligere quae nostrae occurerint memoriae aliquam ex dissonantia quam habere
videntur quaestionem contrahentia, quae teneros lectores ad maximum inquiren-
dae veritatis exercitium provocent et acutiores ex inquisitione reddant.) (*Sic et
non*, tr. 99/103)

The "dissonances" in Scripture do not block but rather *call* readers — and
provoke their attention to the very processes of textual teaching; so too the
contradictions of the *Sic et non*, whose theoretical introduction makes the
reading process an explicit meta-exegetical issue.[41] Read under Abelard's
rules, the opposed texts thus do not block "the path of reason," as John of
Salisbury's warnings and Abelard's own career might lead us to think, but
rather make movement on it possible.[42] Abelardian ideal readers are not,
like John's negative ones, "forever studying, but never acquiring knowledge" (querentes semper, sed numquam ad scientiam peruenientes) (*Met.*
2.7; tr. 89/72); they are equipped, rather, with a master key to wisdom:
"For assiduous questioning is defined as the first key of wisdom. . . . For
by doubting we come to enquiry, and by enquiry we perceive the truth"
(Haec quippe prima sapientiae clavis definitur assidua scilicet seu frequens
interrogatio. . . . Dubitando enim ad inquisitionem pervenimus; inqui-
rendo veritatem percipimus) (*Sic et non*, tr. 99/103).[43] The intellectual activity touched off by contradictory teaching is thus controlled by rules for
reading and justified by its incorporation into a dialectical approach to
something beyond both logic and *verba* — wisdom.[44]

However, Abelard is not calling for a radically subjective interpretation
of Scripture; his student-reader, he says, should be first guided by God in
his search for truth. The pedagogical audacity of the text, however, quickly

follows this orthodox declaration: for Abelard, this search must be dialectical, based on the question and built from contention.[45] His book forces its
imagined readers, trained in philology, conversant with the canon of the
authorities, and reading in accordance with what Augustine called their
intus magister (*De magistro* 12.40), to devote their own multiple *verba* and
sensus to the labor of interpretation.

For all the Augustine and Jerome passages cited in the *Sic et non*'s
preface, there is little—at least on the *superficies litterae*—of those readers'
almost plastic delight in scriptural language here, little of the poetics of
exegesis. What we have instead is a text every element of whose austere
structure seems designed to force us to read. For, to quote Abelard himself,
a solution must be found: unlike other medieval compilations of scriptural
oppositions, the *Sic et non* does not resolve the *quaestiones* that it so aggressively raises.[46] The *Sic et non* makes especially clear what is the case in
all exegesis, poetic or not, monastic or scholastic: finding solutions, finding meaning, is a labor of *invention*, and the exegetical dialectic that Peter
Abelard constructs, delimits, and sets to work in the *Sic et non* demands
such inventiveness. Thus, though the *Sic et non* does indeed summon dialectic's *either/or*, it does far more than that. In the frequent adoptions of
this text as a metonymic representative of "medievalness," few metonym-
izers read the title closely, read the *copula* of the title.[47] The work does not
proclaim itself to be *Yes or No* (*Aut sic aut non*), a command to choose one
or the other, but *Sic et non*, a recognition of both sides of the *quaestio*—as
much *both-and*, that is, as *either/or*.[48]

Is Abelard violent or generous as a reader? Does he divide or multiply?
William of St. Thierry was sure that the *Sic et non* was a monstrously divisive text, though he had not read further than its title:

There are, I am told, smaller works written by the man, whose titles are: *Sic et
non* and *Scito te ipsum*. And there are others of which I fear that their dogmas are
as monstrous as their titles. But they hate the light and are not to be found when
sought.

(Sunt autem, ut audio, adhuc alia ejus opuscula, quorum nomina sunt, *Sic et non*;
Scito te ipsum; et alia quaedam de quibus timeo ne, sicut monstruosi sunt nomi-
nis, sic etiam sint monstruosi dogmatis: sed, sicut dicunt, oderunt lucem, nec
etiam quaesita inveniuntur.) (*PL* 182: 532D–533A) [49]

Abelard was in fact often accused of doing violence to Scripture—"vio-
lating it to its core," as Hugh Metellus put it in a letter to him.[50] The
conjoined multiplicity of the *Sic et non*, this most proverbially schizoid of

medieval texts, should suggest to us that something more is going on here than meets the eye. In his *Theologia "Scholarium,"* Abelard answers such accusations of divisive violence in language whose tone should by now be familiar to us:

> If anyone should accuse me of being an importunate or violent interpreter . . . let him think on the prophecy of Caiphas, which the Holy Spirit brought forth through him, accommodating the prophecy to other meanings than that which the speaker himself would understand. . . . Whence Gregory . . . says: "In the understanding of holy Scripture nothing should be rejected that does not go against faith. For as from a single chunk of gold, some make necklaces, others rings, others bracelets for adornment, so too from one statement of holy Scripture the expositors compose, so to speak, ornaments through innumerable interpretations, for all these things are useful for the adornment of the heavenly Spouse."

> (Si quis autem me quasi importunum ac uiolentum expositorem causetur . . . attendat illam Cayphe prophetiam quam spiritus sanctus per eum protulit, longe ad alium sensum eam accommodans quam prolator ipse senserit. . . . Unde Gregorius . . . : "In intellectu sacre scripture respui non debet quidquid sane fidei non resistit. Sicut enim ex uno auro alii murenulas, alii annulos, alii dextralia ad ornamentum faciunt, ita ex una scripture sacre sententia expositores quique per innumeros intellectus quasi uaria ornamenta componunt; que tamen omnia ad decorem celestis sponse proficiunt.")[51]

While the austerity and rigor of the *Sic et non*'s style—in both thought and expression—are quite different in flavor from the extravagances of monastic exegetes like Gregory or the rich rhythms of Augustinian prose, Abelard is not so far removed from the exegetes we studied in Chapter 1 as might appear at first blush. He is a monk and a poet, after all, as well as a logician. The preface's valorization of active reading and the attendant redefinition of mastery recalls the *Historia*'s one moment of fruitful confusion: the erotopedagogical idyll of the early days with Heloise. It repeats on a chastely intellectual level the mutual mastery and pleasurable play with the letter that took place in that erotic experiment.[52] The letter should not be tortured on the rack, says John of Salisbury, but treated in a friendly fashion (*Met.* 3.1); from the letter, we are reminded again and again by monastic readers, flows infinite sweetness, and from scriptural multiplicity, infinite pleasure. And for this last, our monastic authority is none other than Peter Abelard—exegete and dialectician, monk and teacher, passionate reader above all:

> The triple meaning of Scripture is a meal of diverse courses; the rich table of Holy Scripture abounds in multiple delights.

(Triplex intelligentia
Diversa praebet fercula.
Delitiis habundat variis
sacrae mensa Scripturae fertilis.) [53]

Abelard's refectory metaphor here brings us back, through the intellectual machinations of dialectic, to the poetics of exegesis, to the charged erotic language of a contemplative interpretation invented and performed —as is Abelard's rough and contradictory *Sic et non*—in the image of Scripture. Surprising as it might seem to suggest an erotics in the cool and anxious rigor of Abelardian logic, to do so is to follow good medieval precedent. After all, commentators from Origen forward tell us, of all the books in the Bible, the one that best represents logic is the *Song of Songs*, with its exalted discourse and erotic *mysterium*. Isidore of Seville writes:

Now, the Holy Scriptures are also involved in these three branches of philosophy. For they are given to discussing either nature, as in Genesis and Ecclesiastes; or behavior, as in Proverbs and in general throughout the Bible; or *logic, in place of which our Christian writers appropriate theology*, as in the Song of Songs and the Gospels.

(In his quippe tribus generibus philosophiae etiam eloquia diuina consistunt. Nam aut de natura disputare solent, ut in Genesi et Ecclesiaste; aut de moribus, ut in Prouerbiis et in omnibus sparsim libris; *aut de logica, pro qua nostri theologicam sibi uindicant*, ut in Cantico Canticorum, et Euangeliis.) [54]

Logic and theology, Aristotle and the Song of Songs; unlikely bedfellows in any time but the Middle Ages. Their conjunction produces some very strange and beautiful offspring. Abelard himself, as textualized in his own and others' writing, is one of them. There are other textual offspring of this conjunction, which, as their subject matter moves into fields whose riches are less easy Egyptian gold for theological appropriation, get stranger and stranger. To read their strangeness, we will need every hermeneutical maneuver exegesis and dialectic can teach us, plus a good dose of monastic tolerance for ambiguity. We will also need a sense of the erotics of contradiction, for these texts have learned as much from Ovid as they have from Aristotle and from the Bible. I refer to the medieval *ars amatoria*, that odd and preachy genre, which teaches the seducer both seduction and damnation, and calmly unteaches its own *doctrina*.

Chapter 4

Sophisticated Teaching
The Double-Talk of Andreas Capellanus

Safety in numbers!—Fight on, add up the sum of my precepts;
  Pile up the numerous grains, mountains of counsel arise.
But since the ways we react seem to differ as much as our features,
  Do not trust me too far.

—Ovid, *Remedia amoris*

Medieval writers learned much of what they knew about the literary *doctrina* of love from Ovid, a situation that the Roman poet's narrator does everything possible to encourage. The narrator of Ovid's *Ars amatoria* and *Remedia amoris* dubs himself quite literally the Master of his subject: "I am Cupid's preceptor" (Ego sum praeceptor Amoris), he boasts, not three breaths into his first book (*Ars* 1.17). He says that he can teach anything about love between men and women to both men and women: how to find a woman, how to get her, how to keep her; how to find a man, get a man, keep a man; how to dump him or her and get over it quickly.

Ovid's *Ars* and *Remedia* were core texts of the central medieval curriculum, in part because their ready music could teach young clerics the basics of Latin versification.[1] One need look no further than Abelard's chilly selection of Heloise as his lover ("first of all, work to find what you want to love," advises Ovid's narrator (principio, quod amare uelis, reperire labora) (*Ars* 1.35) to see that medieval students learned rather more from Ovid than how to make their elegiacs limp with proper elegance. Heloise, who should know, called Ovid "teacher of disgrace" (turpidinis . . . doctor) even as she cited him as her authority in a theological argument.[2]

Ovid taught medieval writers so well and so much that for one of them, the thirteenth-century Frenchman Guiart, he seems to have become fused with the Philosopher himself. Henri d'Andeli, in the earlier *Lai d'Aristote*, had imagined Aristotle in love and in trouble, his book learning untaught by Amor.[3] Guiart imagines that the Philosopher put some of that unlearning to educational use, writing a book to teach these things to needy clerics, instructing them in both erotic sophistry and disambiguating erotic dialectic. The resulting pleasant textbook is equal parts *Art of Love* and *Sophistical Refutations*:

Aristotle teaches in his book that a cleric can deceive his girlfriend by fallacy; in the same book he teaches how to know the truth from this falsehood.

> (Aristote en son livre nos aprent a savoir
> Qu'un clerc puet par fallace son amie decevoir,
> En cel meïsme livre aprent a parcevoir
> De cele fausseté a conoistre le voir.)
> (Guiart, *Art d'amors*, lines 21–24)

Guiart has in fact imagined Aristotle after himself—he has imagined Aristotle writing a medieval "art of love" for a medieval Christian clerical student.[4] When we remember that the writers of the medieval arts of love were, like Guiart, themselves trained clerics, who learned to read the Bible as they learned their syllogisms and their elegiacs, we must add another master to the mix, the Bible. This is a provocative curriculum for a teaching-textuality.

The Ovidian pedagogical renaissance of the central Middle Ages has, then, a "fundamental ambiguity" about it. The expression is John Baldwin's, and he asks, "How could Ovid's candidly hedonist doctrine be adapted to the rigors of Christian chastity, in particular the schools' mission to lead clerics toward a life of celibacy?" ("*Ars amatoria*," 21). I hope to leave this question open, for to give it an answer would be to arrest the assiduous questioning provoked by the medieval *ars amatoria*'s juxtaposition of clerical and secular, holy and carnal. The medieval *ars* is a *quaestio*, to be studied and understood rather than answered.

A student of the genre presided over by Guiart's oddly composite Aristotle (part lover, part logician) needs to know how to handle a *quaestio*, for, when asked if human love is good, the medieval arts of love answer vociferously both *sic* and *non*, and with abundant argument to support both propositions. Like the dialectician and, perhaps surprisingly, the reader of Scripture, the reader of medieval erotodidacticism is taught in opposition, must learn to work opposition for its *doctrina*. Unlike the exegetical and logical texts we have so far examined, however, the *ars* moves in an explicitly literary space, for it seems to be concerned only with letters and bodies. Its relation to *res* is even more troubling than that of dialectic, because the *ars* is, ultimately, fiction, and as such serves the truth of things only by indirection. "Do not trust me too far" (non sunt iudiciis omnia danda meis), Ovid's preceptor declares disingenuously (*Rem.* 426; tr. Humphries, 194). The medieval *ars* will lead us to the same conclusion since, for all its insistence on service to truth, its teaching discourse is ultimately less placid demonstration than ambiguous double-talk.

The literary space of the medieval *ars amatoria* is somewhere—or something—in between the exegesis of Scripture's *res* and the word-bound secularity of dialectic, partaking of both.[5] In the contrary things of the medieval *ars amatoria*, opposition is worked into a poetics of didacticism as intellectually and sensually rich as that of exegesis, as rigorous as that of dialectic. The multiple, apparently contradictory discourse that Scripture generates by divine *mysterium*, and from which dialectic collects materials for its arguments, is created in the *ars amatoria* by mortal, even fictional fiat. Like scriptural and dialectical *doctrina*, this contradictory instruction has as much to teach about teaching and reading as it does about its ostensible subject.[6]

One of the most provocative of the medieval reworkings of Ovid has long been Andreas Capellanus's *De amore* (c. 1185), partly because its first two books seem to lay down the precepts of that fascinating "doctrine" that Gaston Paris called "amour courtois" ("Études sur les romans," 519) and partly because that doctrine is so difficult to extract from the many competing teachings represented in and performed by the text. Paris took the *De amore*'s first two books as a textbook for "courtly love." He did not seem to notice that the third book offers itself as quite the opposite: a textbook argument *against* its own previous teaching. These multiple teachings led Donald Monson to observe, "One of the things Andreas seems to be doing in the *De amore* is assembling all the pertinent opinions on any given question. His work may thus be viewed as a kind of summa on love, in the tradition of Abelard's *Sic et non* and Peter Lombard's *Sentences*" ("*Auctoritas* and Intertextuality," 77).[7] I will argue here that the *De amore* resembles the *Sic et non* not only in its assemblage of divergent teachings but also in its endlessly provocative structure, which juxtaposes one teaching (that erotic love is the source of all good) with its opposite (erotic love is the source of all evil). Both the *Sic et non* and the *De amore* aim not only to teach us but also to teach us to read—starting with their own contrary, contradictory selves. However, where the *Sic et non*'s preceptive frame teaches us to resolve *quaestiones* by mediating their yes and their no, the *De amore*'s reading instructions seem to leave little room for such mediation, demanding instead that readers embrace one proposition and reject the other. Though the logic of the *De amore*'s exposition forces one to respond to its doctrine *aut sic aut non*, its textual practice shows its opposite propositions to be deeply embedded one in the other. Abelardian hermeneutic rules offer little help in a text like this, in which opposing propositions are at once mutually exclusive and mutually coimplicated. The *De amore* demands another sort of reading, and Andreas himself will tell us so: it is an "assiduous reading" (assidua lectio) that, unlike Abelard's "assiduous questioning" (assidua interrogatio), finds no exit from the oppositions of the text itself.[8]

We have already met our stand-in in this constant and puzzled reading; he is Walter, the friend whose loving disposition and need for instruction inspire Andreas to make this teaching text:

My revered friend Walter, the assiduous insistence of my love for you compels me to publish for you in my own words and to instruct you by my own hand how the condition of love can be maintained inviolate between lovers, and equally the means by which those whose love is unrequited can shift Venus' shafts lodged in their hearts.

(Cogit me multum assidua tuae dilectionis instantia, Gualteri venerande amice, ut meo tibi debeam famine propalare mearumque manuum scriptis docere qualiter inter amantes illaesus possit amoris status conservari, pariterve qui non amantur quibus modis sibi cordi affixa valeant Veneris iacula declinare.) (*De amore*, Praef. 1; 30)

If Walter knows his Ovid, as Andreas's historical audience of lettered clerics surely did, he will recognize structural echoes of the Ovidian *Ars* and *Remedia* here (*Ars* 1.35–38; *Rem.* 43–44).[9] However, this new Ovid will deliver far more—and, perhaps, rather less—than what it promises. In addition to the instruction announced here, the *De amore* contains a series of eight dialogues in which men and women of various social classes match wits in amorous disputation, twenty-one erotic *quaestiones* together with their solutions, two sets of love's commandments, and two short romances. Most maddening of all, it concludes with a third book that unteaches all that has gone before, raging with sudden and most un-Ovidian violence against everything the rest of the work has praised, most notably erotic love and women.

The *De amore* then delivers two absolutely opposed judgments about the *amor* that appears in one form or another in most of the manuscript titles: one in favor (Books 1 and 2), one against (Book 3).[10] The narrator himself says as much in a declaration as evasive as it is matter-of-fact: "So if this *doctrina* of mine which I send you within the covers of this little book is carefully and faithfully examined, it will present to you a double *sententia*" (Haec igitur nostra subtiliter et fideliter examinata doctrina, quam tibi praesenti libello mandamus insertam, tibi duplicem sententiam propinabit) (3.117; my translation).[11] Andreas's *doctrina* (and here we should read the word in its active sense, as process more than content of instruction) offers a "double *sententia*," he says, and in this little phrase lies much of the head-scratching mystery of the *De amore*.[12] We have seen the word *sententia* before, when Hugh of St. Victor spoke of the multiple *sententiae* or "deeper meanings" in a single passage of Scripture (*Did.* 6.11; tr. 149–50/128). In rhetoric, the term indicates a discourse's *res*, its content as opposed to its linguistic form; in dialectic and law, a judgment.[13] The term is thus a sort of hypertext button, where discourses of interpretation and judgment cross and coincide—much like the *De amore* itself, which goes between exegesis, dialectic, Ovid, and the law with a confounding if not completely meretricious enthusiasm.

Readers of the *Duplex Sententia*

> Let us concede that the reader is being placed in inevitable anxiety
> when it becomes clear how necessary it is to make a determination
> between two syllogismic propositions that seem to be opposites.
>
> —Peter Abelard, *Logica ingredientibus*

One of the few points upon which *De amore* scholarship unanimously agrees is that the text's structure and argumentation bear the mark of contemporary dialectical practice. It follows that one way to construct an interpretation of the book's two competing propositions would be the method suggested by John of Salisbury, as we saw above in Chapter 2: "When inherent agreement is doubted, it is necessary to search for some middle term whereby extremes may be copulated" (*Met.* 3.9; tr. 187/152). This is the path followed, for example, by Irving Singer, who argues that Andreas is attempting to harmonize the competing discourses of love available to a Northern French writer by positioning "courtly love" as a third term between *caritas* and *cupiditas*.[14] Similarly, this argument would run, within the love dialogues of Book 1 and the love problems of Book 2, Andreas consistently reaches for judgments to lay discussions to rest. However, such rest is at best temporary, at worst illusory, and these mediating readers are hard pressed to account for Book 3's discursive and logical violence.

Another reading strategy would see the book not as a logical solution but as a logical problem. Its apparent violation of the principle of non-contradiction certainly is a call to questioning: How is one to make sense of a text that poses the *quaestio* "the love of women is the source of all happiness, *et contra*, the source of all damnation," and in response delivers a double verdict at once for and against each opposing side?

This hermeneutic anxiety is as productive in the *De amore*'s reception history as it is in the logical and exegetical works of Andreas's contemporaries. Since the earliest preserved manuscript testimonies, the *De amore* has clearly produced richly multiple rereadings and rewritings. The many copies, translations, and imitations of the text respond to its provocative structure in multiple ways, each of which remakes the *De amore* and in a very material sense answers its *quaestio*.[15] It is a testimony to Andreas's didactic sophistication that such individual answers are never definitive enough to allay that hermeneutic anxiety completely. Beginning with the text's thirteenth-century copyists, a significant group of readers has tended to take one of the text's two "propositions" as true and the other as false. The problem has long been determining which is which.

The three-book structure that we know as the "complete" *De amore* is well attested in the textual transmission of both the Latin and vernacular versions. Equally strong, if not stronger, in the tradition are partial recastings and florilegial citations that respond to the book's hermeneutic anxiety by isolating one of the *sententiae* as if its opposite proposition had never existed at all.[16] Thus Albertano of Brescia's *De arte loquendi et tacendi* calls solely upon Book 3 in its discussion of love, and the fifteenth-century Castilian cleric Alfonso Martínez de Toledo does the same in his own passionately contradictory *reprobatio amoris*, the *Arçipreste de Talavera*.[17] The Catalan translation, on the other hand, contains only Books 1 and 2, and seems to have been used to adjudicate love games in the late-fourteenth-century Aragonese court.[18]

A postmedieval analogue to this "florilecture" (Dagenais, *Ethics of Reading*, 169) may be found in interpretations that take the *De amore* as a textbook for that troublesome construct "courtly love." Gaston Paris did this in the celebrated (and now perhaps notorious) article in which he coined the term "amour courtois," referring to the *De amore* as a "manuel du droit amoureux" and ignoring completely the doctrinal about-face of Book 3 ("Études sur les romans," 526). The title of John J. Parry's widely diffused English translation, *The Art of Courtly Love*, continues in the same vein, though Parry does discuss and translate Book 3. Reading from Parry or Paris, one might find Book 3's *reprobatio amoris* appended merely for "symmetry and safety," its empty conventionality requiring no critical effort beyond that of shutting the book (Jackson, 4).

Equally concerned with hermeneutic closure, and equally medieval in their precedents, are readings that, rather than excising one part of the double *sententia*, choose one part as the master discourse and read the other through it. The duplicity is only apparent, then. For these readers, the *De amore* is a teaching text with a single *sententia* expressed in two ways: seriously and ironically—or, to use terms more familiar to a medieval reader, literally and figuratively. Thus D. W. Robertson, Jr.: "the subject of the *De amore* is *fornicatio* used with its full connotations as the opposite of *caritas*, and Andreas does nothing but condemn it" ("Subject of the *De amore*," 161). What does not seem on the face of the letter to be condemnation must thus be condemnation made figurally through a discourse of opposites—*anti*phrasis, that is, irony.[19] A conclusion absolutely opposite in content but identical in structure is reached by another group of readers, following Pio Rajna's 1891 suggestion that Book 3 is to be read not literally but parodically. For readers like Betsy Bowden, Bruno Roy, and H. Silvestre, Books 1 and 2 are the literal (even obscene) *sententia* and Book 3 the *sententia*'s parodic and impious verification.[20]

Though opposed in terms of content as neat contraries, both sacred and scabrous readings are deeply exegetical (and, of course, it must be added, deeply medieval). As we have seen, for Christian exegetical readers, the Bible is knit together by a loose but sturdy web of figuration. What is said figuratively in one place is said literally in another; the process of scriptural teaching is thus *duplex*, as Aquinas would later observe: "Holy Scripture manifests doubly the truth that it teaches: by the words, and by the figures of things" (sacra Scriptura veritatem quam tradit, dupliciter manifestat; per verba, et per rerum figuras) (*Quaestiones quodlibetales* 6.a15). Thus, these apparently opposing readings of the *De amore* are identical in their figuralizing exegetical method, if not in their conclusions. Taking the impossibility of didactic double-talk as an axiom, they diligently seek ways to allay the hermeneutic anxiety that the *De amore* causes. Robertson's moral reading dissolves the possibility of "doctrinal inconsistency in the *De amore* as a whole" ("Subject of the *De amore*," 161); Roy states with almost audible relief that an obscenely punning reading of the *De amore* "permits us to surmount its basic contradiction" ("Obscenité," 87).

"Apparent contradictions undermine totalizing interpretations," observes John Dagenais, "and much twentieth-century criticism may be seen as a search for some critical position outside the text . . . from which the contradictions may be viewed as harmonizing to form a coherent and consistent whole" ("Como pella a las dueñas," 1). The problem with solutions to the *De amore* like Robertson's or, contrariwise, Bowden's or Roy's is not that they are "wrong" or "anachronistic"—they are neither. The problem is that they look for a wholeness that is more modern than medieval, failing to see that both their "solution" *and* its apparent opposite are prefigured in the *De amore* itself, whose "duplicity is, *faute de mieux*, the source of whatever integrity may be found in Andreas' text" (Mackey, 348).

It is clear, then, that this odd book offers itself handily, even enthusiastically, to judgments as opposed in nominal doctrine as they are identical in process. The *De amore* is, in short, "less a book than a problem of interpretation, a work constituted by its fundamental internal contradictions and the moral dilemma that results from them" (P. Allen, "*Assidua lectio*," 1). Our task is now to read those contradictions.

Reading the *Duplex Sententia*

> Without moderation, everything falls into contraries, for utility is
> undone by subtlety.
>
> —John of Salisbury, *Metalogicon*

That readers of the *De amore* have been led to such extreme conclusions is highly appropriate, for the conclusions—and, more importantly, the methods used to reach them—are insistently represented in the text itself. Both the preceptor and his characters habitually argue their opposing theses with this same exclusive logic. The first two books take as axioms that worldly love is a good and that all good things flow from it. "What a remarkable thing is love," says the preceptor, "for it invests a man with such shining virtues, and there is no one whom it does not instruct to have these great and good habits in plenty!" (O, quam mira res est amor, qui tantis facit hominem fulgere virtutibus, tantisque docet quemlibet bonis moribus abundare!) (1.4.1; 38). Like the preceptor, the suitors in the dialogues of Book 1 take the virtuous nature of love as a given and argue demonstratively from it. Says the nobleman in the sixth dialogue:

Loving is *either* a good *or* an evil. It is hazardous to assert that it is an evil, because all are agreed on the clear truth which the *doctrina* of Love proves to us— that neither woman nor man can be regarded as happy in this world, nor can anyone perform any acts of courtesy or any good, unless love's kindling inspires such deeds in him. *So you must necessarily conclude that loving is therefore a good and honorable thing.*

(Nam amare *aut est bonum aut est malum.* Quod sit malum non est assere tutum, quia satis omnibus constat et est manifestum, et amoris hoc nobis doctrina demonstrat, quod neque mulier neque masculus potest in saeculo beatus haberi nec curialitatem nec aliqua bona perficere, nisi sibi haec fomes praestet amoris. *Unde necessario vobis concluditur ergo bonum esse amare et appetibile.*) (1.6.305; 126; emphasis added)

The preaching teacher in Book 3 will argue precisely the opposite—using the same logical machinery. "Proper and careful investigation," relying on the double authority of Holy Writ and constant experience (*assidua experimenta*) (3.31; 296), here "demonstrates that there is no sinful transgression which does not result from love" (Recte namque intuentibus et vestigantibus rem diligenter nullius criminis notatur excessus, qui ex ipso non sequatur amore) (3.29; 294). Even more logically formidable is this declaration, also from Book 3, reasoned under the rigorous dialectical rule of the *lex contrarietatis:* "Clean living and bodily restraint are counted amongst the virtues, *and so* their contrary, sexual indulgence and the pleasure of the flesh, are *necessarily* accounted vices" (Honestas et continentia carnis inter ipsas adnumerantur virtutes; *ergo et* eius contrarium, luxuria scilicet et carnis voluptas, *necessario* inter vitia computantur) (3.24; 294; emphasis added).[21]

The *De amore's duplex sententia* about women also juxtaposes its opposites by the book. Woman, in the *De amore*, is either "the cause and source of all good things" (causa et origo bonorum) (1.6.403; 158), as the courtly reasoning of Book 1 and 2 assumes, or the single source of all worldly evil, according to the clerical misogyny of Book 3.[22] Such exclusive reasoning is taken to the limit in the antifeminist third part's repeated claims of universal applicability:

Every woman is by nature not only miserly but also an envious backbiter of other women, a grabber, a slave to her belly, fickle, devious in speech, disobedient, rebellious against prohibitions, marred with the vice of pride, eager for vainglory, a liar, a drunkard, a tongue-wagger who cannot keep a secret. She indulges in sexual excess, is inclined to every evil, and loves no man from the heart. . . . This rule of thumb is never found misleading; there are no exceptions to it.

(Ad haec mulier omnis non solum naturaliter reperitur avara, sed etiam invida et aliarum maledica, rapax, ventris obsequio dedita, inconstans, in sermone multiplex, inobediens et contra interdicta renitens, superbiae vitio maculata et inanis gloriae cupida, mendax, ebriosa, virlingosa, nil secretum servans, nimis luxuriosa, ad omne malum prona et hominem cordis affectione non amans. . . . Et haec non reperitur regula fallax sed omni exceptione carere.) (3.70, 72; 308)

Far from resolving the *quaestiones* raised therein, the logic deployed throughout the *De amore* inextricably implicates the text in an *either/or* dialectical world of almost Manichaean rigor. In such a world, for example, a lady must choose either "pure love" (amor purus) or "mixed love" (amor mixtus), as if there were no other possibilities open to her (1.6.475; 180); a man must take his pleasure in either the upper or the lower half of his lady's body (1.6.533–49; 198–204); a woman must choose between two suitors of equal class and virtue (2.7.13; 254) and between love and marriage (1.6.397–98; 156 and passim). Finally, in Book 3, Walter is shown that he must choose between Amor and Sponsus — either the God of Love or the Heavenly Bridegroom.

In both the theory of its central propositions and the practice of its dialogues, the *De amore* would seem to offer no "middle term whereby extremes may be copulated." We recognize this exclusive reasoning, having seen John of Salisbury wrestle with it and Abelard be undone by it. Andreas certainly learned such logical extremism in school. In his text, it grows inevitably from the way in which the treatise's central term is constructed and defined. Such a close relation between matter and manner is not surprising, for love, the *De amore*'s source of good and evil, is also (and for once unequivocally) the source of the text itself, providing both its subject matter and, as we shall see, the motive for its production.

We should read the *De amore*'s definition of love remembering what John of Salisbury discovered, to his chagrin, about excess and contrariety. "Without moderation," said John, "everything falls into contraries, for utility is undone by subtlety" (*Met.* 2.8; my translation/74).

Love is an inborn passion which results from the sight of, and uncontrolled thinking about, the beauty of the other sex. This feeling makes a man desire before all else the embraces of the other sex, and to achieve utter fulfillment of the commands of love in the other's embrace by their common desire.

(Amor est passio quaedam innata procedens ex visione et immoderata cogitatione formae alterius sexus, ob quam aliquis super omnia cupit alterius potiri amplexibus et omnia de utriusque voluntate in ipsius amplexu amoris praecepta compleri.) (1.1.1; 32) [23]

Though the preceptor backs away from some elements of this definition (most notably when he shows his seducers coolly *choosing* their ladies), he stresses one part of it again and again. Love, in the *De amore*, can grow only from "assiduous thought" (*assidua cogitatio*) (1.2.2; 34, my translation), which absolutely excludes moderation: "Any casual meditation is not enough to cause love; the thought must be out of control, for a controlled thought does not usually recur to the mind, and so love cannot arise from it" (Non quaelibet cogitatio sufficit ad amoris originem, sed immoderata exigitur; nam cogitatio moderata non solet ad mentem redire, et ideo ex ea non potest amor oriri) (1.1.13; 34). The disputing men and women of Books 1 and 2 quote this definition as authoritative (revealing themselves, in one of Andreas's sly *mises-en-abyme*, dutiful readers of the text in which they appear).[24] It remains an axiom even when the narrator has changed his persona from *praeceptor amoris* to preacher: the lover still "cannot observe moderation" (nescit habere modum) (3.62; 304).

John of Salisbury's experience with such extremism demonstrated that it inevitably falls into contraries. Thus it should come as no surprise to find that love, as the *De amore* defines it, should drive the book's argument into cleanly opposing propositions. Equally prefigured are the opposing positions assumed by readers in their judgments of the author and his book. The *De amore*'s excesses thus seem the work of "either an ironist or a nasty fool" (Muscatine, 39), an author "at the same time and contradictorily too daring and too cowardly" (Payen, 53). Such judgments are inevitable responses to the *De amore*, an excessive text "too serious to be funny, too funny to be moral, and at the end too moral to be serious" (Bowden, 67).

Immoderate Imitation

Readings of the *De amore* structured by the logical exclusivity of *either/or* and the paradoxical excess of too much/not enough are thus prefigured by and imitative of the text itself. Such imitative repetition is not particularly surprising, given the way the book defines its topic and puts that definition into discursive action. Love, though innate, is also a mimetic response to already written precepts, and its consummation is less an act of natural desire than the imitative putting into practice of an act of reading:

The whole impetus of the lover is towards enjoying the embrace of his beloved, and this is what he thinks of continually, longing to fulfill with her all the commands of love found included in the treatises on the subject.

(Ad hoc totus tendit conatus amantis, et de hoc illius assidua est cogitatio, ut eius quam amat fruatur amplexibus; optat enim ut cum ea omnia compleat amoris mandata, id est ea quae in amoris tractatibus reperiuntur inserta.) (1.2.2–3; 34)

The *De amore* will later reveal itself as the sourcebook for these very precepts, "said to have been pronounced by the king of love from his own lips, and to have been committed in writing by him to all lovers" (quas ipse rex amoris ore proprio dicitur protulisse et eas scriptas cunctis amantibus direxisse) (2.8.1; 270). It is, we learn, authorized by Amor himself, who lists the *De amore* as supplemental reading: "There are other less important precepts of love as well . . . which you will find in the book addressed to Walter" (Sunt et alia amoris praecepta minora . . . quae etiam in libro ad Gualterium scripto reperies) (1.6.269; 116).

Since lovers are defined as readers of love treatises, the *De amore* included, it is not surprising that theoretical precepts quoted by the narrator should recur in the discursive practice of his characters. One suitor calls upon "the *doctrina* of the lover Andreas, chaplain to the royal court" (amatoris Andreae aulae regiae cappellani . . . doctrina) (1.6.385; 152) to help him refute his lady's argument; others adopt the preceptor's magisterial pronouncements on the nature of nobility and love's effects on speech, morals, and perception as expedient *topoi* on which to build a discourse of seduction.[25]

Imitative links between narrator and characters also draw the apparently contradictory sections of the book together in alarming ways. Several readers have noticed this linkage between Books 2 and 3, seeing the love judgments of the former as preparation for the ecclesiastical judgments in the latter.[26] I would argue, rather, that these co-incidences are not so much proleptic as synchronic: the same patterns of thought are repeated in different contexts, acquiring each time meanings that continue to resonate in their next appearance. Take, for example, this argument:

But to offer love is a grievous offense against God, giving rise to dangers of death for many. Then too it seems to cause boundless pain and daily torture without respite for the lovers themselves. What good, then, can there be in a situation in which the Heavenly Bridegroom is displeased, one's neighbor harmed, and the lovers themselves seen to undergo the dangers of death and the torture of constant pains?

(Amorem autem exhibere est graviter offendere Deum, et multis mortis parare pericula. Et praeterea ipsis amantibus innumeras videtur inducere poenas et assidua parare quotidiana tormenta. Quod ergo bonum esse potest in eo facto in quo coelestis sponsus offenditur, et ipse proximus laeditur, et ipsi auctores mortis inde noscuntur pericula sustinere et poenis cruciari assiduis?) (1.6.411; 160)

The speaker here is one of the reluctant noblewomen of the "pro-love" Book 1, but the language will be repeated nearly word-for-word by the preaching narrator of Book 3, who argues that God is offended by lovers (3.3–4; 286) and that love subjects men to intolerable suffering in life (3.22; 292), harms one's neighbor (3.3; 288), and distracts one from service of the Heavenly Bridegroom.

Therefore you must accept, Walter, the salutary *doctrina* I set before you, and utterly renounce the empty things of this world, so that when the Bridegroom comes to celebrate the greater marriage . . . you may well be prepared to meet him with your lamps adorned and in His company make your way to the divine marriage.

(Sumas ergo, Gualteri, salubrem tibi a nobis propinatam doctrinam et mundi penitus vanitates omittas, ut quum venerit sponsus nuptias celebrare maiores . . . sis praeparatus cum lampadibus occurrere sibi ornatis secumque ad nuptias introire divinas.) (3.120; 322)

Returning to the amorous dialogue of Book 1, we can now see that the noble suitor's response adopts a similar ecclesiastical discourse to force an equally extremist, *either/or* choice upon the lady:

God has not purposed that a man should have his right foot on the earth and his left in heaven, for no man can properly serve two masters. Now it is clear that you have one foot in earthly things, because when men come to you, you give them a smiling reception, exchange courtly words with them, and encourage them to perform deeds of love. So I believe that it is more advantageous for you to devote yourself effectively to love than to lie to God under the cloak of some pretext.

(Non enim Deus voluit aliquem dextrum in terris pedem et in coelo tenere sinistrum, quia nemo potest duorum intendere competenter obsequiis. Unde quum alterum vos pedem in terrenis habere ex eo sit manifestum, quod ad vos venientes hilari receptione suscipitis et curialitatis verba secum adinvicem confertis et amoris eis opera suadetis, credo vobis esse consultius efficaciter amori vacare quam Deo sub alicuius coloris palliatione mentiri.) (1.6.415–17; 162)

Supporting himself on the unimpeachable authority of the Gospel (1 Corinthians 7.34, Matthew 6.24, Luke 16.13), the suitor uses exclusive, *either/or* logic to accuse the lady of hypocritical divided loyalty. That the man's own discourse about God and the flesh partakes of a certain duplicitous hypocrisy does not escape the woman. In fact, she imitates his reasoning when she replies that his clerical profession and amorous vocation place him in exactly the same untenable position: "Granted, however, that both these kinds of love [sc. 'pure' and 'mixed'] win approval, it does not befit you to seek service in either. A cleric ought to devote himself solely to the duties of the church, and renounce all longings of the flesh" (Sed licet uterque amor sit electus, vos tamen neutrius decet affectare militiam; clericus enim ecclesiasticis tantum debet vacare ministeriis et omnia carnis desideria declinare) (1.6.478; 182).[27] You cannot serve two masters, the characters say to each other; the preceptor says the same to his student-reader.

What, then are we to do with this doubled teaching? How are we to respond to the *quaestio* in which the *De amore* entangles us? Perhaps we are in training, and our hermeneutic discomfort is directed toward the philosophical goal of the *Sic et non*: *assidua interrogatio*, provoked by difficult reading and directed through inquiry to truth. But if so, the truth toward which the *De amore* points is neither represented nor taught within the text itself. Both the obviously fictional characters in the *De amore* and the earnest preceptor himself move in the same discursive world, echoing each other in a complicated web of citations and cross-references. When the characters quote the narrator and repeat his discursive practices, and when the narrator echoes his characters and repeats their discursive practices, they all apply theoretical axioms in a practice devoted less to *veritas* than to verisimilitude. What matters to these speakers is not the truth or falsehood of an argument but its utility, and when the arguments recur, one cannot help remembering how they were used in their previous appearance.

The *Duplex Cor* of "Andreas Capellanus"

> All this discourse is spoken in duplicity of heart and revealed with ambivalent mind.
>
> —Andreas Capellanus, *De amore*

The *De amore*'s narrator is not immune from such discursive chicanery, for he imitates his characters as much as they him. The preceptor is no impersonal, objective communicator of nominal doctrine. He is, after all, a lover himself (1.6.385; 152), and as such, he is prey to the immoderation engendered by amatory *assidua cogitatio*. Like the Ovidian *praeceptor amoris*, the narrator of the *De amore* teaches not only with official dispensation from the God of Love but also from personal experience. As the *De amore* presents it, that experience is, like that of Ovid's preceptor, intense, even violent.[28] The preceptor testifies from personal experience that love is obsessive (*De amore*, Praef., 3; 30) and that poverty kills it (1.2.7; 36); he confesses himself paralyzed by unrequited love (2.6.22; 244). He explodes with unexpected anger in Book 2 at a man who loves a two-timing woman, calling him "worse than a corpse" (homine defuncto deterior)

(2.6.19; 244); he rages against women in Book 3, repeating the charge of faithlessness with bitter insistence.

Less violent but equally intense and equally generative of the *De amore*'s peculiarly cathected teaching-textuality is another of the narrator's experiences, with another, though wholly analogous, sort of love—that between Andreas and his book's principal addressee, as was cited above: "My revered friend Walter, the assiduous insistence of my love for you compels me to publish for you in my own words and to instruct you by my own hand how the condition of love can be maintained inviolate between lovers, and equally the means by which those whose love is unrequited can shift Venus' shafts lodged in their hearts." Though the word *amor* is never used to describe this relation, the vocabulary associated with Walter is rich with amatory connotations.[29] Because of the strength of the *dilectio* binding the two men ("sedulous and insistent affection," translates Walsh), Andreas cannot refuse Walter's request for instruction in love (Praef. 4; 30), and fulfills his promise in a clerical love-vigil:

> So, dear Walter, by lending a diligent and attentive ear to the advice which I have composed in nightlong meditation at your pressing request, you can become fully acquainted with the art of love. It was because of my feeling of great affection that I sought thus to assent to your prayers, having produced in this little book detailed *doctrina* on love.

> (Si haec igitur, quae ad nimium tuae petitionis instantiam vigili cogitatione conscripsimus, Gualteri amice, attenta curaveris aure percipere, nil tibi poterit in amoris arte deficere. Nam propter nimiae dilectionis affectum tuis penitus cupientes annuere precibus confertissimam plenamque amoris doctrinam in hoc tibi libello edidimus.) (3.1; 286)

His love (*dilectio*) for Walter thus makes the preceptor, like his literary lovers, both educator and seducer. As his lovers instruct each other in the fine points of *doctrina amoris*, so Andreas teaches them to Walter in Books 1 and 2; as his male characters attempt to persuade their unwilling ladies to love them, so the preceptor in Book 3 attempts to persuade Walter to love not *domina* but *Dominus*, to leave the lady for the Bridegroom.

When the narrator pauses at the opening of Book 3 to explain once again his didactic plan and purpose, this programmatic doubling comes explicitly to the discursive surface. Remembering the persistent analogies we have so far observed between narratorial and fictional discourse, the assiduous reader should be armed with more than a little hermeneutic suspicion:

In the first part of the book I was seeking to comply with your ingenuous and youthful request . . . hence, as you so eagerly demanded of me, I chart for you the art of love in its full development, and I send it to you set down in the appropriate order. If you wish to practice the art of love in accordance with this *doctrina*, according as the careful reading of my little book will prescribe to you, you will obtain in full measure all bodily pleasures.

(Nam in prima parte praesentis libelli tuae simplici et iuvenili annuere petitioni volentes . . . artem amatoriam, sicut nobis mente avida postulasti, serie tibi plena dirigimus et competenti ordinatione dispositam delegamus. Quam si iuxta volueris praesentem exercere doctrinam, et sicut huius libelli assidua tibi lectio demonstrabit, omnes corporis voluptates pleno consequeris effectu.) (3.117–18; 322)

A promise has thus been made and kept, and Walter is assured of his teacher's pedagogical and amicitial faith, and of the utility of his teaching. What follows, however, repeats the claims to utility and faith in an entirely different register:

In the second part of the book I was more anxious to consult your interests, and though you in no way requested it I have on my own initiative appended a full discussion for your benefit on the condemnation of love, with the intention of benefiting you perhaps against your will.

(In ulteriori parte libelli tuae potius volentes utilitati consulere, de amoris reprobatione tibi nulla ratione petenti, ut bona forte praestemus invito, spontanea voluntate subiunximus et pleno tibi tractatu conscripsimus.) (3.119; 322)

Like a faithful lover, the preceptor keeps his word, but he also exceeds it, doing both what he promised and precisely the opposite. Both responses, however, are faithful demonstrations of his love for Walter, and both are useful, one for carnal enjoyment and one for spiritual salvation. Andreas has thus written his narrator (and his teaching text) into John of Salisbury's pedagogical *aporia*, that moment in the *Metalogicon* when nominal doctrine empties out under pressure from the ineluctable processes of twinned affirmation and negation. "What one claims to teach with faithfulness and utility, another claims to unteach with equal faithfulness and utility" (*Met.* 3.1; tr. 148/122).

Let us then consider the *duplex sententia* of the *De amore* through this troubling coincidence. The paratactic way in which Andreas presents his narrator's (de)doctrinal about-face has one assured result: it sends the assiduous reader back to Books 1 and 2 in search of signs of the narrator's faith—good, bad, or indifferent. Perhaps Andreas hints at a dedoctrinal fulfillment of his promise as early as the first chapters of Book 1, when the narrator confesses his lack of confidence in Amor's justice and promises to return to the problem at some later point (1.4.3–5; 38). If this is so, the preceptor would seem to have been up to something rather diabolical:

The Devil promises his knights many pleasant things, but their subsequent rewards are most bitter. He always does the contrary of what he promised, for he was a liar from the beginning, and did not stand in the path of truth.

(Diabolus enim suis militibus multa promittit atque suavia, postmodum eis nimis solvit amara et promissis semper contraria facit, quoniam ipse ab initio mendax fuit et in veritate non stetit.) (*De amore* 3.39; 298)

Although the preceptor's activity is not fully Satanic (he *does* do what he promised, as well as its opposite), the opening of Book 3 certainly indicates that the narrator of Books 1–2 had something in mind beside what the surface of the letter would indicate. That "something else," by Augustine's definition, would make him certainly "a liar from the beginning": "The liar has one thing in mind and expresses another either in words or in some other signs. Whence it is also said that the liar has a double heart; that is, a double thought" (ille mentitur, qui aliud habet in animo et aliud uerbis uel quibuslibet significationibus enuntiat. Unde etiam duplex cor dicitur esse mentientis, id est, duplex cogitatio) (*De mendacio* 3.3; 415).[30] Such double-dealing in matters of the faith, Augustine will conclude, has a catastrophic effect, "for once the authority of *doctrina* is corrupted, no progress toward or return to the chastity of the soul is possible" (Corrupta enim auctoritate doctrinae nullus aut cursus aut recursus esse ad castitatem animi potest) (*De mendacio* 19.40; 461).[31] The authority of the preceptor's teaching in Book 3 demands that the first two books be dismissed as illusions, but, as Peter Allen observes, "the reader still knows that he or she entertained them and cannot help questioning the relationship of trust that the preceptor created."[32] Returning to one section after finishing the other, one finds that the line between the preceptor and the characters becomes ever more indistinct. One cannot be "so certain of [Andreas's] promise that [his] intention and purpose with regard to that promise are not found to be changed in next to no time" (nec ulla posset . . . te facere tanta promissione securum, cuius voluntas et propositum non inveniatur brevi momento circa promissa mutari) (3.84; 312); everything in the *De amore* seems "spoken in duplicity of heart and revealed with ambivalent mind" (cuncta quae loquitur in duplicitate cordis enarrat et mentis plica fatetur) (3.86–87; 312). The preceptor hurls both of these accusations at women in Book 3; his textual teaching shows his own heart to be equally double.

Sophisticated Teaching

A large part of my works is made up and mendacious.

— Ovid, *Tristia*

If Andreas's heart, like his *sententia*, is double, how are we to take his *doctrina*? The earliest explicit response to this irksome question is that of Stephen Tempier, the bishop of Paris who, in 1277, condemned the *De amore* in his introduction to a list of 219 philosophical and theological errors. That he means the three-book *De amore* is plain, for he names it precisely and quotes its opening and closing passages.[33] Less clear, however, is the nature of the error involved: the condemnation does not specify what exactly Stephen found so objectionable in the *De amore*, and its vagueness has given rise to much scholarly disputation. Stephen could have read the work as advancing one or more of the propositions condemned in his list of errors, and offered it as an example of the dangerously useless reading popular among university students who wasted school time discussing "certain manifest and execrable errors, or rather vanities and false absurdities" (quosdam manifestos et execrabiles errores, immo potius vanitates et insanias falsas) (in Denifle, 543).[34]

More tantalizing is the possibility that he placed Andreas among those who "even say that things are true according to philosophy, but not according to the Catholic faith, as if there were two contrary truths, and as if there were in the sayings of damned pagans a truth against the truth of holy Scripture" (dicunt enim ea esse vera secundum philosophiam, sed non secundum fidem catholicam, quasi sint due contrarie veritates, et quasi contra veritatem sacre scripture sit veritas in dictis gentilium dampnatorum) (in Denifle, 543). Much ink has been spilled over the question of whether Stephen is here referring to the so-called doctrine of the double truth, and whether that "doctrine" is professed in the *De amore*.[35]

Although recent historians have tended to see the "double truth" as a historiographic red herring, the error that Tempier condemns bears such striking structural similarities to the *De amore* that it warrants closer examination.[36] Tempier condemns those who say that a thing may be true according to one authority (the pagans) and false according to another (Christ). In contrast, while both of the *De amore*'s propositions—its *sic* as well as its *non*—claim demonstrative truth *ex auctoritate*, they argue their contrary truths from pagan and Christian alike, often using exactly the same quotation for contrary purposes. In exegetical terms, we would say that the *De amore*'s characters deploy their authorities *in bono* and *in malo*; unlike orthodox exegetes, however, they argue without a clear anchor as to *quid sit bonum*. The echoes, citations, and repetitions between the part of the text that serves God and the part that serves Amor tend more to analogize the two "contrary" teachings than to separate them.[37] Dispensing with what was for Abelard the final check on interpretive movement, namely the appeal to canonical hierarchy, Andreas thus makes the apparently contrary parts of his book mutually ironic instances of unteaching, *eque fideliter et utiliter*, in John of Salisbury's words (*Met.* 3.1; tr. 148/122). Both are true; both are false. If the *De amore* teaches at all, it teaches (through) this duplicity.

If the *De amore* is a dangerous text, its heterodoxy is rooted here, *in the way it teaches*, rather than in its espousal of any particular nominal doctrine. Thus the *De amore*'s presence in the 1277 condemnations should not be taken as an unequivocal indicator of immanent heresy. Rather, it is the record of one person's reading of the text, an interpretation that responds to the book's logical and theological problems by condemning it in its entirety. Instead of taking one section as true and one as false, one as literal and the other as figurative, as have many readers medieval and modern, Tempier finds them both dangerous, both false. In this he was certainly correct, for the *De amore*'s repeated fictionalizing of truth makes it not ultimate referent but textual effect.[38]

Despite the text's repeated appeals to the true/false opposition, then, another reading strategy is needed. Bishop Tempier's suggestion that the work, if it teaches at all, teaches only "vanities and false absurdities" (in Denifle, 543) points the way, and one of Andreas's characters offers unexpected support. The noblewoman in the central dialogue E not only resists her suitor but refuses love entirely, because, she says, it is an imprisonment like that of Hell (*De amore* 1.6.214; 100). Her suitor tries to disabuse her of this notion (to be echoed in Book 3); he answers her vision of Love's court as Hell with an erotic *contrafactum* of the Christian afterlife, complete with the judgments of God, the blessings of the elect, and the gruesome punishments of the damned (1.6.229–73; 104–18). The suitor's goal in this allegorical *tour de force* is, of course, to convert the lady to worldly love. To that end, he appropriates the high style of biblical visions. At the end of the Apocalypse, Christ says to the visionary: "I, Jesus, have sent my angel, to testify to you these things in the churches" (ego Iesus misi angelum meum testificari vobis haec in ecclesiis) (Apocalypse 22.16). Our suitor, too, is sent out to testify. Says Amor to this visionary: "You have been granted sight of our great works so that through you our glory can be revealed to those who do not know it, and so that the vision you experience may be the opportunity of salvation to many ladies" (Nostra tibi sunt concessa videre magnalia, ut per te nostra valeat ignorantibus gloria revelari, et ut tua praesens visio sit multarum dominarum salutis occasio) (*De amore* 1.6.267; 116).

Like Walter, the woman of the dialogue is on the receiving end of intense conversionary rhetoric. While the narrator repeatedly instructs Walter how he is to respond to such discourse, he *represents* the woman's response, which is considerably more skeptical than the one he has in mind for Walter:

If your assertion is true, it is a splendid thing to devote oneself to the services of Love, and highly dangerous to set oneself against his commands. So *whether your account is true or false*, your narrative of fearful punishment terrifies me.

(Si vera sunt quae tua proponit assertio, amoris est gloriosum deservire ministeriis, et eiusdem est periculosum valde refragari mandatis. *Sive igitur vera sint sive falsa quae proponis*, terribilium me deterret poenarum relatio.) (1.6.276; 118; emphasis added)

Less a dialectician than a reader of fiction, the lady thus neatly sidesteps the true/false, *either/or* structure in which her suitor sought to trap her by taking the story she has heard as just that: a story.[39] Whether the suitor's account is true or false is less important than its effect, which is, as the man had hoped, to produce a conversion through fear. Her suitor's concern was simply to create enough verisimilitude to persuade (and convert) his listener.[40]

It would then appear that here—and throughout the *De amore*—this seductive teaching uses a kind of reasoning that is neither demonstrative nor probable:

A philosopher who uses demonstrative logic is endeavoring to determine the truth, whereas one who employs dialectic contents himself with probability, and is trying to establish an opinion. But the sophist is satisfied with the mere appearance of probability.

(Philosophus autem, demonstratiua utens, negotiatur ad ueritatem; dialecticus ad opinionem, siquidem probabilitate contentus est. Sophiste autem sufficit, si uel uideatur esse probabile.) (*Met.* 2.5; tr. 83/68)

Creating the appearance of probability is, of course, a function of language itself, for "as Cicero observes, nothing is so unlikely that words cannot lend an air of probability; nothing is so repulsive that speech cannot polish it and somehow render it attractive, as though it had been remade for the better" (nam, ut Cicero est auctor, nichil est tam incredibile quod non dicendo fiat probabile; nichil tam horrendum et incultum quod non splendescat oratione et quodammmodo mansuescat tamquam si excolatur) (*Met.* 1.7; tr. 27/23). Love, the pretext and *primum mobile* for the production of language among secular poets, works these polar transformations on lovers. One of Andreas's suitors declares, "to a lover love makes even an ugly woman appear most beautiful" (amor enim deformem quoque mulierem tanquam valde formosam representat amanti) (*De amore* 1.6.31; 48). The language of loving and unloving, in Andreas as in his master Ovid, is equally mendacious: "you may soften her defects with names," says Ovid's preceptor, "call her 'tanned,' though her blood be blacker than Illyrian pitch . . . and let a defect hide in its closeness to charm" (nominibus mollire licet mala: "fusca" vocetur, / nigrior Illyrica cui pice sanguis erit / . . . / et lateat vitium proximitate boni) (*Ars* 2.657–58, 662).

We have met this sort of deceptive naming once before (above, Chapter 2). It was, for John of Salisbury, an attribute of the disorderly grammar and dialectic he called unteaching: "The wheel of Fortune, like an empty trick, unteaches the weak, whom she could have taught: she shows false appearances and makes small things seem large and, contrariwise, large things small; she puts adverse faces on things, and gives false names on a whim; she pretends false things are something and true things nothing, so as to block the path of reason" (*Entheticus*, lines 255–62; my translation). Though John directs Boethian complaints at Fortune, he does concede that the sophistry of which he accuses her may, in fact, be of some use:

I am loath to brand knowledge of sophistry as useless. For the latter provides considerable mental exercise, while it does most harm to ignoramuses who are unable to recognize it. "One who knows cannot be deceived." And one who takes no steps to avoid a fall which he foresees makes himself responsible.

(Vnde non facile dixerim eam esse inutilem scitu, que non mediocriter exercet ingenia, et ignaris rerum efficacius nocet, si sit ignota. Dolus enim scienti non infertur; sibique imputet, qui casum declinare noluit quem preuidit.) (*Met.* 2.5; tr. 83–84/68)

Here, then, is how we might interpret Andreas's repeated explanations of his book's multiple utility. In Book 1, he says that Walter, being well versed in the art of love, can better avoid its suffering; in Book 3, he says that he has taught the art so that, understanding it, Walter may better shun it (*De amore*, Praef., 4; 30; and 3.2; 286).[41] The legal tag "one who knows cannot be deceived" thus aptly describes the lesson Walter has learned about love, and it just as neatly describes what Andreas has taught about his preceptor. Recognizing the preceptor's own duplicity, we return to the text, as Andreas directs, in continual rereading.

Teaching the *duplex sententia*

The *duplex sententia* of the *De amore* is not the nominal doctrine of the book. It is not any particular informational "lesson" that the *De amore* might teach us, but rather an active *doctrina* by which we are textually instructed—instructed in nothing more and nothing less than how to make sense of textual teaching. Two metadiscourses of medieval teaching lie ready to Andreas the Chaplain's hand; he has taken them up, and taken from them, and made a teaching text that teaches both as they do and as they never anticipated. In the *De amore*, Andreas has given us the structures of exegesis without exegetical transcendence, and applied the structures of dialectic to the issue of transcendence itself: the health of the reader's soul.

Like Scripture, the *De amore* consists of two interfingered yet separable parts in tense unity. When the Christian Bible is asked whether the Messiah has come, one part says yes, the other no; when Walter asks the *De amore* about the moral worthiness of earthly love, one part says yes, the other no. Christian exegesis says that both biblical testaments are parts of the same singularly multiple discourse, a discourse whose *sententia* is constantly and plurally (re)generated in reading. Remember Hugh of St. Victor:

The divine deeper meaning can never be absurd, never false. Although in the sense, as has been said, many contrary things are found, the deeper meaning admits no conflict, is always harmonious, always true. Sometimes there is a single deeper meaning for a single expression; sometimes there are several deeper meanings for a single expression; sometimes there is a single deeper meaning for several expressions; sometimes there are several deeper meanings for several expressions. (*Did.* 6.11; tr. 149–50/128)

Scripture, Aquinas will later say, teaches doubly, its netting of figural and literal a kind of holy and redeemed duplicity.[42] The *De amore* calls upon such double and continuous teaching; the parallels are insistent, but the differences equally—and troublingly—marked.

Structural parallels with the Christian Bible might lead us to read Andreas's Book 3 as a fulfillment of Books 1 and 2, in a secular version of exegetical typology. Similarly, Books 1 and 2 can be read, like the Old Testament, as a fleshly letter; Book 3's teaching would then tend toward Spirit. However, if we read assiduously, as the text instructs us to do, we find that the opposite is also—and very carefully—true. Insistent mutual analogies between the carnal seductions of Books 1–2 and the spiritual seduction of Book 3 weave the two sections together. Reading assiduously, we hear the demonstrative argumentation of Book 3 in the arguments of Books 1–2, even as we hear the sophistical and seductive discourse of the suitors in the preceptor's attempt to woo Walter for the Heavenly Bridegroom in Book 3. In fact, the suitor of Book 3 is less the divine Sponsus than the earthly *capellanus*, who tries to seduce his beloved Walter with discourse as insistent (and, one suspects, as unsuccessful) as that of any of the sophistical suitors of Book 1.

The contemplative practices of *lectio divina* set up conditions wherein the response to contradictory teaching is a hermeneutic not so much *either/or* as *both-and*. Andreas's narrator, however, is no exegete. His precepts allow no *both-and* in this doubled instruction: the most important (and most cathected) of his precepts is "No one can be bound by two loves" (Nemo duplici potest amore ligari) (*De amore* 2.8.44; 282). We are taught again and again, both by example and by explicit textual precept: you cannot serve two masters; you cannot have two lovers; you cannot be husband and lover to your wife, nor lover and wife to your husband; you cannot serve both God and Mammon; you cannot serve both God and Woman.[43]

Of course, the preceptor himself serves (and serves up) two teachings, while teaching throughout his book that duplicity is the most intolerable of moral and intellectual conditions. We are commanded to choose, to cleave either to one proposition or to the other, yet the process of textual teaching interweaves the two propositions so closely that we cannot do so, because one proposition is always already in the other.

It would seem, then, that the preceptor is intent on making an Abelard of Walter. He subjects Walter to the painfully exclusive *either/or* of dialectic, slicing off his dedication both to one thing and to the other, just as Abelard's life story mutilated him in his own doubleness—monk and teacher, philosopher and husband, man and not-man. Like our stand-in

Walter, we are commanded to read *either/or*, but are impelled by Andreas's textual practice to read *both-and*, in what can only be described as a dialectical *contrafactum* not only of scriptural structure but also of scriptural teaching textuality.

I have taken some pains throughout this discussion to separate "Andreas," the flesh-and-blood person who composed the *De amore*, from "the preceptor," who is as much a fictional character as any suitor, lady, or fairy in the text.[44] Now I hope it is clear why I have done this. The preceptor teaches *either/or*. Andreas makes him teach that way, and also sets that *either/or* teaching in a structure that makes its practice, though not impossible, certainly an active assertion of readerly will over a complex, dialogic, and willfully contradictory text.

Andreas's textual *quaestio* teaches reading as questioning, perhaps to the same end that, as we saw in Chapter 3, Abelard set for his collection of contrary things: "For assiduous questioning is defined as the first key of wisdom. . . . For by doubting we come to enquiry, and by enquiry we perceive the truth" (*Sic et non*, tr. 99/103). Or, if Andreas is not so bold or so serious or so ambitious as to direct our eyes toward Truth, at least toward something truthlike, which must be actively constructed by a reader from the contradictory shards, the doubling and dividing of Andreas Capellanus's teaching text. Not much else is possible even in theology, as Abelard himself declared: "I do not set out to teach Truth, to which I believe neither myself nor any other mortal to be adequate, but rather to propose something verisimilar, close to human reason yet not contrary to holy faith" (Nos docere veritatem non promittimus, ad quam neque nos neque mortalium aliquem sufficere credimus, sed saltem aliquid verisimile atque humane rationi vicinum nec sacre fidei contrarium proponere) (*Theologia "Scholarium"* 2.18; 414).

Like the *Sic et non*, the *De amore* uses contradictory teaching, uses contradiction *as* teaching, and sets that teaching in a process of intense intellectual and spiritual activity.[45] Where Abelard's oppositional structure is designed to provoke an *assidua interrogatio* with a guaranteed epistemological and spiritual payoff, Andreas's assiduous reading process, like the reasoning of John of Salisbury's logicians, is sealed within the text's own processes and bounds. Andreas's is indeed an *assidua lectio*, a repeated and careful reading of the *sic* in the *non* and the *non* in the *sic*, of one thing in the other, of one thing *through* the other.

The *doctrina* of Andreas's *duplex sententia* thus creates not a hierarchical, "typological" relationship between its propositions but rather a lateral,

mutually relativizing, dialogical one. Andreas has crossed biblical structures with Ovidian ones, and set them talking with each other according
to the discursive habits of exegesis, which embraces both one proposition
and the other, and dialectic, which sets both in motion, in order to determine the truth of either one or the other. We are instructed with Walter
to wait for the Bridegroom, but until that apocalyptic Last Moment, we
keep reading, commanded that we must choose either earthly or heavenly
love, but unable, the more assiduously we read, to distinguish one from
the other.

Chapter 5

Between One Thing and the Other

The *Libro de buen amor*

Does not Desire, performing many miracles, to use antiphrasis, change the shapes
of all mankind. Though monk and adulterer are opposite terms, he forces
both of them to exist together in the same subject.

—Alan of Lille, *De planctu Naturae*

It is absolutely clear to medieval Christian theologians and exegetes—including even the duplicitous preceptor of the *De amore*—that the love of God and the love of the flesh are two different, even opposed things. Augustine had written, after all, that Scripture teaches nothing but charity and condemns nothing but cupidity (*DDC* 3.10.15). Origen, characteristically, had been quite emphatic in his distinction, and his emphasis was passed on to medieval clerical readers through St. Jerome's translation: "thus there is a certain carnal love that comes from Satan, and another love of the spirit, proceeding from God. And no one can be possessed by two loves" (sic est quidam amor carnalis a Satana veniens, alius amor spiritus, a Deo exordium habens. Et nemo potest duobus amoribus possideri) (*PL* 23: 1121C). Although the discourses of carnal and spiritual love are webbed together in the *De amore* by citation, echoes, and analogy, it is clear that the preceptor's teaching depends upon their being two recognizably different things. Andreas is only exaggerating good orthodox precedent when he has the preceptor declare in Book 3, "We know beyond all doubt on the testimony of scripture that God himself is the fountainhead and source of chastity and sexual virtue, but that the devil is the creator of love and sexual indulgence" (Praeterea ipsum Deum sine omni dubitatione castitatis et pudicitiae caput esse scimus atque principium; diabolum vero amoris et luxuriae auctorem esse scriptura referente cognovimus) (3.38; 298). The weaving together of the *De amore*'s propositions about *caritas* and *cupiditas* that I have just carried out—with Andreas's help, I might add—is thus very much against the preceptor's will, and against a long tradition of Christian thought that would put fleshly love and spiritual love under a moral rule of noncontradiction, declaring that the two must not obtain in the same subject at the same time.

Our next contrary thing is another thing altogether. Where Andreas's preceptor insisted on *either/or* distinctions, the first-person narrator of the fourteenth-century Spanish *Libro de buen amor* (Book of good love) seems intent on collapsing senses rather than distinguishing them. His book's titular "good love" (*buen amor*) is, ultimately, both *caritas* and *cupiditas*, both one thing and its opposite. As we shall see, such collapsing of opposites is the programmatic concern not only of the narrator but also of the poet. This is a text delighting in the in-between: it is at once deeply Latinate and enthusiastically vernacular, sacred and secular, funny and intensely serious. The *Libro de buen amor* is a dialectical problem in the image of Scripture, a secular text of universal didactic utility in which the sign can — nay, *must* — be construed in opposite directions, to the edification of the "good love" that the book serves. In the *Libro de buen amor*, the good love of God and the good love of the flesh gloss each other so intimately that it is nearly impossible — even if we are well educated in both one love and the other, and well read in both multiplicity-savoring exegesis and disambiguating dialectic — to pin down the difference without which, the dialecticians taught, no definition can be made. It is plain that, like the Bible and like Aristotle, this text teaches by positive and by negative example, *in bono* and *in malo*; the intellectual and moral challenge lies in understanding which is which.

Ad nostram doctrinam scripta

But what things soever were written were written for our learning.

— Romans 15.4

The *Libro de buen amor* (1330/1343) is a generous collection of fables, lectures, songs, jokes, and parodies loosely hung upon a tale of the amatory adventures of a first-person speaker calling himself Juan Ruiz, Archpriest of the Castilian town of Hita.[1] When the narrator talks about his book (as he constantly does), he claims to have made a text of inexhaustible and universal didactic utility. Both jokebook and textbook, lectionary and electuary, the *Libro* accommodates itself to all comers:

It is a very big doctrinal book about a great deal of holiness, but it is a small breviary of fun and jokes; . . . may it be for you a brief jest, a delight, and a sweet
confection.

> (De la santidat mucha es bien grand liçionario,
> mas de juego e de burla es chico breviario;
>
> . . .
>
> sea vos chica fabla, solaz e letuario.)
>
> (*Libro*, S 1632abd)[2]

We know that the *Libro de buen amor* teaches; the narrator, whom I'll
call the Archpriest, tells us so himself. "Listen to a worthwhile fable!"
(¡Oy fabla provechosa!) (*Libro*, S 320d), he says; "Ladies, give ear, listen to a good lesson" (Dueñas, aved orejas, oíd buena liçión) (*Libro*, SG
892a); "Understand my words correctly and ponder their meaning" (entiende bien mis dichos e piensa la sentençia) (SG 46a). What this book
teaches, however, is hard to determine exclusively, particularly when we
take *doctrina* postmedievally as solely the nominal content of the didactic
act. Profoundly modern is the unease apparent in the scholarly tendency
to divide neatly on whether or not, like the *De amore*, the *Libro de buen
amor* is didactic, as if the problem were a simple question of *either/or*.

The case of the *Libro de buen amor* is especially striking in this regard.
Though few scholars still take the *De amore* as a transparent social docu-
ment, it is not yet completely canonized as "literature," much less "French
literature."[3] In contrast, it is hard to imagine a class in Spanish medieval
literature or a list for a Spanish master's examination without the *Libro de
buen amor*. Because the *Libro* has been canonized as "art" and inducted
into a national literature as the *De amore* has not been, its didacticism has
been all the more contested ground.[4] Scholarly attempts to identify the
Libro's nominal doctrine strain to account for its obvious and cacophonous multiplicity. A recent editor put it this way: "Juan Ruiz wanted to
mark his work with a comic, colloquial and uninhibited tone . . . in order
to teach and to delight. But to teach what?" (Ruiz, *Libro*, ed. Blecua, xliii).

To pitch the critical question toward the *Libro*'s nominal doctrine as
this editor does is to walk directly into one of its many traps, for the book
by its own admission aims to teach everything—from the catechism to
canon law, from the art of love to the art of versification to the art of dying.
The contradictory abundance of its nominal doctrines alerts us to what is
consistent throughout: the book's focus on active doctrine, on teaching as
act and as process. In this, the *Libro* shares in the contradictory teaching
and metadidactic reflection of both scriptural exegesis and medieval dia-

lectic, discourses built upon theoretical consideration not only of the ways to teach the W/word but also of the ways the W/word teaches. Thus a question more attuned to the active as well as nominal nature of *doctrina* in the Middle Ages would not be "What does this text teach?" but rather "What does this text teach about teaching?" or, better yet, "What does it teach about the teaching text?"[5]

In via hac qua gradieris

> Let us, therefore, pray that those things which are closed to us be opened, and let us in no manner be cut off from the pursuit of reading; for even David, although he was continually occupied with the law of the Lord, nevertheless cried out to the Lord, saying, "Give me understanding, that I may learn thy commandments."
>
> —Cassiodorus, *Institutiones*

If the narrator of the *De amore* is obscure in the laconism of his reading-instructions (what does he mean by *duplex sententia*? how exactly are we to read "assiduously"?), the narrator of the *Libro de buen amor* is obscure in his didactic and exegetical *generosity*. We know that he teaches; he will tell us what he teaches in the prose sermon that introduces the text in the Salamanca manuscript.[6] If what we are looking for is single and generalizable nominal doctrine, transparently communicated, the precision of the *Libro*'s narrator is not much help, for this sermon has a disorienting multiplicity of explicit purposes, expressed in a disorienting multiplicity of first-person voices. Its *thema* is drawn from Psalm 31, verse 8: "I will give thee understanding, and I will instruct thee in the way in which thou shalt go" (Intellectum tibi dabo, et instruam te in via hac qua gradieris). We are set on our way here, but it is not yet clear whether we are on the disambiguating dialectical road that Alan of Lille thought led to the secrets of Sophia (*Anticlaudianus* 3.70–71), or at the misty crossroads that Augustine saw when he thought of obscurity and ambiguity (*Dial.* 7; 105).

The speaker develops his theme in a conventional if not completely rigorous way, glossing the three clauses of the verse with the three powers of the Augustinian soul: understanding, will, and memory (*De Trinitate* 10.11.17–18). Of these, understanding is most important for our purposes, for the preacher assigns it the dialectical job of distinguishing good from its contrary: "For with good understanding, man understands the good, and from this he knows the bad" (Por el buen entendimiento entiende onbre el bien, e sabe dello el mal) (*Libro*, tr. 4/105). If all three powers are sound, the preacher says, they will direct the soul to choose as Andreas commanded Walter to choose, despising the mad love of this world (el loco amor de este mundo) and desiring its opposite, the good love of God (el buen amor de Dios). However, since fallen human nature is crippled with a lack of good understanding and a poverty of memory, human will is as likely to oppose the good love of God as it is to harmonize with it (tr. 6/107).

The *Libro*'s prose preface thus implies that the oppositions that will multiply vertiginously in the book to follow are products of a fallen world, for, as Peter Lombard observed in a graver homiletic context, the Fall threw humanity into contraries:

I, man, created in honor, cleave to the Father by memory; to the Son by intellect; to the Holy Spirit by dilection. For the uncreated Trinity placed in man a created trinity, but, wandering from the blessed and highest Trinity, he fell into a foul and horrible trinity: . . . concupiscence of the flesh, concupiscence of the eyes, pride of life. . . . This trinity is the land of unlikeness, where memory is scattered, intellect blinded, will fouled.

(Homo ego conditus in honore, memoria adhaesit Patri: intellectu Filio: dilectione Spiritui Sancto. Increata enim Trinitas homini indidit trinitatem creatam, sed transmigrans a Trinitate beata et summa, incidit in trinitatem horrendam et foedam . . . concupiscentiam carnis, concupiscentiam oculorum, superbiam vitae. . . . Haec trinitas . . . est regio dissimilitudinis, ubi memoria dissipatur, intellectus caecatur, voluntas foedatur.)[7]

Hugh of St. Victor wrote that scriptural teaching, directed into the *regio dissimilitudinis* by divine fiat, was designed to restore the student-reader's similitude with God (*Did.* 1.7; tr. 47/6). Working the same theme as the Lombard, St. Bernard had glossed the intellectual fall thus: reason's is the dialectical task of distinguishing truth from falsehood, good from evil, proper from improper; in human practice, however, "it is blinded by such a mist that it often judges contrariwise, taking bad for good, false for true, noxious for proper" (tanta modo caligine caecatur, ut saepe in contrarium ducat judicum, recipiens malum pro bono, falsum pro vero, noxium pro commodo) (*De varia Trinitate*, in *PL* 183: 667C).

The *Libro* will work precisely this blinding upon its readers, to a dialectically and exegetically serious purpose. As in Scripture, here key words and images signify both *in bono* and *in malo*, often at the same time: we shall find as we read that "good love" (buen amor) points sometimes to charity, sometimes to cupidity, often inextricably to both at once. Like

Abelard's sequence of *quaestiones*, the *Libro*'s unresolved titular equivocation is designed to provoke the rational soul's dialectical activity, within a
context that puts equal stress (in both senses of the word) on the health of
the understanding and the health of the soul. *Contrafactum* of Bible and
logic the *Libro de buen amor* may well be, but it is a contrary image that
illuminates rather than undercuts its models.

Our narrator will do more than expound Scripture. Now, having
rooted his work in and from the fallen world, he undergoes the first of his
many metamorphoses: the preacher addressing a listening public becomes
a writer addressing a reading audience and introducing a text beyond the
sermon:

Therefore I . . . made this little writing in the memory of what is good, and I
composed this new book in which are written down some of the ways and tricks
and deceitful wiles of the mad love of this world, which some people employ to
commit sin.

(Onde yo . . . fiz esta chica escriptura en memoria de bien, e conpuse este nuevo
libro, en que son escriptas algunas maneras e maestrías e sotilezas engañosas del
loco amor del mundo que usan algunos para pecar.) (*Libro*, tr. 8–10/109)

The book, the Archpriest says, will be useful to those of good understanding, who will choose the path of salvation winding through it, and to
those of little understanding, who will recognize themselves in its fictional
sinners and so be led to change their ways:

And if these be read or heard by any man or woman of good understanding, who
wishes to be saved, he or she will make a choice and carry it into effect. And he
or she will be able to say with the psalmist: "I have chosen the way of truth, et
cetera." Likewise those of little understanding will not be lost, for on reading or
pondering the evil that they do or have in their will to do, and the published revelation of the many deceitful measures that those who persist in their wicked arts
use for sinning and deceiving women, they will bestir their memory and will not
disdain their good repute . . . and they will rather love themselves than sinfulness.

(Las quales, leyendo las o oyendo las omne o muger de buen entendimiento que
se quiera salvar, descogerá e obrar lo ha. E podrá dezir con el salmista: "Viam veritatis, e çetera." Otrosí, los de poco entendimiento non se perderán, ca leyendo e
coidando el mal que fazen, o tienen en la voluntad de fazer, ⁺los porfiosos de sus
malas maestrías, e descobrimiento publicado de sus muchas engañosas maneras
que usan para pecar e engañar las mugeres, acordarán la memoria e non despre-
çiarán su fama. . . . E querrán más amar a sí mesmos que al pecado.) (*Libro*, tr.
10/109–10) [8]

Still more guarantees of didactic utility are forthcoming. Instructed by the *Libro* in the arts of amatory deceit, careful readers can better guard against them: the book thus has the practical prophylactic utility that both Andreas's preceptor and his seductive characters invoke for their teaching texts (*Libro*, tr. 12/110; cf. *De amore* 1.6.220; 102). But the speaker continues, and makes himself now a master poet as well. The *Libro*'s multiple verse forms and clever wordplay have much to teach aspiring writers, he says: "And I likewise composed the book in order to give to some people lesson and example of rhyming and composing lyrics" (E conpose lo otrosí a dar {a} algunos leçión e muestra de metrificar e rrimar e trobar) (tr. 12/110–11).[9] The *Libro*'s didactic enthusiasm, pushed to its moral limit, ultimately accommodates nothing less than the sinful practice of carnal love itself. The preacher is also, it seems, *praeceptor amoris*: "However, because to sin is a human thing, if any should choose—which I do not advise them to do—to engage in mad love, they will here find a few methods for it" (Enpero, por que es umanal cosa el pecar, si algunos, lo que non los conssejo, quisieran usar del loco amor, aquí fallarán algunas maneras para ello) (tr. 10/110).

The stories of sin to follow in the *Libro* are thus integrated into a global instruction that, like the *De amore*, teaches both virtue and vice and advises that the better of the two be chosen. The Archpriest's advice, however, makes mistier reading than the sermon would seem to promise:

> The text speaks to everyone in general: people of good sense will discern its wisdom; as for frivolous young people, let them refrain from folly: let him who is fortunate choose the better.
>
> (En general a todos fabla la escriptura:
> los cuerdos con buen sesso entendrán la cordura;
> los mançebos livianos guarden se de locura;
> escoja lo mejor el de buena ventura.)
>
> *(Libro, SG 67)*

Like readers of Scripture, the *Libro*'s readers will construe their target text according to their differing wills, memories, and understandings; like readers of Scripture, they will also, the Archpriest guarantees, come away the better for it. However, since one reward for a good reading of the *Libro de buen amor* is a pretty girlfriend (*SG* 64d), what exactly "the better" is, is not entirely clear. Properly understood, the *Libro de buen amor* will be all things to all people; all readers may quote the sermon's *thema* to the very letter, though the sense of the line will vary according to the path the interpreter has chosen, whether it be the *via veritatis* or the road to the other place, with all its well-intentioned pavement:[10]

And so this book of mine, to every man or woman, to the wise and the unwise, to whomsoever may understand the good and choose salvation and do good works loving God, and likewise to whomsoever may desire mad love, on whatever road he might walk, each one can truly say, "I will give you understanding, et cetera."

(E ansí este mi libro a todo omne o muger, al cuerdo e al non cuerdo, al que entendiere el bien e escogiere salvaçión e obrare bien, amando a Dios; otrosí al que quisiere el amor loco; en la carrera que andudiere, puede cada uno bien dezir: "Intellectum tibi dabo, e çetera.") (*Libro*, tr. 10/110)[11]

Ars Backwards

> He always accused others of what he himself did most frequently; he blamed others for things he praised in himself.
>
> —Juan Ruiz, *Libro de buen amor*

The games played with structures of address and didactic utility make the introductory sermon less a constative, transparent communication than a discursive performance—a prologue, in short, to a work of fiction. These same fictionalizing pressures come to bear on the narrator himself as it becomes clear that he and the historical author are not seamlessly one and the same subject. Already introduced to us as a Christian preacher, Ovidian preceptor, and master poet, the narrator soon takes on another role: Everylover. "And since I am a man like any other sinner, I have felt great love for women on occasion" (E yo como soy omne commo otro pecador, / ove de las mugeres a las vezes grand amor) (*Libro*, SG 76ab), he says, and proposes to tell us all about it, adding that his experience has exemplary, dialectical value: "for a man to try out all things is not the worst course, nor to know good and evil, and practice that which is better" (Provar omne las cosas non es por ende peor; / saber bien e mal e usar lo mejor) (SG 76cd).[12] This explanation will feel more than a little sophistical as the text proceeds and the narrator shows that he is not able to distinguish good from bad, much less "practice that which is better."[13]

As the prologue warns, much of the *Libro* is in fact given over to the *ars amatoria*, but as the sermon's teaching is subject to the poet's wit, so too is the *doctrina* of the *ars*. The *Libro* will, in fact, play as many games with the teaching of love as it does with the teaching of Scripture, bringing forward the competing voices embedded in both discourses. Juan Ruiz appropriates structures from the *ars*, as he appropriates scriptural exegesis, "to turn them inside out."[14]

As the *De amore* devoted the bulk of its first book to the dialogue of seduction, so, too, the *Libro*'s art of love begins with a few affairs; as Andreas's men were consistently unsuccessful in their attempts to win their ladies, so, too, the Archpriest's first attempted liaisons are unmitigated failures. "I have always striven to serve the ladies I have known," he says, but adds, "many ladies have I done much service to; yet nothing have I accomplished" (Sienpre puné en servir dueñas que conosçí, . . . a muchas serví mucho, que nada non acabesçí) (*Libro, S* 153bd). Disappointed, the Archpriest takes refuge in the *reprobatio amoris*.

> For, as I have told you, my luck is such that, whether my astral sign causes it or my clumsy behavior, I can never accomplish half of what I long for: this is why I sometimes quarrel with love.
>
> > (Ca, segund vos he dicho, de tal ventura seo
> > que, si lo faz mi signo o si mi mal asseo,
> > nunca puedo acabar lo medio que desseo;
> > por esto a las vegadas con el amor peleo.)
> >
> > (*Libro, S* 180)

Where the *De amore* performed a condemnation of love, the *Libro de buen amor stages* it, making the condemnation a fictional as well as rhetorical performance. Amor himself pays the disgruntled Archpriest a visit, and in the dispute that follows, the Archpriest begins where Andreas's narrator left off, quite literally—that is, figurally—unteaching Amor to his very face. Then, when Amor responds (*Libro, SG* 423), the Archpriest becomes his Walter, an eager and decidedly needy student. The Archpriest is thus both Walter and his preceptor, both student of love and teacher of the *reprobatio amoris*. Emptyings and inversions of stock oppositions characterize this intensely dialectical fiction "on love"—Andreas's *ars* backwards.

After his initial greeting, Amor cannot get a word in edgewise for some 960 lines, for the Archpriest lets go a torrent of moral recrimination against the god he has served for so long with so little reward. Like the preacher he sometimes is, and like Andreas's preceptor before him, he accuses Amor of being the source of all the deadly sins and destroyer of bodies and souls.[15] The most significant difference, however, is the *Libro*'s insistence on the worldly motives driving the speaker's tirade. There is even less chance here than in the *De amore* of taking the narratorial for the authorial "I."[16] "I am always in trouble whenever I listen to you," he whines (Sienpre me fallo mal cada que te escucho) (*Libro*, *S* 246d), and drops his preacherly persona long enough to demand, "Answer me: what have I done to you? Why didn't you bring me happiness with any of the ladies I have loved, not even from the saintly one?" (Responde, ¿qué te fiz? ¿Por qué me non diste dicha / en quantas que amé, nin de la dueña bendicha?) (*S* 215ab). The protagonist's persona-shifting sets ecclesiastical and Ovidian didacticism in conversation one with the other, and makes it hard to tell which is which. Who speaks here? Is it the lover-Archpriest, in search of *ad personificationem* vengeance? The preacher-Archpriest, in search of a textual pulpit? The poet-Archpriest, in search of a convenient frame for a collection of versified fables?

The Archpriest allows narrative pleasure to dominate his *reprobatio*, illustrating the capital sins with exemplary stories. These preacherly exempla often seem only tangentially related to the sin the Archpriest means them to illustrate;[17] more importantly still, many of them empty out and confuse the poles of didactic opposition: teacher/student, preacherly corrector/corrected sinner. One such exemplum is the celebrated parody of the canonical hours (*Libro*, *SG* 373–87, plus a few stanzas in *T*). The Archpriest introduces this as an example of Love's deceptive and blasphemous speech (*SGT* 373d), but its macaronic mixture of God-loving liturgical Latin and seductive Romance in fact repeats his own program of discursive and linguistic confusion. A line from Psalm 109, redeployed here in Latin, teaches rather differently than it does in the mouth of the psalmist:

I never saw a sexton who could ring for vespers better; you play all instruments easily; any lady who comes to your vespers, no matter how smartly she rolls up her sleeves [to resist], with "the scepter of thy power" you compel her to remain.

> (Nunca vi sacristán que a vísperas mejor tanga:
> todos los instrumentos {tocas} con la chica manga;
> la que viene a tus vísperas, por bien que se {arremanga},
> con "virgam virtutis tue" fazes que + aí {rremanga}.)
> (*Libro*, *SG* 384)[18]

Another exemplum is even more revealing of the way in which the *Libro* works on stock oppositions. It is a doubly didactic story of yet another dispute, a trial this time; it is told to teach Amor about his own hypocrisy—and to teach country lawyers a thing or two about how to handle a case (*Libro*, *SGT* 371d).[19] The wolf brings suit against the fox for stealing a rooster. The fox replies that the wolf has no business accusing her, for he does the same thing himself: "he always accused others of what he himself did most frequently; he blamed others for things he praised in himself" (lo que él más fazía, a otros lo acusava; / a otros rretraía lo quél en sí loava) (S 322ab). Their case comes before the mayor of the town, the monkey don Ximio, who is to determine which of them is telling the truth and which of them lying, and thus decide whether the fox is guilty or innocent. Faced with the two conflicting arguments, he passes sentence (sentençia) (SG 347d). Both accusations, he says, are correct, and he sets both accuser and accused free through a legal loophole (SG 352).

We shall return to the wider importance of don Ximio's *both-and sentençia*; for the moment, let's consider its strategic importance in the Archpriest's dispute with Amor, of which it is an image *en abyme*. The tale is clearly an indictment of hypocrisy, but, as don Ximio's judgment does not distinguish between one crime and the other, so the speaker identifies both accuser and accused as figures for Amor: "When you spy a pretty girl you ogle her foxily" (Do vees la fermosa, oteas con rraposía) (*Libro*, S 319d), he tells Amor before launching into the tale, but the next stanza makes Love's stand-in not the fox but the wolf, an identification repeated in the tale's conclusion:

Of all the good that you preach, you yourself perform nothing; you delude everybody with your fair words; you want what the wolf wanted of the fox.

> (De quanto bien pedricas, non fazes dello cosa:
> engañas a todo el mundo con palabra fermosa;
> quieres lo que el lobo quiere de la rraposa)
> (*Libro*, S 320abc)

You, Love, are like the wolf: you censure what you yourself do, you express amazement at others for being in the mud that you lie in; you are a dreadful foe to all to whom you give pleasure; you speak with great simplicity, by which means you snare many a one.

> (Tal eres como el lobo, rretraes lo que fazes;
> estrañas {a los otros}+ el lodo en que yazes.
> Eres mal enemigo a todos quantos plazes;
> fablas con grand sinpleza por que muchos {enlazes}).
> (*Libro*, SGT 372)

The speaker's explanation of his fable makes it a perfectly open allegory. By evacuating the disputants of stable allegorical identification, he ensures that Amor will see himself in both of the guilty parties. What remains unspoken, but nonetheless abundantly clear, is that this strategy also ensures that the tale will apply just as well to the speaker as to Amor.

The allegory is open enough for the Archpriest to fall into, and fall into it he does; though in keeping with his comic blindness, he fails to recognize himself in his characters. Like the fox, he draws attention to another's guilt in order to excuse himself; like the wolf, he condemns in others what he himself does; like don Ximio, he delivers a *sententia* that is not so much *duplex* as no sentence at all.[20] In the fables deployed in the dispute with Amor—and, as we shall see, throughout the *Libro*—narrative positions are empty, roles are reversible: the litigating wolf and fox and the disputing Archpriest and Amor are neat serial and simultaneous images of each other.

Alieniloquium: One Thing for the Other

> They make dark out of light by turning a fur piece inside out.
>
> —Juan Ruiz, *Libro de buen amor*

At a misty crossroads in Scripture, Augustine recommended the most careful of readings: otherwise, "taking one thing for the other," readers will be "deceived by many and multiple obscurities and ambiguities" (multis et multiplicibus obscuritatibus et ambiguitatibus decipiuntur . . . aliud pro alio sentientes) (*DDC* 2.6.7; my translation). Augustine trusted that in that mist were certain signs put there for the reader's benefit: "by following certain traces he may come upon the hidden sense without any error, or at least he will not fall into the absurdity of wicked meanings" (quibusdam uestigiis indagatis ad occultum sensum sine ullo errore ipse perueniat aut certe in absurditatem prauae sententiae non incidat) (*DDC*, Prologue 9). There are certain traces of such immanent sense in the *Libro* too, but they are not nearly so sure:

The utterances of good love are veiled; set to work where you find its [or their] certain signs. If you understand the meaning of what is said or hit upon the sense, you will not speak ill of the book which you now censure.

> (Las del buen amor son rrazones encubiertas:
> trabaja do fallares las sus señales çiertas.
> Si la rrazón entiendes o en el sesso açiertas,
> non dirás mal del libro que agora rrefiertas.)
>
> (*Libro*, SG 68)

"Certain signs" here indicate deictically the sites of the interpretive act, pointing out as brooches do the juncture point of veil and body, letter and sense. Although these certain signs are surely signs of meaning, there is yet one difficulty, for the possibilities of understanding the *Libro*'s discourse or hitting upon its sense, cast as they are in the sly conditional "if" that introduces them, seem set just beyond readerly grasp.

The *Libro* delivers this sneaky co-incidence of promise and evasion within a carefully constructed preceptive framework that at once guides interpretations of the book's discourse and, through reiterated insistence, emphasizes the mist that makes such guidance necessary. On the one hand, the Archpriest repeatedly guarantees the usefulness of exegetical instruments for his book's interpretation; on the other, he repeatedly embodies those instruments in contradictory ways that reverse, then evacuate the oppositions—sense and letter, inside and outside—upon which their proper hermeneutical functioning depends.

We have seen that the exempla that the Archpriest deploys against Amor in their dispute are little fables in which one or the other or both disputants are perfectly justified in saying to the other, *ad tua res loquitur*, this tale speaks to your affairs. In reading the exempla allegorically, I am following the road indicated by the Archpriest himself, in his persona as professor of *Libro de buen amor* studies:

I have made you a little text-book, but I do not think the gloss is small, but it is rather a good big piece of prose; for in respect to each tale something else is to be understood, apart from what is said in the pretty wording. It is a very big doctrinal book about a great deal of holiness, but it is a small breviary of fun and jokes; . . . may it be for you a brief jest, a delight, and a sweet confection.

> (Fiz vos pequeño libro de testo, mas la glosa
> non creo que es chica, ante es bien grand prosa,
> que sobre cada fabla se entiende otra cosa,
> sin la que se alega en la rrazón fermosa.
>
> . . . .
>
> De la santidat mucha es bien grand liçionario,
> mas de juego e de burla es chico breviario;
>
> . . . .
>
> sea vos chica fabla, solaz e letuario.)
>
> (*Libro*, *ST* 1631–32)

The Archpriest here assures us of the prefigured necessity of some Other meaning over and above his words, something else alien to or at least independent from them. This *otra cosa* is, of course, the *aliud* of allegory. "Allegory is other-speaking," says Isidore of Seville: "one thing sounds and another is understood" (Allegoria est alieniloquium; aliud enim sonat, aliud intelligitur) (*Etymologiae* 1.37.22).

The allegorical glossing that the speaker expects his book to produce will in fact work on two different levels, and when he teaches his imagined reader how to accomplish it, he speaks out of both sides of his mouth. We, the *Libro*'s glossators, are advised that *aliud—otra cosa*—is superimposed over every episode. Because the alien gloss is conceived as the target's opposite,[21] if we read according to the oppositions of these instructions, we must overlay figural holiness upon literal folly, surely, but also figural folly upon literal holiness.

To get even this far, however, we must be able to distinguish one from the other. It is in this context that we should take the Archpriest's request in the sermon that we "understand well and judge well my intention in writing it, and the meaning of what is said there, and not just the ugly sound of the words" (bien entender e bien juzgar mi entençión por qué lo fiz, e la sentençia de lo que ý dize, e non al son feo de las palabras) (*Libro*, tr. 10/110). This clear separation between *sentençia* and sound suggests that one strategy for making sense of *B/buen A/amor*—both concept and book—draws on the exegetics of the integument.

The commonplace that Scripture and secular letters do not signify in the same way (for example, *Pol.* 7.12) did not prevent commentators on secular authors and modern writers with ambitions of *auctoritas* from appropriating for their human fictions the veiling and multiple discourses characteristic of Scripture.[22] Thus the integument, defined in the twelfth century as "a kind of demonstration of truth under a fabulous narrative, veiling the meaning, whence it is also called a veil" (genus demonstrationis sub fabulosa narratione veritatis, involvens intellectum, unde et involucrum dicitur).[23] The Archpriest will urge us repeatedly in the stanzas that follow the sermon to look through the book's veiled surface at its meaning or lesson, its *sentençia* (*Libro*, tr. 10/110). While the *De amore*'s narrator tells us that he teaches a *duplex sententia*, the Archpriest seems blithely confident that his *sententia* is unitary. If the *Libro* deploys *sententia* singularly, however, it does so with deep duplicity: its repeated appeals to the integument will subject that trope's oppositional axis (sentence/sound, inside/outside) to multiple inversions and set it against other means of inventing good doctrine from the text.

These inversions are performed in a series of meta-allegories that, like the stories we examined in the Archpriest's dispute with Amor, fuse and confuse apparently opposing positions.[24] In one tale, the Archpriest courts —through gifts of poetry—a lady described in terms very much like those used for the ideal reader of the *Libro* itself: she is prudent and wise, endowed with ample good sense (*Libro*, S 168cd). So good, in fact, is her good sense that she rejects the Archpriest's advances, a turn of events that he illustrates with a story: a burglar breaks into a house and, to dispose of the guard dog, throws him a loaf of bread in the center of which is hidden a poison (S 174–78). The dog wisely refuses the poisoned bread, as the lady refused the Archpriest's proffered poems—the implication being, of course, that their sweet crust hides a poisonous crumb.

Another lady, the nun Garoça, perhaps the wisest of the beleaguered women of the book, also refuses the Archpriest's affections, choosing instead the safety of her cloister. The Archpriest's go-between criticizes her choice, comparing her to the rooster who found and ignored a sapphire in the dunghill. The tale's *sententia* shifts suddenly from fiction to metafiction, making the foolish rooster a figure not only for doña Garoça but also for the peevish or inattentive reader of her story:

There are many who read the book and keep it in their possession, who don't know what they are reading and can't understand it; they own some valuable and precious things, but do not give them the honor they deserve.

> (Muchos leen el libro toviendo lo en poder,
> que non saben qué leen, nin lo pueden entender;
> tienen algunas cosas preçiadas e de querer,
> que non les ponen onrra la qual devían aver.)
> (*Libro, SGT* 1390)

Thus, while the *Libro* declares that it contains both dung and sapphire, the two opposing poles are valorized alternately as purely bad and purely good.

Juan Ruiz's habit of "implying the negative pole at precisely the moment when he is asserting the absolute validity of the positive one" (J. Burke, 210) is apparent even when he calls upon the integument directly. The first time he does so, he glosses his own book's textuality with the same figural exuberance we have seen exegetes use when they speak of Scripture:

Do not think that this is a book of foolish nonsense, and do not take as a joke anything that I recite in it, for, just as good money can be stored in a worthless purse, so in an ugly-looking book lies wisdom that is not uncomely. The fennel seed, on the outside blacker than a cooking pot, is very white inside, whiter than ermine; white meal lies within a black covering; sweet white sugar lies within the humble sugarcane. Under the thorn lies the rose, a noble flower; in ugly letters lies the wisdom of a great teacher; just as under a bad cape lies a good drinker, so under a bad cloak lies good love.

(Non tengades que es libro neçio de devaneo,
nin creades que es chufa algo que en él leo,
ca, segund buen dinero yaze en vil correo,
ansí en feo libro está saber non feo.

. . . .

El axenuz de fuera más negro es que caldera;
es de dentro muy blanco, más que la peña vera;
blanca farina está so negra cobertera;
açucar {dulçe} e blanco está en vil caña vera.

. . . .

Sobre la espina está la noble rrosa flor;
en fea letra está saber de grand dotor;
commo so mala capa yaze buen bevedor,
ansí so el mal tabardo está {el} buen amor.)

(*Libro, SG* 16–18) [25]

The oppositional evaluations are clear here: the inside is good, sweet, and white; the outside ugly, black, and bad. Later occurrences of the trope within the fiction itself, however, invert the oppositions and confuse their key terms. The Archpriest, in his role of frustrated lover, will suggest that what lies under the bad cape is not *buen amor*, as here, but bad old Amor himself, whom the Archpriest accuses of "always plotting, covered by a bad mantle" (urdiendo sienpre cobierto so mal paño) (*Libro, S* 216d, my translation). Amor himself gives the screw one more turn when he gives the Archpriest the following advice about selecting a go-between:

Of all those old women, this one is the best; beg her not to lie to you, show her good love, for a good broker is able to sell plenty of bad cattle, and a lot of bad clothes can be covered by a good cloak.

(De aquestas viejas todas, ésta es la mejor;
rruegal que te non mienta, muéstral buen amor,
que mucha mala bestia vende buen corredor,
e mucha mala rropa cubre buen cobertor.)

(*Libro, G* 443)

The promise that good love lies under a bad cloak (*SG* 18cd) leaves the integument untouched, but subjects to racy redefinition the "good love of God" so praised in the sermon. Amor's advice meddles with both, equating the truth-veiling integument with the cover-up of sophistry: a good cloak covers up bad clothes, just as a good salesman unloads a bad beast.[26] Thus, a good bawd will be able to offer assurances that a lady looks as good without her clothes as with them (*S* 435cd), but is equally likely to trade in damaged goods, as here, or to blow her client's amorous cover (S 921cd). The best way to avoid such calamity is, of course, to show her good love: neither the good love of God nor the good love hidden under the tunic, but social good love—that is, flattery.

The *Libro* tampers with hermeneutical oppositions in an even bolder way in the pause introducing the book's first comic fable. We have just seen the poet reverse the evaluative oppositions of integumental allegory; now he turns the integument itself inside out:

And since a person cannot laugh at sensible things, I will insert a few jokes here; whenever you hear them pay attention only to the way they are put into song and verse.

> (E por que de buen seso non puede omne rreir,
> avré algunas {burlas} aquí a enxerir;
> cada que las {oyeres}, non {quieras} comedir
> salvo en la manera del trobar e del dezir.)
> (*Libro, SG* 45)

Here the poet advises that we should read his foolishness not for the kernel of truth that it hides but for the very "ugly sound of the words" which the prologue had begged us to reject. The dung is the sapphire, the shell the kernel. The *sententia* of the jokes is precisely that there is no exegetical *sententia* at all; they will indeed teach, but only about the shifting attractions and pleasures of verse.

The very next stanza, however, seems to invert the rule again. It promises, in the burlesque fable to follow, a kernel within the shell, a *sententia* that we must understand:

Understand my words correctly and ponder their meaning: may it not happen to me with you as it happened to the wise man from Greece with the ignorant Roman hoodlum and his little wisdom, when Rome petitioned Greece for learning.

> (Entiende bien mis dichos e piensa la sentencia;
> non me contesca con tigo commo al doctor de Greçia
> con {el} rribaldo rromano e con su poca sabiençia,
> quando demandó Roma a Greçia la çiençia.)
> (*Libro, SG* 46, following *S*)

Many readers, taking the poet's hint, have found hiding beneath this tale's witty surface "the very kernel of the *Libro*'s structure."[27] It thus bears a brief retelling. The Romans ask the Greeks for their laws; the Greeks, not trusting that the Romans have a good enough understanding to deserve them, propose a disputation, which both parties agree will be conducted in sign language. On the appointed day, the disputation takes place, various hand gestures are exchanged, and the Greek sage concludes that the Romans do indeed deserve the gift. From the subsequent explanations of this encounter, we learn that the Greek understood the contest as a theological discussion, and took the Roman hoodlum's signs as indicating agreement with his own. The Roman, on the other hand, understood it as a semiotic feud, and read the Greek signs as physical threats, to which he responded in kind.

Now, the introduction to the tale encouraged us to take it as an allegory of reading, to recognize ourselves in one of the characters, and to interpret accordingly. The problem is that both the declarations leading up to the story and the manuscripts themselves offer conflicting indications as to which character is, in fact, our stand-in. Stanza 46 in the Salamanca manuscript tells us not to be like the Roman: "may it not *happen to me* with you as it happened to the wise man from Greece" (non *me contesca* con tigo commo al doctor de Greçia); that is, as stanza 16 warned, not to mistake high intent for foolery. Stanza 46 in the Gayoso manuscript, on the other hand, advises precisely the opposite: "let it not *happen to you* as it happened to the wise man from Greece" (non acaesca *con tigo* commo al dotor de Greçia) (my translation); that is, as stanza 45 warned, do not mistake folly for high doctrine. Like the positions of the litigants in the case of Fox versus Wolf, the opposing positions in this mirror game are empty, to be filled in turn by either author or reader, or both.

Not only an allegory of readers, the tale is also a multiple allegory of readerly strategies. First, it represents both of the book's contrary deployments of the integument—looking for truth beneath apparent folly and taking apparent folly at face value—and brands both as misreading: the first, as spiritual overreading; the second, as carnal underreading. At the same time, the fable mirrors the *Libro*'s other didactic strategy, the mimetic one sketched out in the prologue's advice to recognize our sinning selves in the fiction and emend accordingly. The tale of Greco-Roman misinterpretation exemplifies the dangers of exactly this sort of specular reading of oneself in the text of another, for each disputant construes the other's signs in the image of his own intention, failing to understand the intentional and intellectual alterity of the text before him.

Another tale of mimesis and deception a bit later in the *Libro*, however, teaches the opposite lesson. Like the story of the Greeks and Romans, the tale of the painter Pitas Payas is framed with paradoxical reading instructions and assurances of didactic utility. It begins with a conditional, if equivocal, acknowledgment of the tale's frivolity—"if you perceive that it is a joke, tell me another one just as big" (si vieres que es burla, di me otra tan {maña}) (*Libro*, *S* 474b)—but the conclusion—"don't be a Pitas Payas" (non seas Pitas Pajas) (*S* 485b)—offers a moral instead of a punch line. In the tale, Pitas Payas paints a lamb on his wife's belly before he leaves on a business trip. In his absence, his wife takes a lover, and their lovemaking wears the lamb away. Before the painter's return, the lover replaces the image with a painting of a big old ram with a fine set of horns (*S* 480ab). Pitas Payas notes the change, but accepts his wife's explanation that the lamb simply grew up during his absence.

Pitas Payas is certainly the butt of the joke here, not so much because he is sexually naive as because, like the Greek philosopher, he is laughably obtuse about his own profession. A painter tricked like the audience of Zeuxis into identifying the painted with the real, Pitas Payas yet remains blind to another, more significant correspondence of representation and reality. His naïveté is hermeneutic, for he fails to read the horned beast on his wife's belly as his own allegorical portrait. The lesson in interpretation here, then, is precisely the opposite of the one taught by the Greeks and Romans: failing to see your own image in a text is pure foolishness.

It would seem, then, that whatever we choose to think about the *Libro de buen amor* is wrong. So the poet himself tells us: "until you understand my book, don't speak either well or ill of it, for you will understand one thing and the book will say something else" (fasta que el libro entiendas, dél bien non digas nin mal, / ca tú entenderás uno e el libro dize ál) (*SG* 986cd, my translation). However, we have it on the authority of the book itself that precisely the opposite is true:

I, this book, am akin to all instruments: as you play well or badly, so, most assuredly, will it speak; in whatever way you choose to speak, stop there and hold fast; if you know how to play me, you will always hold me in mind.

> (De todos instrumentos, yo, libro, só pariente:
> bien o mal, qual puntares, tal te dirá çiertamente.
> Qual tú dezir quisieres, ý faz punto, ý, ten te;
> si me puntar sopieres, sienpre me avrás en miente.)
> (*Libro*, *SG* 70)[28]

The book thus suggests, even imposes, two opposed didactic reading programs: one, the book is a "morally neutral object" (Gerli, "Recta voluntas," 501) to be construed in the image of the reader's understanding; and two, the book is a repository of hidden and authoritative truth.

Both are alternately—and, in the case of the Greeks and Romans, *simultaneously*—evoked and denied. Whatever approach one takes to the book is both always wrong and always right; like Scripture, the *Libro* is at once the image of its reader and utterly different from him or her. As the Archpriest himself advises us, "Where you think it is lying, it speaks the greatest truth" (Do coidares que miente, dize mayor verdat) (*Libro, SG* 69a).

Even readers with the temerity to think that they know what Juan Ruiz is up to, readers well-read enough to know that mistaking lie for truth—or sound for sense—is the rashest of readerly errors, even these readers cannot help but take one thing for the other here. The fact that such misreading may well be caused by following to the letter the Archpriest's own reading instructions does not make any less awkward the position in which we now find ourselves. Puzzled, we might remember the *De doctrina christiana*:

For care must be taken from the start lest you take figural expressions literally. The Apostle's statement is pertinent here: "The letter killeth, but the spirit quickeneth." For when a thing said figuratively is taken as if it were meant literally, it is understood carnally. . . . To this observation that we should beware taking figural expressions literally, another should be added, lest we take literal expressions as if they were figurative. Therefore a method must be established whereby we might discover whether an expression is literal or figural.

(Nam in principio cauendum est, ne figuratam locutionem ad litteram accipias. Et ad hoc enim pertinet, quod ait apostolus: *Littera occidit, spiritus autem uiuificat.* Cum enim figurate dictum sic accipitur, tamquam proprie dictum sit, carnaliter sapitur. . . . Huic autem obseruationi, qua cauemus figuratam locutionem, id est, translatam quasi propriam sequi, adiungenda etiam illa est, ne propriam quasi figuratam uelimus accipere. Demonstrandus est igitur prius modus inueniendae locutionis, propriane an figurata sit.) (*DDC* 3.5.9; 3.10.14; my translation)

We are no better off than we were when we started, for all that rereading Augustine has done here is to reiterate what the *Libro* has already taught us, and "understand well" is not particularly helpful advice.

In the In-Between

> Good and bad are two contraries, and you put them together as if they were the same thing!
>
> —*Roman de la poire*

While the introductory sermon clearly casts negotiation of the *Libro*'s equivocations and obscurities as a dialectico-moral problem, the text offers no consistent rules for resolving it—unlike Augustine in the *De doctrina christiana*, or Abelard in the *Sic et non*. Perhaps what we need is a third term to mediate between the oppositions that both fuse and multiply throughout the text. Such mediation would permit readers to differentiate between the spirit of *sententia* and the veil of the letter long enough to avoid the *Libro*'s prefigured interpretive perils of misunderstanding the book or badmouthing it (*SG* 68).

Aspiring *Libro* exegetes will perhaps not be surprised to find our dilemma represented within the text itself. We, too, have a stand-in here, and he is as perplexed and put off by his undertaking as we are. Our allegorical double is the unlucky Archpriest himself, in his dispute with Amor. "Why haven't I succeeded?," he complains, and Amor tells him that he needs an amatory third term—in Spanish, a *tercera*:

Make sure, as best you can, that your go-between is well-spoken, subtle, and familiar with her job; that she knows how to tell beautiful lies and stay on the trail, for the pot boils hardest with its cover on.

> (Puña en quanto puedas que la tu mensajera
> sea bien rrasonada, sotil e costumera;
> sepa mentir fermoso, e siga la carrera,
> ca más fierbe la olla con la su cobertera.)
> *(Libro, G 437)*

Amor's wife, Venus, later concurs:

Therefore hunt for a good go-between who knows how to tread this road wisely, who can understand well the nature of both of you: let your trotter be as Sir Love described her to you.

> (Por ende busca una buena medianera,
> que sepa sabia mente andar esta carrera,
> que entienda de vós anbos bien la vuestra manera,
> qual don Amor te dixo, tal sea la trotera.)
> *(Libro, S 645)*

Here, in Venus's speech, Juan Ruiz the poet is freely translating the anonymous twelfth-century Ovidian comedy *Pamphilus*. In this work, Venus advises, "let there be always an interpreter between you who carefully reports your individual desires" (et placeat uobis interpres semper utrisque, / qui caute referat hoc quod uterque cupit) (lines 137–38). The *interpres* has a long lexical pedigree—translation from one language to another in the Middle Ages is *interpretatio*;[29] so is dialectic, which, as John of Salisbury wrote, "serves as an interpreter of both words and meanings" (vocum et intellectuum interpres est) (*Met.* 2.3; tr. 78/64). Thus it is no surprise to find that the words associated with the *Libro*'s go-between — to understand (*entender*), to reason (*rrasonar*), road (*carrera*), covering (*cobertera*), subtle (*sotil*) — should be those associated with the judgment of difficult texts, and with the *Libro* in particular. Like dialectic, the erotic *interpres* points out the road to union, if not with Sophia, then with some other, mortal, girl; equally, the *Libro* will show readers the way on whichever road they choose to travel. As the book, quoting Scripture, gave its readers understanding, so lovers reach *their* understanding through the go-between's agency. As the good go-between is subtle and well-covered in her speech, so too is the *Libro de buen amor*: "The manner of the book must be understood by you as subtle; for you will not find one among a thousand troubadours who knows how to speak good and ill, cryptically and gracefully" (La manera del libro, entiende la sotil; / que saber bien e mal dezir encobierto e doñeguil, / tú non fallarás uno de trobadores mill (*SG* 65bcd, following *S*).[30]

In his obvious enchantment with his text's subtlety, the Archpriest here sounds like a boasting poet of the *trobar clus*. Equally striking is the resonance between this self-praise of the subtle "discourse of good love" (razones de buen amor) (*Libro, SG* 68ab, my translation) with Abelard's praise of the titular discipline of his *Dialectica*:

The more subtle it is, the more difficult; the more difficult, the more rare; the more rare, the more precious; the more precious, the more worthy of the exercise of great study. But because the long labor of this *doctrina* fatigues these readers with assiduous reading . . . they turn the praise of subtlety into an accusation.

(Quanto subtilior est, tanto difficilior; quanto autem difficilior, tanto rarior; quanto autem rarior, tanto pretiosior; quanto pretiosior, tanto maioris studii digna exercitio. Sed quia labor huius doctrinae diuturnus ipsos assiduitate legendi fatigat lectores . . . subtilitatis laudem in crimina vertunt.) (Abelard, *Dialectica* 4, Prologue; 470)

The Archpriest, too, anticipates that his book's subtlety will likely be the source of some ill-tempered accusations from readers not assiduous enough to follow his trail (see, e.g., *Libro SG* 68d). You must be smart when you use an *interpres*, because it can double-cross you: this advice applies to users of dialectic, users of go-betweens, users of the *ars amatoria*, and, finally, users of the *Libro de buen amor*. You must take care in choosing the go-between, advises Venus, appropriating as she does so the language of wisdom and free choice that the Archpriest called upon to describe the proper reading of the *Libro*:

The prudent man of good sense should ponder all things, he should choose the best and shun the harmful ones; for carrying love-messages, people of dubious character are never good or helpful.

> (El cuerdo con buen seso pensar deve las cosas:
> escoja las mejores e dexe las dañosas;
> para mensajería, personas sospechosas
> nunca son a los omnes buenas nin provechosas.)
>
> (*Libro, SG* 696)

Sneaky intermediaries that aim to promote various sorts of "understandings," the book and the go-between are figures of each other.[31] The go-between makes the analogy explicit when she renames herself, saying to the Archpriest:

Never utter a bad name or an ugly one; call me "Good Love" and I will be loyal to you, for everyone around takes pleasure in good words: nice speech costs no more than senseless words.

> (Nunca {digades} nonbre malo nin de fealdat;
> llamat me Buen Amor e faré yo lealtat;
> ca de buena palabra paga se la vezindat;
> el buen dezir non cuesta más que la nesçedat.)
>
> (*Libro, S* 932)

The book follows suit. As it had appropriated to itself the words of the Good Book, so, too, it takes over the words of Good Love: "For love of the old woman and to speak the truth, I named this book 'Good Love' and her too from this time on" (Por amor de la vieja, e por dezir rrazón, / "buen amor" dixe al libro, e a ella toda saçón) (*S* 933ab). Like the red sky with which John of Salisbury attempted to elucidate the *lex contrarietatis* (*Met.* 4.34; tr. 257/204), the *Libro*'s titular *B/buen A/amor* by now has acquired a signification at once perfectly proper and perfectly ambiguous.[32]

After applying the phrase *buen amor* to the love of the flesh as well as that of God, the poet packs both meanings into the name he gives his book. In his farewell to us and to his book, he tells us what we can do with it:

Since it is of good love, lend it gladly; don't deny it its name and don't give it censure; don't give it for money, either by sale or by rental, for, purchased, it has no delight or grace.

(Pues es de buen amor, enprestad lo de grado:
non desmintades su nonbre, {nil} dedes rrefertado;
non le dedes por dineros, vendido nin alquilado;
ca non ha grado nin graçia nin buen amor conprado.)
(*Libro, ST* 1630; following *S*) [33]

The best things in life are free, it seems. St. Paul told us that good *caritas* "seeketh not her own" (non quaerit quae sua sunt) (1 Corinthians 13.5); similarly, many medieval writers remind us that good carnal love is not the kind you pay for, either. Even Andreas's preceptor would agree that there's no delight or grace in the love obtained by money (*De amore* 1.9–12).

We are, it seems, in a dreamy world of the in-between: "We have already become acquainted with the interpretive rule according to which every element in a dream can, for the purposes of interpretation, stand for its opposite as easily as for itself. We can never tell beforehand whether it stands for the one or the other; only the context can decide" (Freud, *Interpretation*, 508). *B/buen A/amor*, then, means both one thing and the other, multiply signifying like a figure in Scripture or an image in a dream. The Cistercian Aelred of Rievaulx (d. 1167) warned against exactly this ambiguity, which folds the opposed emotions *caritas* and *cupiditas* into the same word, *amor*.[34] Similarly, in the *De amore*, a noblewoman asked to compare extramarital and marital love refuses to do so, reducing the question to a logical equivocation (*fallacia secundum aequivocationem*):[35]

Feelings in marriage and true love between lovers are accounted utterly different, and take their source from completely different impulses. So the ambiguous nature of the language employed makes comparisons impossible, but causes them to be associated though they are different in kind. When things are expressed ambiguously, any comparison of greater or less disappears if the comparison is referred to the common term, in relation to which they are called ambiguous.

(Maritalis effectus et coamantium vera dilectio penitus iudicantur esse diversa et ex motibus omnino differentibus suam sumunt originem. Et ideo inventio ipsius sermonis aequivoca actus comparationis excludit et sub diversis ea facit speciebus adiungi. Cessat enim collatio comparandi per magis et minus inter res aequivoce sumptas, si ad commune nomen, cuius respecte dicuntur aequivocae, comparatio referatur.) (*De amore* 2.7.21–22; 258)

This same equivocation, so inimical to the *either/or* logic of the *De amore*'s preceptor and his characters, is enthusiastically practiced by the Archpriest (and the poet himself) who, after using the phrase *buen amor* to point to both *caritas* and *cupiditas*, packs both meanings into the name he gives his book.

The good love of God (buen amor de Dios) and the mad love of this world (loco amor de este mundo) were plainly opposed in the opening sermon, but as the *Libro* progresses, the differences between them become more and more obscure, wrapped in such a dense mist that even the rashest reader cannot find anything to interpret falsely, so insistently are both figural and literal readings represented, prescribed, and performed in the text. For Augustine, the last recourse in a case of such obscure ambiguity is, of course, an appeal to the arbitration of divine charity (*DDC* 3.15.23). By folding opposed terms into his titular equivocation, Juan Ruiz has counterfeited the rule of charity so central to Augustinian exegesis.[36] As Scripture, interpreted by the methods of charity, accommodates itself to all possible readings, in a polysemy as lush as a peacock's tail and as virtuously wanton as a redeemed courtesan, so, interpreted thus by the methods of *buen amor*, the letter of its *Libro* eagerly accommodates itself to all of the multiple misreadings possible to the misguided human will.

The End of Ambiguity

In summoning and destabilizing hermeneutic oppositions of letter/sense, inside/outside, kernel/shell, and so on, the *Libro* may seem to be transgressing, but in fact is imitating and *performing* the teaching processes of scriptural interpretation. As we have seen, in exegetical practice these oppositions are something of a fiction, for the poetics of exegesis ultimately collapses them. Gregory the Great, after all, likened the meanings of Scripture to all the ornaments that can be made from a lump of gold: for him, as for the reader of "good understanding" constructed by the *Libro*, "external" ornament and "internal" meaning are one and the same: "As, from a single lump of gold, some make necklaces, some rings, some bracelets, and all for adornment, so from one understanding of Holy Scripture, the expositors, through innumerable meanings, compose as it were various ornaments, which all serve to adorn the beauty of the celestial Spouse" (*PL* 77: 668AB).

If the *Libro* is transgressive, its transgression lies not in collapsing exegetical polarities but in imitating scriptural *doctrina* and performing it in secular fiction. Secular letters cannot signify like Scripture, we are told again and again by medieval readers and writers. In secular letters, says John of Salisbury, "not things but words merely have meaning" (non res sed dumtaxat uerba significant) (*Pol.* 7.12; tr. 264/2: 144). Aquinas agrees, stating flatly that poetry's only function is to signify.[37] Where does all this leave the *Libro*?

In one argumentative story told by the present study, *Contrary Things*, I have, I confess, been casting the *Libro de buen amor* as a sort of utopia: a parodic transfer of the poetics of exegesis into a secular world of verbal, intellectual, and literary play, a letting loose of exegetical reading upon the plains of secular fiction, taking the delights of the wanton letter of Scripture to their logical and meretricious lengths.[38] But is this the whole story I want my book to teach?

Well, yes and no; *sic et non*. Utopian the *Libro* may well be in my narrative, but we need to remember what "utopia" means. If the *Libro* is utopian, it is so to the very letter: its joyously meretricious appropriation of the *both-and* of exegesis was, in the mid–fourteenth century, literally no place. Not so much utopia, then (the word is after all a Renaissance coinage), as a region of unlikeness, mimicking in its oppositions, contraries, and contradictions not only the divine discourse of Scripture but also the beautiful and deceptive dissonances of the fallen world:

> Just as these contraries opposed to contraries make the beauty of a discourse, so the beauty of the course of this world is built up by a kind of rhetoric, not of words but of things, which employs this opposition of contraries. This is very clearly stated in the book of Ecclesiasticus as follows: "Good is set against evil, and life set against death; so the sinner is set against the godly. And so you are to regard the works of the Most High: two by two, one against the other." (Augustine, *De civitate Dei* 11.18; 3: 496)

The *doctrina* of Scripture, Hugh of St. Victor wrote, is meant to lead readers out of this region of unlikeness (however beautiful it might be) into some restored similitude with the divine (*Did.* 1.7; tr. 47/6). Does the *Libro*'s imitation of scriptural teaching-textuality extend to the ontological reeducation that Hugh imagined? In order for this to occur, we should, under the Archpriest's guidance, renounce what Peter Damian called the "consequences of exterior words" (*PL* 145: 603D), the "ugly sound of the words" (*Libro*, tr. 10/110) that the *Libro*'s puns and wordplay love so well, and direct our attention toward the divine *res*. Our narrator is incapable of the renunciation such transcendence requires, but there are signs that he knows it must come, even begs for it to happen. Playful the *Libro* may be, but its play is not free.

A hint of what is to come appears quite early, in another of the *Libro*'s meta-allegories: the story of the five astrologers (*SG* 129–39). This tale, like that of the Greeks and Romans, is framed by instructions and apologies: there, the Archpriest justified his interweaving of jest and earnest; here he justifies the autobiographical and erotic subject matter of those jests

by blaming his passions on the stars. However, the links between the episodes go deeper, for while the fable of the Greeks and Romans dramatized
the incorrect interpretation of ambiguous signs at the root of an ancient
translatio legum, that of the astrologers treats interpretation and ambiguity
to a much grimmer end. The signs at issue here are natural ones; the hermeneutic discipline, neither exegesis nor dialectic, but astrology.[39] While
John of Salisbury doubted "that there exists such a close relationship between [celestial] signs and that which is signified, that the one necessarily
follows from the other" (non equidem signorum signatorumque eam co-
herentiam arbitror, ut alterum ex altero necessario consequatur) (*Pol.* 2.25;
tr. 120/1: 136), this story proves the opposite proposition, and proves it
with a vengeance.

A prince is born, and five astrologers are called in to cast his future:

When they had plotted the instant at which he was born, one master said: "He
will be stoned to death." The next one said: "I predict that he will be burned
to death." The third said: "The boy will be cast down to his death from a high
place." The fourth said: "He will be hanged." Said the fifth master: "He will die
in water by drowning."

> (Desque vieron el punto en que ovo de nasçer,
> dixo el un maestro: "Apedreado ha de ser."
>
> . . . .
>
> Judgó el otro e dixo: "Este ha de ser quemado."
> El terçero dize: "El niño ha de {ser} despeñado."
> El cuarto dixo: "El infante ha de ser colgado."
> Dixo el quinto maestro: "Morrá en agua afogado.")
> (*Libro, SG* 130cd–131)

Reading the same set of natural signs, the sages produce five different
and apparently mutually exclusive interpretations. Logically, their propositions cannot all be true at the same time; logically, the king condemns
them as manifest liars (*SG* 132d). Then one day, the prince goes hunting,
and in a single terrible storm, he is pounded by hail, struck by lightning,
snagged by his clothing as he falls from a bridge, and eventually drowned
in the rising flood. The laws of logic, it seems, were suspended: "The five
aforementioned prognostications were fulfilled, the wise natural scientists
turned out to have been telling the truth" (Los çinco fados dichos, todos
bien se conplieron; / los sabios naturales verdaderos salieron) (*SG* 138cd).

What the astrologers read were "sure signs" (çiertas señales) (*Libro, SG*
128c), the Archpriest assures us. Things seem providentially arranged so
that, as Hugh of St. Victor said, "teaching might be multiple, the truth

remaining the same" (*PL* 176: 678D). Diverse but not adverse, all readings of these signs are correct, and, like the multiple certain signs of Scripture, all indicate a single truth. And in this single truth the similarity between Good Love and Good Book ends, for the *Libro*'s one unequivocal truth is not *caritas* but death.

The explosive entrance of death as a major preoccupation in the second half of the book makes explicit the eschatological stakes of the *Libro*'s *doctrina*. First one, then another of the Archpriest's ladies dies (*S* 943–44, *SGT* 1506); but his tone remains almost flippant until the passing of Buen Amor herself, the go-between. At this point, the Archpriest's cool naturalism seems to fail him, and the narrative comes to an abrupt halt in another poetic set-piece, a long and detailed lament (*SGT* 1520–1544; *ST* 1520–1575).

Though the lament begins with a joke and ends with a parodic epitaph for the dead go-between, more is going on here than grim nose-thumbing at the inevitable. Death is represented as the destroyer of everything the book seems to treasure most. It is certain, yet absolutely resists understanding: "we should feel certain of, and not secure from, Death" (devemos estar çiertos, non seguros, de muerte) (*ST* 1580a); "your woeful arrival cannot be understood" (la tu venida triste non se puede entender) (*Libro*, *SGT* 1523c). It destroys both corporeal and intellectual sense (*ST* 1547b); the dying man "quickly loses his speech and his understanding" (pierde luego la fabla e el entendimiento) (*SGT* 1535a). There is no ambiguity in death, nor any possibility of interpretive play with or after it; its unreadable certainty casts a cold light on worldly games, those of reading and teaching included: "bear in mind that tomorrow you may die, for life is a game" (tened que cras morredes, ca la vida es juego) (*SGT* 1531d).[40]

The end of ambiguity has been hovering over the Salamanca manuscript from the very beginning, for this version of the *Libro de buen amor* begins with an impassioned *contrafactum* of the *ordo commendationis animae*, the ritual for the dying (*S* 1–10). The following sermon, whose dialectically demanding play with readerly understanding we studied at the beginning of this chapter, takes its *thema* from the Psalm read in that same rite of passage.[41] Having begged God at the poem's very beginning, "deliver me from this anguish, from this wretched prison" (saca me desta lazeria, desta presión) (*S* 2d), Juan Ruiz devotes much of the rest of his book to entangling his readers, no matter how good their understanding, in a discursive performance of that very earthly prison.[42] The didactic cacophony produced by the *Libro*'s insistent multiplicity of instructional discourses stresses *doctrina*, at once underlining and frustrating medieval textual teaching.

We have seen that the *Libro de buen amor* is without doubt a teaching text, that it mobilizes and fuses the teaching strategies and theories of both exegesis and dialectic. The question is still unanswered: To what end? What does the *Libro de buen amor* teach us? The *Libro*'s own answer is: Everything. That's a good answer. The best modern answer I have yet heard was made by an undergraduate in class discussion. "Why make reading a book so hard?" I asked them. "Why didn't the author just come out and say what he meant?" From the back row, a hand shot up, that of a student who had been chatty but disengaged and vaguely surly all semester. Her answer came in a rush: she said that she had less invested in a task if it was easy, and that making her work for whatever she found in the *Libro* was the author's way of making her make the book her own. "He wanted to teach us to think," she said of Juan Ruiz.

I have never heard a better or more medieval way of reading the *Libro de buen amor*. Inventive in the premodern sense, this student found meaning in the *Libro* that she understood as both already there in some sense and very much of her own making. Without having read or even heard of St. Augustine or Peter Abelard, she saw the book through their eyes. Difficulty inspires questioning, Abelard's "first key of wisdom" (prima clavis sapientiae) (*Sic et non*, tr. 99/103), and as Augustine knew well, "what is sought with difficulty is discovered with greater pleasure" (cum aliqua difficultate quaesita multo gratius inueniri) (*DDC* 2.6.8).

Conclusion
Teacher's Manual

A representative member of a late-twentieth-century university community is reading a modern edition of a book written in the European Middle Ages. I imagine him or her sitting up straight at the desk, a dictionary close at hand, pencil sharpened, highlighter uncapped. The book, our reader has been assured, has much to teach. Perhaps someone told her the book was "influential"; perhaps he has to read it for his master's exams. Perhaps excited, but mostly puzzled, each one reads anxiously, looking for meaning made by or, more likely, hidden in every sign on the page. "Should I look up this word?" she wonders. He worries, "This must make sense, or they wouldn't have put it on the list. I must be missing something." They look hard at this obscure textual object, and they take good notes.

We can all imagine this scene. Those of us who teach not only imagine it but see its results written on the furrowed brows of our students: "It *must* mean, or she wouldn't make me read it, but it means so strangely." Paul Zumthor imagined such a scene himself in 1972, at the beginning of his monumental essay on medieval poetics:

When a reader of our century confronts a twelfth-century work, the time span separating them distorts and even destroys the relationship that is normally produced by a text's mediation between author and reader. Such a relationship cannot be said to exist anymore. What is a true reading, if not an activity involving both the reader and the culture to which he belongs, and corresponding to the activity of production involving the author and his own universe? In dealing with a medieval text the correspondence ceases to be spontaneous. The very perception of the forms becomes doubtful. Metaphors become opaque, and the vehicle of the comparison parts company with the tenor. (Zumthor, 4)

What Zumthor—and the anxious student-readers I have just imagined— take as a "spontaneous" relation under "normal" (that is, familiarly modern) conditions is anything but spontaneous when we read these medieval texts, if it ever can be spontaneous at all. Author and reader, like a medieval erotic couple, must leave negotiation of their mutual understanding to an *interpres*, a go-between whose manuscript or printed words cannot be fully understood or completely trusted. When that aspiring reader-lover is of a scholarly inclination, like Zumthor, my imaginary master's student, myself, and my own readers, a great deal hangs on the interpretation of the go-between's words, for we read within an institutional frame assuring us that these signs, however contradictory or obscure, both have and make abundant sense—that they do, in fact, have something to teach us.

Medieval readers read from this position too; we have company here:

> So it is little wonder that if we lack that Spirit, by whose agency these writings were written and dictated, and communicated directly by it to the writers, we may fail to understand their actual writings. The greatest barrier to our understanding is the unusual style and the fact that very often the same words have different meanings, when one and the same word has been used to express now one meaning, now another. For each person has an abundant supply of words, just as of thoughts. (*Sic et non*, tr. 87/89)

This medieval reader is Peter Abelard. Like Zumthor, he writes about obstacles between reader and read: loss, alterity, historical change. Unlike Zumthor, however, he sings no elegiac song for the loss of imagined community between target text and readers. Abelard's target text, Scripture, is always already radically other, ever and simultaneously both image of its readers and their determined and resistant other. Abelard does not lament these obstacles on the *via veritatis* of reading; in fact, the text he is here introducing will perform them insistently, willfully placing its own obstacle—contradiction—between reader and read, between student and doctrine.

Readers of the contrary things in Walter's library can, I imagine, stand next to the crippled readers Abelard hopes to teach, for we (post)moderns stand before medieval texts as medieval readers stood before Scripture. I do not mean to mystify medieval texts by this comparison, but rather to point out the analogous pressures brought to bear on the two reading scenes. Both the medieval and the scriptural text are products of a lost era and irrecuperable authorial intention; both have been subject to centuries of translation, emendation, and textual drift; both require a daunting amount of erudition before their study can even begin. Both canons, too, are riddled with lacunae and full of contending voices, and both readers are burdened with the difficult yet urgent task of constructing from such noisy discontinuity an interpretation that will *make sense*. Augustine, John of Salisbury, Abelard, Andreas Capellanus, and Juan Ruiz would certainly agree that the ability to read a book like this is no spontaneous or natural gift, and they all set out to teach us how to read such books, which, they know, teach us so abundantly.

For some time now I have begun each semester by asking students to write a short essay on the topic "How to Read a Book." These essays have taught me much about the ways we read now—postmedieval, postmodern—and the stories we tell ourselves about the reading we do. Some writers are put off by the topic, suspicious of the legislative quality they hear in the assignment; others give themselves over to it, and hand in sets of numbered rules, sometimes subdivided by category. The reading lessons are particularly detailed on matters of physical surroundings and the conduct of the reader's body: where to sit, how to sit, what to hold in your hand, what to listen to, what to drink, what to do if you fall asleep. These lessons, and their attendant scene-setting, consistently construct two modes of reading: reading for yourself and reading for school, "pleasure reading" and "homework." For "pleasure reading," the instructions are luxurious, even pandering: choose a nice fat armchair, put your feet up, turn the lights down, slip and slide about in the text however you please. But for textbooks (that is, anything presumed to be edifying), the instructions are ascetic, almost punishing: Sit up straight. Use your highlighter. Stay focused. Don't go to sleep.

These students teach us that reading a teaching text—or *any* text, so long as the context of reading is presumed to be instructive—is the farthest thing possible from pleasure, closer to punishment than delight, subject to eternal vigilance, ramrod posture, and a fresh highlighter. They would never be confused with Charles Horton Cooley's benighted medievals who "read textbooks and thought they were literature" (Cooley, 171). Yet medievals *did* read in a way that collapsed into one complicated process what postmedieval Western culture has taught us to understand as the mutually exclusive opposites of textual teaching and literary pleasure. The medieval teaching texts we have studied here certainly do this, and take a great deal of pleasure in doing it. But when my students read such a teaching text, they look, "naturally," for the information it communicates—its nominal doctrine. They are frustrated when, as in the *Libro de buen amor*, their textbook is not forthcoming on what precisely its nominal doctrine is, or, as in the *De amore*, when that nominal doctrine appears to be double, and they cannot see which of the two teachings they are "supposed" to take as true. Frustrated, and sometimes illuminated. They come to the *De doctrina christiana* expecting dogma, and are surprised to find that what they get is questions and speculation. What they get is the theory and practice of how to read—and *teach*—a book. Especially a difficult, obscure, and contradictory book. "But those who read rashly are deceived by many and multiple obscurities and ambiguities, understanding one thing instead of another; indeed, in certain places they do not find anything to interpret erroneously, so obscurely are certain sayings covered with a most dense mist" (*DDC* 2.6.7; my translation).

Mist, the *De doctrina*'s trope for the obscuring veil of language 'round the Word, appears in another work attributed to Augustine: a work that treats not the Logos but logic. Book 7 of the *De dialectica* uses mist as a blanket figure for all kinds of semiotic undecidabililty. Our puzzled reader, according to the *De dialectica*, is like a traveler standing at an unmarked crossroads in the mist. In the mist, we cannot see into our surroundings, and the path is obscure. When the mist burns off, we find ourselves at the crossroads: the proper road still unmarked, we must choose between one thing and the other (*Dial.* 7; 105).

Distinguishing one thing from another is of course the very foundation of sense-making, but sense is *made*, after all, and it is made even more abundantly when such dialectical discrimination is difficult to effect. Thus the titular *Buen Amor* of the book and bawd who bear its name, is flagrantly both *caritas* and *cupiditas*, while reminding readers that the difference between the two loves is urgently consequential. Thus the multiple and varied textual transmission of the *De amore*'s doubled and divided *sententia*, which attests to medieval readings as different among themselves as they are from the modern edited text we now call *De amore*. Thus the clamoring voices of the dialectical revolution in twelfth-century Paris; thus too, in exegesis, the endless and delicious production of meaning from the misted words of Scripture.

These puzzling places between affirmation and negation, between *either/or* and *both-and*, are amply represented for us in these medieval teaching texts. They are places into which, as into Walter's shoes, modern readers may step, our historical alterity and particularity intact, but with the uncanny feeling that our predicament has been anticipated, even prewritten. We have a stand-in in one of the beleaguered ladies in Andreas's love dialogues, who has just endured a long allegory from her suitor—a double discourse in which he means one thing and says another. Rather testily, she presses him: "This description of yours is much too obscure for me, and your words too cryptic, unless you explain them and make them clear" (Hi mihi sunt nimis sermones obscuri nimisque verba reposita, nisi ipsa tua faciat interpretatio manifesta) (*De amore* 1.6.224; 102). Her suitor responds by teaching her the correspondences between the ideas in his head and the words on his tongue, connecting one thing with the other. As we have seen, Andreas Capellanus is not like this suitor, and is not so forthcoming with a gloss of his own seductive teaching text's disjunctive signification. Andreas offers no *interpretatio manifesta*, only reading instructions whereby an interpretation might be constructed. A reader of the *De amore* must be assiduous, at least in part because she or he is working in the dark.

Sometimes in medieval classes I vary the How to Read a Book exercise by asking students to write little essays on How to Read an Old Book. In these, the split between pleasure and study is even more pronounced than it is when I pose the question without regard to textual antiquity. This last semester, only a few writers mentioned either imagination or pleasure; the rest issued anxious commandments, listing things we "must" do to achieve full understanding and avoid misinterpretation. For these students, the greatest obstacle to reading old books (besides the received wisdom about them) is the opacity of medieval language. "I think," one wrote, "that the solution will be to read lots of old books until their language becomes transparent to me."[1]

I have not told this student yet that she will be disappointed, for when the mist lifts, she will still find herself at a crossroads, able to see the signs but still forced to use her own *intellectus*, her own *buen entendimiento*, to figure out what to do with them. I have not told her yet that I suspect that the opposite is true: the more she reads old books, the harder it will be to see transparency. In fact, reading old books may teach her that the language of twentieth-century novels is just as opaque as that of medieval lyric; modern opacities, being familiar, simply pass, unnoticed, for transparent. Reading an old book, especially one as dedicated to making things difficult as the contrary things we have read here, violates and defamiliarizes assumptions, and thus has a great deal to teach us about how we read in general, "new" books or "old," for work or for pleasure, textbooks or jokebooks. There is no one way to read an old book, just as there is no one way to read a new book. Unless it be, as Andreas Capellanus reminds us, assiduously.

The poetics of contrary teaching in the Middle Ages are built on an insistent (even assiduous) return to Augustine's dialectical crossroads where, when the fog lifts, the way is marked with mutually noisy signs. The poetics of medieval didacticism teach us to read in the space between contraries, where "textbook" and "literature" are indistinguishable, where *both-and* laps over *either/or*. Poetic teaching, which focuses as much on the making (*poiesis*) as it does on the thing made, teaches us to read interpretive difficulties like contrariety and contradiction as provocations to the invention of meaning rather than merely as obstacles to its re- or discovery. For, as Abelard taught, the key to wisdom is assiduous questioning, and true teaching—medieval and modern—aims less to reproduce a doctrine than to instigate *doctrina*: the doubled movement of constative and performative that instructs both *de arte*, about an art, and *ex arte*, through the art, about and through the very process of teaching.

Reference Matter

Notes

Introduction

1. Work on the *Rose* and on Chaucer has both enriched and provoked this project. On the *Rose*, I have benefited from Paré, *Idées*; Jung; Regalado; Hult, "Closed Quotations" and *Self-Fulfilling Prophecies*; Pelen; P. Allen, *Art of Love*, 79–110; and Dragonetti, 200–225. Kelly, *Internal Difference*, and Burke, *Desire Against the Law*, are very relevant to this project but appeared too late to be taken into account here. On Chaucer, I have been informed by Elbow; Robertson, *Preface*; Rowe; Patterson; Ferster; Frese. Also important at the early stages of this project were Vance, *From Topic to Tale*, and T. Hunt, "Aristotle, Dialectic, and Courtly Literature."

2. "Jest and earnest" is from Curtius (417–35); model and antimodel from Corti. This oppositional model continues to structure work as recent as Thomas Reed's *Middle English Debate Poetry*, in which the "irresolution" is suspended between binary "categories of opposition" (e.g., order/disorder, didactic/recreational; see especially 38–39). More sophisticated, but ultimately equally dualistic, is the Bakhtinian construct of the medieval "two-world condition" (Bakhtin, 6).

3. Robertson, *Preface*, 11; see also Wood.

4. Dahlberg, ix. Similarly concerned with universal(izing) coherence is Rowe, though arguing from a different principle of unity, the *concordia discors* tradition.

5. Elbow, Reiss ("Conflict and Resolution"), and, more recently, Sturges have read the movement as "indeterminacy," which they take as a positively valued term in medieval ethics, epistemology, and hermeneutics. Nichols sees in Romanesque art "contradictory discourses that interrogate each other" (Nichols, 147). Camille, too, has placed himself in this indeterminate, in-between space.

6. I have borrowed this metapedagogical question from Barbara Johnson (iii). Apart from the medieval texts themselves, the works from which I have learned most about approaches to textual teaching are the essays collected in *Yale French Studies* 63 (1982); also inspirational has been the work of Jane Gallop and her col-

laborators (*Pedagogy*). For the terms "constative" and "performative," see Austin, 1–11; my use of the term "performative" also bears the mark of Butler.

7. The Middle Ages' other great teacher about teaching, Plato, is noticeably absent from this list. Though Platonic theories of teaching as remembering were deeply formative in the Middle Ages, they are not the principal shapers of the oppositional teaching-textuality I study here. Plato represents Socrates's teaching practice as dialectical, true, but this is the dialectic of "cooperative discussion" (Crombie, quoted in Stahl, Johnson, and Burge, 105 n. 63) rather than that of disputation and contradiction.

8. Lewis and Short, *Latin Dictionary*, s.v. *doctrina*. Both senses of the word are clear in Romans 12.7–8: "Or ministry, in ministering; or he that teacheth, in doctrine; he that exhorteth, in exhorting" ("sive ministerium in ministrando; sive qui docet in doctrina, qui exhortatur in exhortando"). For uses of the term *doctrina* in early Christianity, see Marrou, " 'Doctrina' et 'disciplina,' " according to whom *doctrina* is reserved for the process or content of teaching in their more theoretical aspects.

9. Thanks to Ana Montero for this memory.

10. The notion of transparent vehicular didacticism is the farthest thing from Augustine's mind as he theorizes teaching in the *De magistro*, where language is in fact an *obstacle* to true teaching and learning. Rita Copeland has recently put it nicely: "the philosophical substance [in medieval writing] has an integrity beyond the accidents of language, and yet paradoxically is constituted by the force of the language that mediates it" (145).

11. Lest these categories of process and product sound too much like the language of twentieth-century pedagogical theory, I should note that they are equally medieval notions. Augustine is notably more concerned with spiritual and hermeneutical process than he is with the ultimate product thereof: "meaning," for example, is "correct" when it has been produced correctly, that is, through a process undertaken faithfully and charitably (e.g., *Conf.* 12.18–20, *DDC* 3.15.23). In secular literature of the central Middle Ages we see this fascination fictionalized again and again in the hermeneutical, enigmatic romances of Chrétien de Troyes, the metasemiotic *Lais* of Marie de France, and the nested, *en abyme* teachings of Juan Manuel's *Conde Lucanor*.

12. Cf. *Did.* 3.7; tr. 91/57–58.

13. Solterer is here speaking of Aristotle's taxonomy of oppositional propositions formulated in the logical square, laid out in *Analytica priora* 2.15 (63b23–30); for Aristotle's treatment of the difference between contradictory and contrary, see *De interpretatione* 7 (17b–18a). For a suggestive general introduction to binary thinking in the West, see Lloyd (on Aristotle and the square, 86–88, 161–69). More technical discussions of Aristotelian oppositions may be found in Bochenski, 57–72, 234–251, and Broadie, 90–112.

14. Dialectic is paraphrasing Aristotle here (*Categories* 10, 11b17–23).

Chapter 1

1. For Paul and the Jews, see especially Romans 2.28–29 and Galatians 2.15; on the relations between the Old and New Testaments in medieval exegesis, the best introduction is still Smalley, *Study*.

2. I am using an example of scriptural contradiction offered by the fourteenth-century Spanish prince Juan Manuel in his *Libro de los Estados* 2.5; 308. There is a long tradition in Christian apologetics of compiling catalogues of scriptural contradictions, together with ways to answer the skeptics who adduce them. Julian of Toledo's *Antikeimenon* (c. 690) is an early medieval example; the issue has recently been granted the mark of late-twentieth-century celebrity, a World Wide Web site (Tong).

3. The most frequently cited practitioner of seven-fold exegesis is the Carolingian Angelom of Luxeuil. Far from being expelled from interpretation, contradiction is in fact one of Angelom's seven senses, specifically the fifth, or *parabolicus*, "that is, a contradiction with a mystical meaning" (Smalley, *Study*, 42); see also *Exégèse*, pt. 1, 1: 131–38.

4. Peter the Chanter, 103. Giusberti offers a study of the text with his edition of the prologue of the *De tropis loquendi*. Gillian Evans has studied the *De tropis* most deeply; see her "Peter the Chanter's *De Tropis*"; "A Work of 'Terminist Theology'"; *Language and Logic*, 97–100, 148–50; and "Ponendo theologica exempla."

5. Bernard of Clairvaux called the *Song of Songs* a *theoricus sermo* [theoretical discourse] (Leclercq, *Love of Learning*, 126). *Theoria* is a technical term, characteristic of the more mystical forms of exegesis. First coined at Antioch, it there refers to the prophetic vision of scriptural writers; in twelfth-century writers like Bernard, it will mean "contemplation." The most succinct definition (and the most inspirational for a late-twentieth-century theoretician) is offered by an early commentary on Hosea attributed in the *PL* to Rufinus Aquileiensis (c. 410): "*Theoria* is a well-considered or contemplative perception," he says (Theoria est autem . . . considerata perceptio) (*PL* 21: 971C). For more on this usage of *theoria*, see *Exégèse*, pt. 1, 1: 122; Margerie, 1: 189–90.

6. For the poetic and quotidian texture of *lectio divina*, there is still none better than Leclercq, *Love of Learning*; for a briefer but equally evocative discussion, see Leclercq, "Caractères," 36. For a concise introduction to the differences between monastic *lectio divina* and the Scholastic *sacra pagina*, which came into currency in the twelfth century, see Smalley, *Study*, 79; Colish offers a deeply documented comparison of monastic and early scholastic practices of exegesis for the Psalms and St. Paul (*Peter Lombard*, 1.15–226). Illich treats the two more explicitly as reading practices, and is especially eloquent on the subject of their differences, though perhaps unjustly to the detriment of the latter.

7. The Fall as hermeneutical master-story has been explored by Eric Jager, to whose discussion my own is indebted (see especially 1–20). For Adam and Eve's fatal misreading of God, see also Evans, *Language and Logic*, 2.

8. The Christ of Mark is particularly noteworthy for his simultaneous teaching and screening; see, for example, Mark 4.11–12. For the Incarnation and signification, Boyarin's observation is particularly suggestive: "The dual person of Christ in the world is a perfect homology, then, to the dual nature of language and the necessity for allegorical interpretation to fulfill the spiritual meaning of concrete expression" (75). See also Colish, *Mirror*, 40–41.

9. I borrow the term "logological" from K. Burke, 1–2.

10. The *De magistro* aims to prove that "we learn nothing through those signs which are called words" (per ea signa quae verba appellantur, nos nihil discere) (10.34; tr. 45/130), and that true teaching comes from the "inner Truth," i.e., Christ (12.38; tr. 47–48/136).

11. "Therefore Christ is my grammar, who was made man for men" (Mea igitur grammatica Christus est, qui homo pro hominibus factus est) (Peter Damian, Ep. 8, "Ad Bonumhominem," in *PL* 144: 476BC).

12. School of Hugh of St. Victor, *Miscellanea* (*Elucidationes variae*) (*PL* 177: 505A).

13. "Omnis mundi creatura/quasi liber et pictura/nobis est et speculum" (*PL* 210: 579A). The bibliography on this rich image is vast. Classic treatments are those of Curtius, 302–47; *Exégèse*, pt. 1, 1: 119–28; and more recently Gellrich, especially 29–39. See also Leclercq, "Aspects spirituels," 2; Illich, 122–24; Whitman, 123–31; Hanning, 111–12.

14. Augustine, *De civitate Dei* 11.18; 3: 496, my translation. The image resonates through the Middle Ages; cf., for example, Honorius of Autun, *Liber de xii quaestionum* 2 (*PL* 172: 1179B).

15. Abelard, *Commentariam*, Prologue, 41.

16. For "the genesis of hermeneutics," see Jager, 51–98. Jager is arguing from Augustine here, who, as Jager observes, "traces scriptural enigma and allegory back to the 'clothing' necessitated by the Fall" (71).

17. Ezekiel 3.1; Apocalypse 10.9–10. For more on tropes of reading and/as eating, including monastic *ruminatio*, see Carruthers, 164–69; Leclercq, *Love of Learning*, 89–96; Illich, 50–61.

18. Gregory the Great, *Homiliae* 2.5.3; 257.

19. For the range of medieval terms for what we now call exegesis, see Häring, "Commentary and Hermeneutics," 174–80.

20. The *Moralia* of Gregory the Great is a rich source for this sort of rhapsodic praise of Scripture; almost every new book of the text begins in this way. For a catalogue of patristic and medieval poetic evocations of scriptural multiplicity, see especially *Exégèse*, pt. 1, 1: 119–38.

21. Robertson's translation of *DDC* follows the reading from MSS *C*, *V*, and the Maurist/Bibliothèque Augustinienne edition, which I quote here. Martin's edition reads: "non solum ea, quae *intellego* . . . ," with a resulting shift of sense.

22. The Bible, most particularly the Psalms, was the foundation of monastic

Latinity and the text through which Latin and reading were learned and kept in daily practice. *Praxis*, then, as well as *theoria*, makes the Bible and commentary on it the most suitable matter for (meta)didactic reflection in the Middle Ages. For monastic reading and educational practice, see Illich and especially Gehl.

23. Augustine is very cautious about speaking of scriptural contradiction, advising that some conflicts of words (pugna verborum) are better "passed over in silence rather than resolved verbally" (silentia cauenda potius quam uoce pacanda est) (*DDC* 1.6.6). Augustine did, however, turn his hand to verbal resolutions: Peter the Chanter takes him as the explicit model for the solutions in the *De tropis* (105); the underpinnings of Abelard's *Sic et non* are similarly Augustinian.

24. Cf. Isidore of Seville, *Quaestiones in Vetus Testamentum*, Praef. (*PL* 83: 208). This reading of contradiction and other absurdities as pointers to necessary figuration is patent throughout the Church Fathers, and is most famously associated with Origen; see, among others, Pépin, "À propos de l'histoire"; Dawson.

25. Kermode (23–48) stresses this concealment, and the consequent formation of a hermeneutic élite, in his treatment of this question, which he phrases thus: "Why Are Narratives Obscure?" He answers through the Gospel of Mark.

26. Such was certainly Augustine's take on the problem, as Pontet observes: "It is as if, for him, the kernels of resistance found in Scripture contained the rarest of truths" (120); for a fine overview of Augustine on scriptural obscurity, see Pontet, 136–48. This issue is now studied deeply in Stock, *Augustine the Reader*, which was not yet available at my time of writing.

27. Peter the Chanter's *Distinctiones "Abel"* repeats this pleasant justification for obscurity in a more condensed form: Scripture is obscure as a result of original sin; it is also obscure to exercise us, and to give us pleasure (Barney, 91).

28. Thus, most famously, Dionysius the Areopagite's negative theology; for general discussion see Minnis, Scott, and Wallace, *Medieval Literary Theory*, 165–73. For a (Robertsonian) reading of Dionysius's place in medieval readings of contradiction and dissimilitude, see Dahlberg, 55–72.

29. "Providential intermediary between God and humanity, Scripture resembles both one and the other" (Pontet, 120); cf. Augustine, *Enarrationes in Psalmos* 103 (*PL* 32: 1338).

30. One of the most extended versions of this widespread trope (Scripture as house) may be found in *Did.* 6.4; tr. 140/118. Peter the Eater, appropriately enough, calls Scripture a dining room in his *Historia scholastica* (*PL* 198: 1053).

31. For the most programmatic application of Augustinian charity to medieval literature, see Robertson, "Doctrine of Charity." Not surprisingly, the obscure and contradictory texts of Andreas Capellanus and Chaucer (Robertson, *Preface*) and the *Rose* (Fleming, *The "Roman"*; *Reason and the Lover*) formed the canon of Robertsonian "exegetical" reading, a canon still worked in a similar way by Dahlberg. The method produced much polemical discussion (Donaldson; Kaske); for critical reviews, see Patterson, 3–39; Dinshaw, 31–39, 208 n. 3.

32. Following Paul (2 Corinthians 3.6), the letter is troped with the body, and adherence to the literal and to the sign itself is understood at least from Augustine forward as a sort of fornication (see, e.g., *DDC* 3.5.9). Harpham has followed this ascetic thread into a general theory of Western aesthetics (*The Ascetic Imperative*).

33. Perhaps some of the young Eco's blindness to the luxuriance of the exegetical letter is due to his material—this statement comes from his early book on Aquinas, the poetics of whose approach to Scripture has far less *jouissance* about it than that of monastic *lectio divina*. The more recent Eco, however, still shares this restrictive understanding of scriptural exegesis: "Medieval culture, for example, did everything it could to encourage an interpretation that was infinite in terms of time but nonetheless limited in its options" ("Overinterpreting Texts," 53).

34. Cf. John 6.50–56. This somatic troping of holy body, book, and food is not uncommon in the early Middle Ages; see also St. Jerome's observations quoted in Morin, 243 n. 3.

35. The trope of Christ as manuscript is widespread, especially with the rise of mendicant-inspired personal devotion. It is mentioned in Smalley, *Study*, 283; Lochrie, 167, 170; Gellrich, 17; and Curtius, 319. For more, see Leclercq, "Aspects spirituels," 2; Richter; and Ross.

36. Eriugena, *De divisione Naturae* 4, in *PL* 122: 749C.

37. Gregory also states here that his book will not only dip up biblical water but also imitate the Bible's movement in its own textual meandering, rockiness, and flow (*Moralia*, Ep. ad Leandrum 2; 143: 4).

38. Gilbert of Stanford, *In Cant.*, quoted in *Exégèse*, pt. 1, 1: 352 n. 4. Origen had imagined the Bridegroom's kiss as the moment of interpretive illumination, when the reader-Bride lifts the text's veils; see Astell, 3–4.

39. Gregory the Great, Ep. 76, "Ad Domitianum metropolitanum" (*PL* 77: 668AB).

40. For more on exegesis and pleasure, see Robertson, *Preface*, 52–64; and Jager, 84–86. Arguing from Peter the Chanter, Barney finds exegesis characterized by a "delight in the technology of interpretation" (107).

41. Canon "B.," letter, fol. 84v; cf. *Moralia*, Ep. ad Leandrum 4; 143: 6. "B.'s" text has been partially edited by Omont (24–27) and treated briefly by Jeauneau ("Nani gigantum," 94–95). I am now preparing a study and edition of this text as part of a book on theories and practices of the letter in the Middle Ages.

42. Commenting on the "enormous riot" of Gregory the Great's *Moralia in Job*, Ker, for example, sniffed, "beside these allegories the most untamed things in history seem merely respectable. . . . The most appalling, the most deliberate absurdities of false wit, as St. Gregory's expositions must be judged when taken as *mere literature, mere play of figures*" (134; emphasis added). De Lubac begins his monumental florilegium of exegetical theory and practice with a hand-wringing discussion of the disfavor into which theological allegory has fallen in the twen-

tieth century: it is denounced, he says, as "the phylloxera of exegesis" (*Exégèse*, pt. I, I: 12).

43. For versions of this trope, see McNally, 58–59.

44. Eriugena, *De divisione Naturae* 1.2.20 (*PL* 122: 560A). For a useful catalog of tropes on the abundance and multiplicity of Scripture, see *Exégèse*, pt. I, I: 119–28.

45. "And it is often the case that one and the same passage of Scripture, when multiply expounded, says many things to us in one" (Et saepe fit ut una eademque Scriptura, dum multipliciter exponitur, multa nobis in unum loquatur) (Richard of St. Victor, *Benjamin maior*, in *PL* 196: 151C).

46. For the history of the famous formula *diversa, sed non adversa*, which Heer called the twelfth century's *zauberformel* (*Mittelalter*, 194), see Ghellinck, *Mouvement théologique*, 517–23; Paré, et al., *Renaissance*, 284–95; Lubac, "À propos de la formule"; and Silvestre, "Diversi, sed non adversi."

47. Sturges quotes this passage from Hugh of St. Victor to a similar end, stressing the totalizing impulse of exegesis. He is, however, more nuanced in his discussion than either Gellrich or Eco (Sturges, 12–15).

48. Hugh of St. Victor, *De arca Noe morali* 1.4.9 (*PL* 176: 678D).

49. Medieval readers themselves noted the similarities between the discourse of dreams and that of Scripture. John of Salisbury's discussion of dreams in *Pol.* 2.16–17 speaks of their overdetermination and polysemy in terms that Freud would recognize, and compares their discourse to that of the parable (*Pol.* 2.16; tr. 81/1: 94); he is eloquent on the necessity of considering the multiplicity of their meanings, rather than simply one (*Pol.* 2.17; tr. 84/1: 97). Some of the greatest dream interpreters are, after all, John notes, biblical figures: Daniel, Joseph, Moses.

50. I have drawn the *siccus* (dry)/*succus* (juicy) example from another essay by Freud, the fascinating "Antithetical Meaning of Primal Words" (159). Here, Freud reports excitedly on the philologist Karl Abel, whose theories about "primal" language neatly paralleled Freud's work with dreams. Abel argued that early languages packed contrary meanings into the same word, even going so far as anagrammatic pairs, in which words with contrary meanings are metathetic images of each other. The uncanny parallels with Saussure's late work on anagrams are well worth exploring.

51. Medieval discussions of Scripture's multiple and reversible signification often share the delightfully vertiginous quality of Hugh's statement. See, for example, Peter the Chanter, 104. Secular obscurity calqued on Scripture shares its poetics; thus writes Juan Manuel in the mid-fourteenth-century *Conde Lucanor*: "All things look good and are good, and look bad and are bad, and look good and are bad, and look bad and are good" (Todas las cosas paresçen bien et son buenas, et paresçen mal et son malas, et paresçen bien et son malas, et paresçen mal et son buenas) (281).

52. William of Conches, quoted in Jeauneau, "Usage de la notion," 47. Thanks to Jeff Rider for reminding me about this passage.

53. Augustine, *Enarrationes in Psalmos* 126.11 (*PL* 37: 1675).

54. See, for example, *Conf.* 12.31–32.

55. In both sacred and secular commentary, as Dane observed, "the identification of the *res* signified by the words must proceed on the basis of the language of the text and the interpreter's own reconstruction of that language as *veritas*" (205). Barney adds, rather more poetically, that "medieval allegoresis springs from the Bible and finally settles back on it for authority, but its chief business is the acrobatics it performs while in the air" (97).

56. Thibaut offers two important verbs for meaning-making with numbers: *numerum mysteriare* (Lange, 68) and *numerum sacramentare* (106). They seem to be synonyms.

57. Augustine, *Enarrationes in Psalmos* 38.2 (*PL* 36: 413D).

58. See, e.g., Peter Damian, one of whose concerns about dialectical exegesis is precisely that it will sow argument and doubt (*De Divina omnipotentia*, in *PL* 145: 597C); cf. Juan Manuel, *Libro de los Estados* 2.4; 305–7.

59. Smalley wryly observes, "choos[ing] the most arbitrary interpreter of Biblical texts of the Middle Ages would be rather like awarding a prize for the ugliest statue of Queen Victoria" ("Bible and Eternity," 89).

60. Peter the Eater, *Sermo* 2 (*PL* 197: 1755D). The image of blowing Scripture's nose is drawn, Lubac notes, from Proverbs 30.33 (*Exégèse*, pt. 2, 1: 302).

61. Writes Bede, "We press hard on the breasts [of Scripture] when we measure the words of sacred eloquence with a subtle mind" (Ubera fortiter premimus, cum verba sacri eloquii subtili intellectu pensamus) (*Allegorica expositio*, in *PL* 91: 1027D). For a review of these tropes, see *Exégèse*, pt. 2, 1: 301–17. Irvine discusses a related "semiotic anxiety" underlying exegesis as interminable interpretation (*Making of Textual Culture*, 265–71).

62. Wolbero of Cologne, *Commentaria in Canticum canticorum* (*PL* 195: 1076C).

63. This reaction is clear as early as Origen, whose strategy for editing of the Bible when he found contradictory renderings of a locus was to make "double commentaries on double texts without choosing between them" (Smalley, *Study*, 13).

64. Hugh of St. Victor, *De arca Noe morali* 1.4.9 (*PL* 176: 678D).

Chapter 2

1. In Denifle, 1.48; translated in Thorndike, 23.

2. The definition is a medieval commonplace; this version is from *Dial.* 1; 82. For general overviews of twelfth-century dialectic, see Tweedale, "Logic (i)"; Jacobi; and Marenbon, *Early Medieval Philosophy*, 90–142. More technical and

detailed, but very rich, are Rijk, *Logica Modernorum*; Minio-Paluello; and Grabmann.

3. Quoted in Rijk, *Logica Modernorum*, 1.83. For the Aristotelian source, see *De Sophisticis elenchis* 2.165b.2.

4. For Boethius, see especially the articles collected in Gibson; for Boethian logic, see the more technical Stump, "Dialectic," and her *Dialectic and Its Place*. Studies of the practice and teaching of logic before the twelfth century that have been most useful for this study are Kenny and Pinborg; P. Hadot; Owen. Also helpful are the general overviews of pre-twelfth-century pedagogical and educational practice found in Marrou, *Histoire de l'éducation*; Bonner; I. Hadot; and Riché, *Écoles*. Wonderful discussions of the vocabulary of medieval logical education may be found in Weijers (ed.), *Vocabulaire des écoles*; and Rijk, "Specific Tools."

5. Alcuin, *De dialectica* 1 (*PL* 101: 952D–953A); the originator here is Cicero, *Academica* 2.91.

6. Alan of Lille, *Anticlaudianus* 3.70–71; tr. 94/91.

7. Augustine's praise of dialectic is often quoted by clerical writers; see, in addition, Rhabanus Maurus, *De institutione clericorum* 3.20 (*PL* 107: 397C), and John of Salisbury, *Met.* 4.25, discussed below, p. 58. Similarly metadisciplinary is Martianus Capella's Dialectica, who declares, "Whatever the other Arts propound is subject to my authority" (Meique prorsum iuris esse, quicquid Artes ceterae proloquuntur) (*De nuptiis* 3.337; tr. 110/155).

8. See the discussion in Aristotle, *De interpretatione* 7.17b (contraries); 7.18ab (contradictories). These laws are laid out very clearly in Peter of Spain's *Summulae logicales* 1.14. For more technical modern discussions, see Bochenski, 60–63; and Broadie, 91–93.

9. For the pre- and early history of the university, especially the University of Paris, see Rashdall; Paré et al., *Renaissance*; and Ridder-Symoens. Among recent and more specialized studies, Jaeger (on the cathedral schools) should be balanced with Ferruolo (on the city schools and early university).

10. The most evocative treatments of the combative masters of the twelfth century may be found in Roy and Schooner, "Querelles"; Ferruolo; and Luscombe, "Masters and Their Books." Primary sources for life in the urban schools are William of Conches, *Dragmaticon* (pp. 1, 2, 7, 35, 63, 157); the letters of Matthew of Vendôme (see Roy and Schooner, "Querelles"); William of Tyre (in Huygens, "Guillaume de Tyr"); Walter of St. Victor, *Contra quatuor labyrinthos Franciae* (see Glorieux, "Mauvaise action"); Godfrey of St. Victor, *Fons philosophiae*; and abundant letters home from students (see, e.g., Merlet). Thorndike offers a stimulating anthology. For catalogues of masters working in twelfth-century Paris, see Iwakuma and Ebbesen. Works that help a modern reader to imagine the intellectual texture of Paris life in the period include Le Goff, *Intellectuels* and "Quelle conscience"; Southern, "The Schools of Paris and the School

of Chartres"; Southern, *Scholastic Humanism*, 163–232; Delhaye; Baldwin, "Masters at Paris"; Luscombe, "Philosophy and Philosophers"; and Gabriel.

11. Peter the Chanter's *De tropis loquendi* is a beautiful example of a master using exegetical problems to teach dialectic, and vice versa. For the most stimulating recent discussion of the interfertilization of dialectic and theology in this period, see Evans, *Language and Logic*; see also Chenu, *La théologie*; and Landgraf.

12. For reviews of the antidialectical polemics of the eleventh and twelfth centuries, see especially Cantin; Ghellinck, "Dialectique et dogme"; MacDonald, 95–104; *Exégèse* 1.104–5; and Stock, *Implications* (especially on the conflict between Berengar and Lanfranc, 299–309).

13. John presents his academic autobiography in *Met.* 2.10. On his studies, see especially Keats-Rohan, "Chronology"; Poole; Weijers, "Chronology"; and Southern, *Scholastic Humanism*, 214–21. Good overviews of John's work may be found in Riché, "Jean de Salisbury et le monde scolaire"; and Liebeschütz.

14. For pedagogical theory and practice in the *Metalogicon*, see Keats-Rohan, "John of Salisbury and Education"; McGarry, "Educational Theory"; and Aspelin. Dal Pra, *Giovanni di Salisbury*, is especially interesting on the relation of theory and practice in John's thought; Wilks, "John of Salisbury and the Tyranny," studies the conceit of "unteaching."

15. Cornificius has been identified with various innovative Parisian teachers. However, as we shall see, the contradictory presentation of Cornificius makes it next to impossible to identify him with any historical figure; the name is more of a placeholder than anything else. For more on "Cornificius," see Tacchella; Alessio.

16. In this, "Cornificius" the innovator partakes in the charismatic pedagogy of what Jaeger calls the "Old Learning." In the cathedral schools of the eleventh century, Jaeger argues, the student's goal was to transform himself into his master (79). Similar patterns will continue to structure the career of text- and system-centered innovators like Peter Abelard, who, as we shall see, seeks to destroy his masters by *becoming* them.

17. In spite of John's reticence on Alberic's teachings, Rijk (*Logica Modernorum* 1.85–86) and Jacobi have interpreted Alberic's doctrinal about-face after Bologna as the result of the teachings of James of Venice, who rediscovered Aristotle's *De Sophisticis elenchis*. If they are correct, John's accusation of unteaching can be directly associated with Alberic's technical interest in this new text, whose teaching runs counter to John's instrumental view of sophistry as useful, if dangerous, mental exercise (*Met.* 2.5; *Met.* 4.23–24).

18. The rubric of *Pol.* 7.12 announces that it treats "Of the follies of triflers who take words to be wisdom" (De ineptiis nugatorum qui sapientiam uerba putant) (my translation/2: 137). For the opposing, excessively practical response to the same problem, compare the blacksmith Hescelin in *Met.* 3.10, who cannot name the object he makes until it is finished.

19. The distinction is drawn ultimately from Cicero, who uses the terms *de*

arte loqui and *ex arte dicere* (*De inventione* 1.6.8). R. W. Hunt's overview of the *de/ex arte* distinction ("Introduction to the *Artes*") has since been supplemented by Ward, "Date of the Commentary," and Häring, "Thierry of Chartres." For more on theory and practice and the *de/ex arte* distinction, see *Met.* 2.9.

20. Though John clearly presents Bernard as an example of the best of moderate pedagogies, Jaeger has recently pointed out that Bernard's text-centered pedagogy is in fact radically different from the charismatic teacher-centered teaching of the eleventh century. Jaeger uses Bernard as a moderate exemplar of the "new learning" (130–31). See also Carruthers, 85–89.

21. On Bernard's famous image, see Jeauneau, "Nani gigantum"; also useful are Chenu, "Antiqui-Moderni"; Silvestre, "Quanto iuniores"; Guyer, "Dwarf on Giant's Shoulders"; and Stock, *Implications*, 517–21.

22. For a summary of probable logic in John of Salisbury, see Brasa Diez; see also Nederman.

23. None of the *Metalogicon*'s modern editors (Webb and now Keats-Rohan and Hall) has been able to track down analogues or origins of this odd definition of truth. In *Met.* 4.4, John defines the mode as, "so to speak, a certain relation between terms" (quasi quidam medius habitus terminorum) (tr. 209/169). Though Webb seems taken aback by this expression here and in *Met.* 4.33, it seems clear to me that this "intermediate relation of terms" aptly describes logical modality, which Lalande defines as a property of the relations between subject and predicate, e.g., "The whole is *necessarily* larger than the part."

24. *Met.* 1.19; tr. 56–57/47; cf. John of Salisbury, *Entheticus*, lines 31–32.

25. In the immediate scriptural sources for the red-sky image, its ambiguity is not problematic, and in fact serves to point up a much more difficult act of interpretation, that of reading "the signs of the times" (signa temporum) (Matthew 16.2–4; cf. Luke 12.54).

26. For resolution buried in opposing arguments, see John's famous discussion of the universals, *Met.* 2.17; tr. 111–17/91–96. For avowals of incapacity, see his discussion of free will and fate, where he confesses himself unable to resolve the conflict (*Pol.* 2.26; tr. 125/1: 141). And for outright contradiction, see John on harmonizing Plato and Aristotle, *Met.* 2.17; tr. 115/94.

27. Dickinson, introduction to John of Salisbury, [*Policraticus*] *Statesman's Book*, lxxxi–lxxxii.

28. Even the teaching of dialectic in the schools is deeply structured by this self-reflexivity. A student's guide to the disciplines from the University of Paris (c. 1230) explains the parts of dialectic by reference to the elements of the dialectical syllogism (Lafleur, 37).

29. The *De dialectica*'s most recent editor and translator both support the attribution to Augustine. The text certainly feels Augustinian on many points of thought and expression; if it is not Augustine's directly, it was surely composed by someone intimately familiar with his work. For more on the *De dialectica*, see

Marrou, *St. Augustin*, 576–77; Pépin, *St. Augustin et la dialectique*; and Stock, *Augustine*, 138–44.

30. Peter Abelard, that great defender of dialectic, would in fact agree with Peter Damian's point here, though not with its polemical bite. For Abelard, physical science studies things; logic, words (*Dialectica* 3.1; 286). The "dereification" (Jolivet, *Arts de langage*, 350–57) characteristic of Abelard's thought would have given Peter Damian much to worry about.

31. Deschamps, *Un traictié de Geta et d'Amphitrion*, lines 339–41. Deschamps has expanded the Latin considerably (cf. Vitalis of Blois, *Geta*, lines 161–66). For more on logical in-jokes in the twelfth century, see Ziolkowski.

32. Cicero, *Academica* 2.95–96; quoted in Rijk, "Some Notes," 84. For more on the *insolubilia*, see Bochenski, 239–51; Spade, *Medieval Liar* and *Lies, Language and Logic*; and Rijk, "Some Notes."

Chapter 3

1. For general studies of Abelard as a dialectician, see Beonio-Brocchieri Fumagalli, *Logic of Abelard*, and Tweedale, "Abelard and the Culmination"; for his philosophy of language, Jolivet's *Arts de langage* is essential. For Abelard and the schools, see especially Delhaye, "Organisation"; Châtillon; and Verger. Of recent scholars, Eileen Kearney has worked most closely with Abelardian exegesis ("*Scientia* and *Sapientia*"; "Master Peter Abelard"). See also Lohr. Weingart discusses Abelard's exegesis as it enters into the larger picture of his theology. McCallum, though focused on the *Theologia Christiana*, is also useful. Marenbon's deeply documented *Philosophy of Peter Abelard* came my way too late to be included in this study (see especially 54–98, 101–16).

2. The letters attributed to Abelard and Heloise are of course the starting place for any discussion of their lives. Since their case was well known in their own time, contemporary testimonies abound. For Abelard, see the following works focused on professional or intellectual issues: John of Salisbury, *Metalogicon* 2.10 and passim; Otto of Friesing, *Deeds*, 83. More polemical are Bernard of Clairvaux, *Epistolae*, epistles 187–96, especially 190 ("Capitula de erroribus Petri Abaelardi"); William of St. Thierry, *Disputatio adversus Petrum Abaelardum*; and Walter of St. Victor, *Contra quatuor*. Positively vicious are Fulco of Deuil's "consolatory" Letter 16 (*PL* 178: 371B–376B) and the letter from Abelard's old teacher Roscelin (dis-(discussed below, pp. 76–78). Truci's Italian edition—Abelard and Heloise, *Lettere* —offers a very useful collection of otherwise hard to find contemporary texts, unfortunately in Italian translation only (*Lettere*, 281–383). Careful discussion of Abelard's philosophical and pedagogical legacy may be found in Luscombe, *School*, and now Luscombe, "School of Peter Abelard Revisited." For medieval responses, the best place to start is Dronke, *Abelard and Heloise*; see also Dronke, "Orléans, Bibl. Mun. 284 (228)."

3. "Every *quaestio* consists in contradiction" (Omnis enim quaestio contra-

dictionibus constat) (Boethius, *In Ciceronis Topica*, in *PL* 64: 1048AB). On the *quaestio* as a genre, see Paré et al., *Renaissance*, 125–31; Landgraf, 48–50; P. Hadot; and Viola. For Abelard in particular, see Jolivet, *Arts de langage*, 191–204.

4. Here and throughout, I use the terms "identity" and "self" to indicate textual constructions that need not necessarily be direct expressions or representations of the historical Peter Abelard.

5. The "authenticity" of these texts was hotly debated in the 1970s; I fall in with the current consensus that the correspondence between Abelard and Heloise, as well as the *Historia calamitatum*, is basically the work of their signatories, though probably subject to significant editing at the Paraclete, where the correspondence was kept. The most important contributions to the debate are discussed in Marenbon, *Philosophy of Peter Abelard*, 82–93. Newman's biting review of the debate makes its ideological overdetermination clear ("Authority," 123–44).

6. *Historia*, tr. 58/63. Le Goff has noted both Abelard's consistently negative forms of self-definition and their problematic result ("Quelle conscience," 17–18). For these agonistic structures in logically formed pedagogy, and Abelard in particular, see Solterer, 23–30. Clanchy gives a very vivid sense of Abelard's aggressiveness and wit.

7. On William of Champeaux see Michaud (especially 118–44, 220–35); Lefèvre; see also Fredborg; and Jolivet, "Données." For the conflict with Abelard, see Bertola, "Critiche di Abelardo."

8. For replicative relations between students and masters, see Jaeger, 76. The oedipal underpinnings of this desire to stand in the father's place are worth considering, especially given the problems of paternity, generation, and succession raised both in the *Historia* and in Abelard's later career. Lest the word "oedipal" seem anachronistic, here is William of Conches: "In a way, the teacher begets the student in wisdom. That is to say, he confers existence upon the student better than a real father" (Magister quodam modo gignit discipulum in sapientia, scilicet melius ei esse confert quam verus pater) (quoted in Jeauneau, "Deux rédactions," 233). For an analysis of Abelard's Trinitarian doctrine along these lines, see Bloch, 141–49. In an unpublished paper, Judson Allen provocatively studies Abelard's repetitive oedipal positioning with and through Lacan. Thanks to Carolyn Dinshaw for sharing a copy of this typescript.

9. "At Laon, Scripture was read through a preceding erudite study of authorities" (Bertola, "Precedenti," 273); for more on the School of Laon, see Ghellinck, *Mouvement*, 133–48; and Flint. Several books of the *glossa ordinaria* are attributed to Anselm and his school; see Bertola, "Glossa ordinaria." For Abelard and Anselm, see Häring, "The *Sententiae Magistri A.*"; Luscombe, *School*, 173–82; Bertola, "Critiche di Abelardo"; and Châtillon, "Abélard et les écoles," 146–58. Jaeger treats Anselm and Abelard as representatives, respectively, of what he calls the "old" and the "new" learning, that is, charisma and the personal ethic as opposed to intellectualization and systematization (229–40).

10. For the distinction between *usus* and *ingenium* in Abelard's own work, see

his *Dialectica* 4.1, Prologue; 471; and Beonio-Brocchieri Fumagalli, "Conceptes philosophiques," 112.

11. Martianus Capella gives Grammatica a scourge for punishing her students (*De nuptiis* 3.223). Augustine (*Conf.* 1.9.15), John of Salisbury (*Met.* 1.24), and Guibert of Nogent (*De vita sua*, chap. 5) discuss the uses and effects of pedagogical violence.

12. Radice makes the wandering hands here explicitly Abelard's, in spite of the impersonal construction of the clause ("sepius ad sinus quam ad libros reducebantur manus") and the stress on mutuality throughout the passage. Abelard's second letter to Heloise (*Letters*, tr. 147/89) gives a much more negative reading of this eroticized violence.

13. I do not read the violence Abelard describes here as a powerful man's abuse of a helpless woman, as does, for example, Nye; Abelard leads us to expect this, but delivers something more disturbing because less easily explained: a relation mutually constructed through mutual violence. The short lifespan of this passionate exchange and its transgressive undercurrent of violence indicate that resolution of the *Historia*'s larger conflicts will be equally problematic. Kamuf notes Heloise's repeated attempts in the letters to return the relation to this stage, "to revive the erotic confusion where mastery is posited only as a pretext to an evacuation of the controlling hierarchies" (10). My reading owes much to Kamuf, though I would not make the eroticism so utopian.

14. This struggle is especially clear in the conflict over structures of address in the letters between Heloise and Abelard. For more on Heloise's very particular way of constructing and handling multiple subject positions, see Brown, "*Muliebriter.*" Solterer's discussion of gender and mastery in textual conflicts between a male master and a female respondent is particularly illuminating.

15. A little-known manuscript of the correspondence recently studied by Jeudy contains, at this section, a fifteenth-century marginal note marking the *contrarium* of philosophy and family.

16. Robertson quotes Mark Twain's observation in *Innocents Abroad* that Heloise's lecture is "not good sense" (*Abelard and Heloise*, 216). Robertson himself certainly reads it this way, and not without some pleasure at the spectacle of "little Heloise" (51) "completely abandoning logic with a somewhat alarming feminine flair" (53). Feminist readings like those of Kamuf, Kauffman, and Nye have tended to stress and revalorize this "illogic" as a gendered subversion of a "logic" gendered masculine and incarnate in Abelard. Both approaches, to my mind, efface the extraordinary (and vicious) subtlety with which Abelard and Heloise maneuver for power in their letters.

17. Dronke notes that readers of the dossier have long assumed that all the book learning in the relationship flowed from Abelard to Heloise. He suggests, in contrast, that she had a thing or two to teach him, specifically an Italianate *cursus* that dominates her prose and appears less frequently in Abelard's (*Women Writers*, 111–12; see also 140–43).

18. Alexander's mistress, who sets out to seduce and humiliate his chaste teacher Aristotle, boasts that, Love willing, "neither dialectic nor grammar will do him any good against me" (ja contre moi ne li vaudra/dialetique ne gramaire) (Henri d'Andeli, lines 246–47).

19. Luscombe notes that Walter of Mortagne was "reported to have thought of Abelard as Abelard thought of Anselm of Laon" and quotes Walter as saying that Abelard "was a man expansive enough in lecturing . . . but not in the solution of questions" (erat homo in lectione satis diffusus . . . sed non adeo in quaestionum solutione) (*School*, 105). Cf. Abelard's *Historia* on Anselm, who "could win the admiration of an audience, but . . . was useless when put to the question" (mirabilis quidem in oculis erat auscultantium, sed nullus in conspectu quaestionantium) (tr. 62/68).

20. For a useful overview of this complex issue, see Carré. Abelard's own teaching on the matter, discussed by John of Salisbury in his review of the controversy (*Met.* 2.17; tr. 112/92), has been studied by Tweedale, *Abailard on Universals*. See also Stock, *Implications*, 385–403; Boler; Wenin; and Rijk, "Semantical Impact."

21. Bertola offers a text of William's that reflects this revised theory ("Critiche di Abelardo," 516). See also Luscombe, "Peter Abelard," 289–90; and Lefèvre, *Variations de Guillaume de Champeaux*.

22. For a fuller treatment of Abelard's singularity and castration in a different context, see Bloch, 141–46. Nouvet has discussed Abelard's castration in the philosophical terms of accident and impasse; Irvine studies Abelard's constructions of masculinity ("Abelard and (Re)Writing").

23. This pun is not entirely gratuitous: "In med. L. and O.Fr., and in Eng. from Wyclif to 17th cent., regularly spelt *abhominable*, and explained as *ab homine*, quasi 'away from man, inhuman, beastly,' a derivation which influenced the use and has permanently affected the meaning of the word" (*Oxford English Dictionary*, 2nd ed., s.v. *abominable*).

24. Benton observes that the twelfth century's "discovery of the individual" informs the contemporaneous fascination with universals, "the observable reality of personalized differences between individuals who still had *something* in common" ("Consciousness of Self," 282).

25. The only surviving text attributable with certainty to Roscelin is the letter to Abelard, which we will discuss below. For texts possibly by Roscelin or reflecting his views, see Mews, "Nominalism and Theology" and "St. Anselm and Roscelin." Given the scarcity of texts, monographs on Roscelin are few; see, however, Picavet and Kluge. Two fine discussions of Roscelin's letter appear in articles that came my way too late to be included in the argument here: Irvine, "Abelard and (Re)Writing"; and Wheeler, 15–16.

26. Abelard attacks Roscelin in several of his works, including *Dialectica* 5.554–55 (see below, n. 28), and a letter to Gerbert, bishop of Paris, in which he denounces Roscelin's views on the Trinity (Ep. 14, in *PL* 178: 355–58) and states

that his *Theologia "Summi Boni"* was written to refute the older master. This violent rupture with Roscelin conceals an ironic repetition of Roscelin's career in his student's: both men were condemned at Soissons (Roscelin in 1092, Abelard in 1121) for heterodox Trinitarian teachings; both feared being stoned by an angry populace; both, after their condemnations, wandered from place to place. For the argument with Roscelin, see Abelard, *Theologia "Summi Boni,"* 41–46.

27. Roscelin's vicious game of name calling by not- or un-naming replies tit for tat to Abelard's letter about him to the bishop of Paris, which also makes a show of not naming the opponent, and then names him in an insult. Says Abelard: "I considered it superfluous to designate by name this person, whom the scandal of his heresy and his life makes singularly notable" (Nomine designare quis iste sit supervacaneum duxi, quem singularis infamia infidelitatis et vitae ejus singulariter notabilem facit) (*PL* 178: 358B). Then Abelard expels Roscelin from *his* categories by naming him with the epithets *pseudodialecticus* and *pseudochristianus* (358B).

28. In his choice of analogies, Roscelin here may be recalling some of the curriculum Abelard studied with him. In the fifth book of the *Dialectica*, Abelard observes: "I remember that our master Roscelin had the following insane theory, i.e. that nothing consisted of parts; but just as he said that the species was simply a word, so too he said of parts" (Fuit autem, memini, magistri nostri Roscellini tam insana sententia ut nullam rem partibus constare vellet, sed sicut solis vocibus species, ita et partes adscribebat) (5.1; 554–55). Roscelin, he says, would mock those who maintained that the object "house" was composed of other objects as parts, saying that if the wall were part of the house then the wall must be part of itself, which is impossible (cf. Abelard's letter on Roscelin, in *PL* 178: 362B). If Nicolau d'Olwer is correct in suggesting that a version of all five parts of the *Dialectica* was in circulation by 1118 ("Sur la date"), it is likely that Roscelin knew this passage and, in accordance with his contrariwise strategy, was turning his student's reasoning against him.

29. Roscelin's logico-grammatical reading of Abelard's castration draws on a connection of sophistical logic with literal and metaphorical unmanning dating back at least to Augustine. In *DDC* 2.31, Augustine offers such figurative unmanning as an example of sophistry (quoted above, p. 76); similarly, in *De magistro* 8.22, Augustine sharpens Adeodatus's wits by leading him through a line of reasoning whose inevitable conclusion is that Adeodatus is not a man. The connection between dialectic and unmanning is especially fascinating to Northern French clerical writers of the twelfth century; see Vitalis's *Geta* (discussed above, pp. 63–64, 79) and the anonymous comedy *Babio*. Walter Map's "De monacho quodam" presents castration in explicitly grammatical terms (quoted in Bate, *Three Latin Comedies*, 8; cf. *Babio*, lines 441–44).

30. The book in question is most likely the *Theologia "Summi Boni."* Abelard himself makes very clear the correspondence between the book burning and his castration in the *Historia* (tr. 65/71), a parallelism thus mockingly troped by

Roscelin: "But you have very much to fear divine justice, lest the same thing happen to your tongue that happened to your penis: previously, while you could, you were plunging its sting indiscriminately and were deservedly deprived of it due to your indecency. In the same way your tongue, too, with which you now sting, may be taken away from you" (Sed valde tibi divina metuenda est iustitia, ne, sicut cauda, qua prius, dum poteras, indifferenter pungebas, merito tuae immunditiae tibi ablata est, ita et lingua, qua modo pungis, auferatur) (64).

31. Burnett, 152; the cited translation is on p. 153 of this edition. Similarly valedictory is Abelard's poem to their son, Astralabe, which aims to teach the boy what he needs for a happy and virtuous life. What Abelard's advice does, in fact, is to contradict his own biographical practice: be quicker to learn than to teach, he says; hold your tongue; respect your teachers; beware self-contradictory teaching (*Carmen ad Astralabium*, lines 3–6; 17–18).

32. Similar constructions continue in Abelardian scholarship. Southern observes, "Abelard portrays himself throughout [the *Historia calamitatum*] as half-beast, half-monk" (*Medieval Humanism*, 91); see also Clanchy, 23. Most poetic, even if unconsciously so, is Meadows, *A Saint and a Half*. Here, St. Bernard is complete, even excessively so; Abelard is only a fragment.

33. Roscelin wonders the same thing: "Amodo enim neutri generis abiectionem, sicut et suum significatum, penet . . . , et cum hominem integrum consueverit, dimidium forsitan significare recusabit" (80; the ellipsis is the editor's). Reiners renders this contorted sentence thus: "the *nomen* Petrus henceforth will either bear the shame of its signified's neuter gender or refuse to do so."

34. The Abelard of the *Historia* is a tempting subject for late-twentieth-century psychological reconstruction. For readings along this line, see Visser; Amsler; and McLaughlin; for a balancing historicization, see Leclercq, "Modern Psychology." If I were to approach this problem psychoanalytically, I would find it more fruitful to look at the big-picture issues than at the question of Abelard's "personality," which is after all unrecoverable to us. In an essay on classical rhetoric, Barthes suggests one useful approach, which complements what I have been doing here: he discusses what he calls the "the neurotic sense of *disputatio*," and says that the genre is an externalized self-division that grows from a Western intolerance of "all self-contradiction of the human subject" (191).

35. The importance of this hermeneutic anxiety in Abelard's thought is clear when, on the next page, he repeats: "Let us concede that the reader is being placed in inevitable anxiety when it becomes clear how necessary it is to make a determination between two syllogistic propositions that seem to be opposites" (Ut in anxietate inevitabili posito lectore appareat, quanta necessitate determinandum sit, cum in duobus syllogismis propositiones, quae oppositae videntur, concedamus) (*Logica ingredientibus*, 446).

36. All of the surviving manuscripts of the *Historia* include the later letters between Heloise and Abelard. The continuation of Abelard's biography in the let-

ters to Heloise shows him speaking fully from the position of one converted and thus offers a satisfactory closure that stabilizes the cycle of worldly negation structuring the *Historia*. The Heloise of the correspondence, on the other hand, is a far more ambiguous *quaestio*. Heloise is repentant; Heloise is unrepentant: readers continue to puzzle anxiously, searching for resolution.

37. The longest manuscript versions (*K* and *A*) of the eleven preserved contain 158 such *quaestiones*. The *quaestio* I have offered as an example, *Quod nuptiae sint bonae, et contra*, is number 135 in Boyer and McKeon's edition; I have chosen it intentionally to show how biographical issues continue to be worked over in Abelard's philosophical and pedagogical practice. It is interesting to note in this connection that MS *K* also contains Jerome's much-cited *dehortatio nuptiis*, the *Adversus Jovinianum*.

38. Though the *Sic et non* is unique in its lack of commentary and resolution, it is far from the first medieval collection of scriptural contradictions: William of St. Thierry, *De sacramento altaris* (1128); Bernold of Constance, *De sacramentis excommunicatorum* (c. 1100); and Ivo of Chartres, *Panormia* (c. 1096) preceded it. Cf. Gratian's almost contemporary *Decretum* (c. 1140). For this genre, see Bertola, "Precedenti storici." For broad reviews of other medieval approaches to contradiction among authorities, see Ghellinck, *Mouvement*, 472–99; Evans, *Language and Logic*, 79–80, 133–63. For good general discussions of the *Sic et non*, see especially Jolivet, *Arts de langage* 238–51; Jolivet, "Traitement"; and Smalley, "Prima clavis."

39. It does not seem that the *Sic et non* was received this way by those of Abelard's contemporaries who actually read it. In later centuries, the work acquired a scandalous reputation. The *PL* edition reports that D. Martène planned to edit the *Sic et non*, but stopped "after having recognized that this book was more likely to scandalize than to edify the faithful" (*PL* 178: 39).

40. Far from being a fortress to protect scriptural language from interpretation, then, such codifications and systematization rather make such hermeneutic activity all the more necessary. This is certainly the case in the *Sic et non*. For more evidence for this protective anchoring of scriptural interpretation in the disciplines of the trivium, see Giusberti, *Materials*, especially at 96.

41. For the *Sic et non*'s attention to process and its implications, see Reiss, "Conflict and Resolution," 870–71.

42. Cf. Dionysian dissimilitude, in which the abyss of difference between image and referent provokes a search for spiritual truth. See the medieval texts in Minnis, Scott, and Wallace, *Medieval Literary Theory*, 165–96; for discussion, see Dahlberg, 55–72. Whittaker studies explicitly grammatico-rhetorical ways of working theological dissimilitude (8).

43. For sources, see Smalley, "Prima clavis." Though the idea comes to Abelard via Aristotle and Boethius, what is striking is that Abelard turns this doubt to use in theology, taking as his model Christ himself among the doctors (*Sic et*

non, tr. 99/104). Cf. John of Salisbury, who, for all his praise of Academic doubt, was careful to direct it safely away from theological matters (*Pol.* 7, Prologue; tr. 216/2: 93).

44. Abelard's etymology for "logic" takes this alignment of dialectic with wisdom a step further: "Since the Word of the Father, the Lord Jesus Christ, is called *Logos* in Greek . . . that science which is conjoined to him by name and which is called 'logic' as derived from *logos* seems to pertain the more to him; as we are called Christians from the name 'Christ,' so it seems that logic is properly derived from *logos*" (Cum ergo Verbum Patris Dominus Jesus Christus logos Graece dicatur . . . plurimum ad eum pertinere videtur ea scientia quae nomine quoque illi sunt conjuncta, et ea per derivationem quamdam a logos logica sit appellata; et sicut a Christo Christiani, ita a logos logica proprie dici videatur) (Ep. 13, in *PL* 178: 355B; translated in Weingart, 21 n. 1).

45. Contrast this with Augustine, *Quaestiones in Heptateuchum*: "Disputation is not to be sought by means of truth, but rather truth by means of disputation" (Non enim disputatio veritate sed veritas disputatione reperitur) (*PL* 34: 547).

46. Cf. the *Sic et non*'s teaching-textuality with that of the later medieval monument of logical theology, Aquinas's *Summa Theologica*. Abelard's text is mostly citation; Thomas's mostly argument. Though Thomas presents both *sic* and *non* on every question, his discussion is always sealed with an authoritative judgment on the problem. The *Sic et non* offers no such anchors.

47. See, for example, Green, 3–26; and Nepaulsingh, 125–60.

48. The way the title is introduced in the text makes the unitariness of its *both-and* clear: "Here begin the sentences, collected from holy Scriptures, which seem to be contrary. On account of this contrariety this collection of sentences is called *Sic et non*" (Incipiunt sententiae ex divinis Scripturis collectae, quae contrariae videntur. Pro qua quidem contrarietate haec compilatio sententiarum *Sic et non* appellatur) (*Sic et Non*, my translation/113). Compare Aristotle's definition of a dialectical argument as one that *collects* contradiction (*De Sophisticis elenchis*, 2.165b.3–4).

49. It is a tasty irony that William's own *De sacramento altaris* had treated scriptural contradiction in a way so like the *Sic et non*'s as to have been suggested as that text's immediate predecessor (Bertola, "Precedenti," 258–64).

50. "You have deflowered holy Scripture, you have violated it to its core, if it is true what they say of you, that you raised yourself above man and degraded yourself beneath man" (Hugh Metellus, Ep. 5, trans. Truci, in Abelard and Heloise, *Lettere*, 346).

51. Abelard, *Theologia "Scholarium"* 1.180; 394. Cf. Gregory the Great, Ep. 76, "Ad Domitianum metropolitanum" (*PL* 77: 668AB).

52. This sort of transposition is very characteristic of Abelard: its most poetic occurrence is one of the dialectical high points of the correspondence with Helo-

ise, when he responds to her anguished self-portrait as whore and hypocrite and her excruciating memories of their sexual life together with an allegorical exegesis of the erotics of blackness in the Song of Songs (Brown, *"Muliebriter,"* 38–39).

53. Abelard, "In II Nocturno," lines 9–12 (*PL* 178: 1775D).

54. Isidore of Seville, *Etymologiae* 2.24.8; 105 (emphasis added). This elegant conflation of Logos, logic, and theology occurs in all the manuscripts of the *Etymologiae* but one; *K* offers *theoricam* for *theologicam*. I follow Marshall's edition for the reading here, rather than Oroz Reta's. Marshall points out that Isidore is quoting Jerome; Astell (26) traces the formula to Origen. See also Honorius of Autun (*PL* 172: 347, 356).

Chapter 4

1. For the *Ars amatoria* in the schools, see Pellegrin; Hexter; Alton and Worm-well; and McGregor. The *accessus* to the erotic works of Ovid offers another ex-ample of the way these poems were read (see the examples in Minnis, Scott, and Wallace, *Medieval Literary Theory*, 24–28), as does the glossed Old French trans-lation (*Art d'amors*, ed. Roy).

2. Heloise, Letter 5, in Abelard and Heloise, "Letter of Heloise on the Reli-gious Life," 242.

3. For this section of the *Lai d'Aristote*, see above, Chapter 3, p. 73.

4. For a catalog and overview of the medieval arts of love, see Segre. Useful collections of texts may be found in Finoli and in Bigazzi; for an anthology of breezy English translations, see Shapiro.

5. The coincidence of dialectic with secular love casuistry is studied by T. Hunt; see also Vance, *From Topic to Tale*. The best-known "exegetical" ap-proach to the *De amore* is undoubtedly that of Robertson (e.g., "Subject of the *De amore*"), though he is more interested in applying exegesis to the *De amore* than in studying the text's own exegetical structures.

6. Ovid's *Ars amatoria* is up to more than teaching (about) love; for its intense metadidactic and metarhetorical self-awareness, see especially Durling; Shulman; and Blodgett. Fyler and P. Allen (*Art of Love*, 15–58) have read the *Ars*'s literary program thus, and followed its aftereffects into the Middle Ages.

7. Frappier makes a similar, if more sarcastic, comparison, observing that many critics take the *De amore* "for the *Summa Theologica* of courtly love" (176).

8. The theoretical treatment of "assiduous" reading in the *De amore* has been elegantly studied by Peter Allen ("*Assidua lectio*"; "*Ars amandi*"; *Art of Love*, 59–78). My argument here shares much in terms of sympathy as well as evidence with Allen's work, and I am pleased to acknowledge my indebtedness.

9. On the basis of the manuscript tradition, both Roy ("Un art d'aimer: Pour qui?") and Karnein ("*Amor Est Passio*," *"De amore" in volkssprachlicher Literatur*) argue for a primarily clerical (and secondarily notarial) audience for the Latin *De*

amore. Dronke ("Andreas Capellanus") argues for a clerical audience of university students. Readers who construct the *De amore* as a courtly Bible assume a deeply vernacularized court audience; see, for example, Jackson. My own view is that the hermeneutic structures of Andreas's text construct and presuppose a clerical audience; the abundant vernacular translations surely had a more mixed, even "courtly" readership. Drouart la Vache says that his translation of the *De amore* is an act of "courtoisie" (line 55); he says that he did it to please his lady (lines 74–75).

10. For the manuscript titles, see Karnein, *"De amore" in volkssprachlicher Literatur*, 270. Neither the manuscripts nor the work's reception history offer much evidence for the title of Parry's English translation, *The Art of Courtly Love*.

11. One effect of Andreas's Ovidianism is the careful distance he maintains between himself as writer and his textual — even fictional — incarnation as teacher. Thus, throughout, when I refer to "Andreas" I will mean the writer, the artificer; I will refer to his first-person persona as "the preceptor" or "the narrator." For Ovid's play with poet and teacher, see Durling; Wright; and P. Allen, *Art of Love*, 15–37.

12. Walsh's translation coincides with Parry's (*Art of Courtly Love*, 211); both render *duplex sententia* as "two points of view." Robertson, however, hewing more closely to the Latin, combines them into "a double lesson," that is, "a single lesson with two sides" ("Subject of the *De amore*," 146).

13. For the term *sententia*, see Paré, *Idées*, 23–27. The term *sententiare* was used in the arts and medicine faculties at Bologna (late fourteenth century) as a synonym for *exponere* (Maierù, 151). For rhetorical uses, see especially Woods. See also the discussion of hermeneutic keywords in Robertson, "Some Medieval Literary Terminology," 71–72; the inflexibility of Robertson's schema should be balanced with readings in the primary texts themselves (e.g., *Did.*, Books 5–6).

14. Singer, 1294; see also Kelly, "Courtly Love in Perspective."

15. The Italian translations are collected in Battaglia's edition of *De amore*, *Trattato d'amore*. The French version of Drouart la Vache has received more study. See Bossuat; Dembowski; and especially Sargent. The Catalan translation is edited by Amadeu Pagès; for more, see Pagès, "Version catalane du *De amore*." For a synthetic discussion of vernacular translations, see Karnein, *"De amore" in volkssprachlicher Literatur*.

16. There are as many *De amore*s from the Middle Ages as there are manuscripts, ranging from the "fragmentary" to the "complete" three-book version. I have chosen to use the title *De amore* to indicate the three-book versions of the text. Indispensable surveys of the manuscripts of the *De amore* may be found in Karnein, *"De amore" in volkssprachlicher Literatur*, 266–83; Roy and Ferzoco; and Roy, "Un art d'aimer: Pour qui?" Particularly useful is the information these scholars provide about texts copied or bound with the *De amore*. The "fragmentary" transmission of the *De amore* has been most closely studied by Karnein ("Réception," "Amor Est Passio," "De amore et l'enseignement de l'amour," and *"De amore" in volkssprachlicher Literatur*).

17. On Andreas and Martínez, see Brownlee, "Hermeneutics of Reading"; Gerli, "Boccaccio and Capellanus"; and Wise.

18. Pagès's introduction to the Catalan translation of *De amore* places it squarely in the court of King Joan I. For the translation as law book for late medieval Aragonese "courts of love," see Parry's translation, 26.

19. The most "Robertsonian" contemporary reader of the *De amore* is Dahlberg (73–97). See also Frappier; Cherchi, "Andreas's *De amore*" and "New Uses of Andreas's *De amore*." For a useful review and analysis of ironic reading strategies in the *De amore*, see Monson, "Problem of Irony."

20. Bowden's "Art of Courtly Copulation" ferrets out scabrous Latin-French wordplay in the *De amore* and is still the most carefully worked out of these readings. See also Roy, "Obscenité"; and Silvestre, "Du nouveau sur André le Chapelain."

21. Compare this roundly (and circularly) reasoned thesis, also from Book 3: "Whereas it [love] begets all evils, there is in my view absolutely no good which men get from it; because the pleasures of the flesh, which we take from it so greedily, are not counted in the category of the good" (Quum enim ex amore mala cuncta sequantur, nullum penitus hominibus inde video procedere bonum quia delectatio carnis, quae inde multa aviditate suscipitur, non est de genere boni) (*De amore* 3.33; 296).

22. Similarly, woman is defined alternatively and contrarily as paragon of constancy (*De amore* 1.6.455; 174) and fickle monster (*De amore* 3.83; 312).

23. For more on this definition and its reception history, see Karnein, "*Amor Est Passio*." In both courtly and Ovidian discourse, love is above all a generator of contraries. Thus, for example, Alan of Lille: "Love is peace joined to hatred, loyalty to treachery, hope to fear and madness blended with reason. . . . Does not Desire, performing many miracles, to use antiphrasis, change the shapes of all mankind. Though monk and adulterer are opposite terms, he forces both of them to exist together in the same subject" (Pax odio fraudique fides, spes iuncta timori/Est amor et mixtus cum ratione furor. . . . Nonne per antiphrasim miracula multa Cupido/Efficiens, hominum protheat omne genus?/Cum sint opposita monachus mechator eidem/Hec duo subiecto cogit inesse simul) (*De planctu Naturae*, metrum 5, lines 1–2, 21–24; tr. 149–50/842–43). One of the love poems of Walter of Châtillon closes a series of the usual erotic antitheses thus: "A fool, I diligently raise an objection to logicians inasmuch as I am subject to two contraries" (stultus ex industria/logicis obicio, / quod duo contraria/suscipio) (quoted in Ziolkowski, 3).

24. The male lover refers to the *De amore*'s definition of love at 1.6.368; 146; the woman at 1.6.368; 148. The definition is canonized in the Commandments of Love offered at the end of Book 2: "The true lover is preoccupied by a constant and unbroken picturing of his beloved" (Verus amans assidua sine intermissione coamantis imaginatione detinetur) (2.8.48; 284).

25. See, for example, the preceptor's theoretical discussion of love and virtue at 1.4.1; 38; the male suitor echoes him at 1.6.181; 90 (cf. 1.6.31; 48). Cf. Love and speech (preceptor: 1.6.23; 46; suitor: 1.6.74–75; 61); *probitas morum* and nobility (preceptor: 1.6.14; 44; suitor: 1.6.32–33; 48). The judgments delivered in Book 2 are likewise often based upon the preceptor's teachings.

26. Benoît, 19; T. Hunt, 127–28.

27. A similar intercitationality marks the *De amore*'s representations of the afterlife: Book 1's miniature romance contains a parody of the Christian Hell, complete with the weeping and gnashing of teeth (1.6.262; 114) found both in Book 3's more orthodox description (3.22; 293) and in the Gospel itself (Matthew 8.12).

28. Cf. *Ars* 1.29: "Experience directs my undertaking: submit to the experienced bard" (usus opus movet hoc: vati parete perito); later he will receive direct amatory instruction from Apollo himself (*Ars* 2.493–508). The Ovidian preceptor's passionate outbreaks are too numerous to catalogue here; most interesting for this context are his mockery of Pasiphae for two-timing her husband (with a bull, no less) (*Ars* 1.303–10), and his evident erotic obsession with jealousy (*Ars* 2.247–54 and *passim*). Ovid's preceptor, too, is vengeful, and says as much from the very beginning: "the more Love pierce me, the more violently he burn me, the better avenger will I be of that wound" (quo me fixit Amor, quo me violentius ussit, / hoc melior facti vulneris ultor ero) (*Ars* 1.23–24).

29. The erotic link between the writer of love doctrine and his audience is clear in Ovid (e.g., *Ars* 3.309–10) and in Drouart, who translates the *De amore* for his male friends but dedicates it to his *amie* (lines 58–72). Jaeger reads the *De amore* through the male-male pedagogical structures of the "Old Learning's" *cultus virtutum*, but does not develop its homosocial and homoerotic implications (319–22). Nor, interestingly enough, does he discuss Book 3.

30. Andreas clearly was acquainted with the definition, for the woman in dialogue C uses it against her suitor (1.6.130; 76). Should it be objected that in Books 1–2 Andreas is purposely uttering something other than his "true" intention, one should remember that the lie told in the service of Christian truth is, for Augustine, the worst of all lies; he directs the whole of the *Contra mendacium* against it.

31. P. Allen discusses this passage from Augustine, though to different ends (*Art of Love*, 79).

32. P. Allen, "*Ars amandi*" 192. Cf. Brownlee on the *Arçipreste de Talavera*, a text deeply shaped by the *De amore*: "In moving backward and forward through the text, as the reading process necessitates, we find the authority of the clerical misogynistic stance irreparably damaged" ("Hermeneutics," 220–21).

33. In Denifle, 543. For more on the condemnations themselves, see Hissette, "Étienne Tempier et ses condamnations" and *Enquête sur les 219 articles*. For a brief but suggestive treatment of Tempier and the contrary things of Jean de Meun's *Rose*, see Hult, "1277, 7 March."

34. Denomy has made the most systematic effort to prove Andreas a professor of the "double truth." For an opposing argument, see Hissette, "André le Chapelain et la double vérité" and "Une 'duplex sententia' dans le *De amore*?"

35. The term "double truth" is usually used to describe the heretical Averroism of thinkers like Siger of Brabant and Boethius of Dacia. Van Steenberghen has undertaken a critical discussion in "Légende tenace" and " 'Averroïsme' et 'double vérité'."

36. Van Steenberghen dismisses the "double truth" as a "legend" on the grounds that, as it is usually understood, it violates the principle of non-contradiction ("Légende tenace," 555). Dales argues that Stephen misunderstood the perfectly orthodox position that to deny a thing's natural occurrence is not to deny its supernatural occurrence.

37. Most striking are the *De amore*'s uses of the Bible for both seduction and salvation; e.g., Matthew 8.12 (seduction: 1.6.261; 115; salvation: 3.22; 293) and Genesis 3.6 (seduction: 1.6.499 ff.; 189; salvation: 3.81 ff.; 311). Ovid receives the same treatment (seduction: 1.6.7; 42; salvation: 3.89; 314; seduction: 1.2.7; 36; salvation: 3.19; 292; seduction: 1.6.34; 48; salvation: 3.25; 294; seduction: 2.3.1; 230; salvation: 3.12; 290).

38. Very provocative here is Iser's definition of fiction as "an organization of signifiers which do not designate a signified object but instead designate *instructions* for the *production* of the signified" (18).

39. P. Allen comes to the same conclusion about both the *De amore* and its Ovidian model: "The most effective approach, I believe, is to accept the contradictions in the treatises, but to define them—against their instructions—as fiction" ("*Ars Amandi*," 196). The thesis is developed further in P. Allen, *Art of Love*, 59–78. See also Solterer, 36–43.

40. This concern with the *appearance* of truth is part and parcel of the courtly didacticism of Books 1 and 2: in teaching the *ars facundiae amoris*, Andreas is teaching his reader to counterfeit that arch-courtly virtue, *proeza* ("worthiness"). The eloquence he teaches, says the preceptor, "creates a good impression about the speaker's moral worth" (de loquentis facit probitate praesumi) (1.6.16; 44).

41. When asked by a student about the moral issues raised by the *Ars amatoria*'s place in the medieval curriculum, Peter the Chanter (d. 1197) answers in a similar way, saying first that the art is good in itself, but that its use is bad. He concludes, "He who corrupts women through it, uses it, but the teacher teaches it, not for use, but as a warning" (Ille autem qui per eam corrumpit mulieres, utitur ea. Doctor uero tradit eam, non ad usum sed ad cautelam) (in Baldwin, *Language of Sex*, 24 [English], 251 [Latin]). For Baldwin's reading of the *De amore* through and with this text of Peter's, see *Language of Sex*, 16–25. Perhaps not coincidentally, Abelard defends his textual teaching of dialectic with a very similar argument: "If the practice of a thing is bad, knowledge of it may be good: to sin is an evil, but it is good to know sin, for otherwise we cannot avoid it" (Cuius itaque mala est ac-

tio, bona potest esse cognitio, ut, cum malum sit peccare, bonum est tamen pec-
catum cognoscere, quod aliter non possumus vitare) (*Dialectica* 4, Prologue; 469).

42. Aquinas, *Quaestiones quodlibetales* 6.a15; 563B.

43. Guiart's later *Art d'amors* is especially cheeky on this last point, jumping
from the scriptural version of this command to its carnal application: "For Scripture, which should not lie, says that no man can serve two masters well. Thus
one man cannot have two girlfriends" (Car l'escripture dit que pas ne doit men-
tir:/Que nus hons ne puet bien a deus seignors servir./Ausi ne peut uns hons dues
amies avoir) (lines 167–69).

44. Dronke has recently made the most explicit argument I have seen for this
separation ("Andreas Capellanus"). He takes the name "Andreas Capellanus" as a
witty pseudonym, a reference to a now-lost romance of Andreas of Paris and the
Queen of France. The author, for Dronke, is a coarsely cynical player of complicated intellectual games, a medieval cross between Thersites and Borges (62). I
would incline more to the Borges side of this vividly imagined chimera.

45. I coincide here, in the *De amore*'s valorization of readerly *activity*, with
P. Allen (see, e.g., *Art of Love*, 74–78). Allen, however, stresses the ludic qualities
of this engagement and does not move far beyond them: "The *De amore*, in possibility and in imagination, creates a space for itself that is isolated from Christian
morality, and then plays within those limits" (77).

Chapter 5

1. As in Chapter 4 for *De amore*, here I will use "the narrator," "the speaker,"
"the Archpriest," or "the preacher" to refer to the first-person protagonist of the
Libro de buen amor. I will use the name "Juan Ruiz" to refer to its historical au-
thor(s), recognizing that the authorship question, though quieted by Hernández,
is not and may never be conclusively settled. The dates I offer here are those sup-
plied in stanza 1634 by the Toledo manuscript (1330) and the Salamanca manuscript (1343).

2. I cite the *Libro*'s verse passages by stanza number and line letter. I cite the
prose sermon by page numbers in the translation and the original edition. The
three most important manuscripts containing the text—Salamanca (*S*), Gayoso
(*G*), and Toledo (*T*)—differ significantly among themselves. Because editorial
choices play so large a part in constructing any interpretation of the *Libro*, I will
enclose *Libro* editor Gybbon-Monypenny's emendations to his base manuscript
(*S*) in curly brackets and indicate his deletions with a superscript plus ([+]). I will
also follow Zahareas and McCallum's useful practice of prefacing all stanza and
line numbers with the sigla (*S, G,* or *T*) of the manuscripts in which they appear,
using no commas between sigla where more than one is cited; see their synop-
tic edition, *Libro del Arcipreste*. Dagenais returns to the manuscripts in a deeply
innovative manner (*Ethics of Reading*, see especially 118–52). See also Orduna.

3. Useful here is LaCapra's distinction between "worklike" and "documentary" aspects of a text: "The documentary situates the text in terms of factual or literal dimensions involving reference to empirical reality and conveying information about it. The 'worklike' supplements empirical reality by adding to it and subtracting from it" (30).

4. That a text may be deeply funny, intellectually demanding, *and* didactic is something that the Middle Ages knew well and that we poor (post)moderns are only gropingly realizing. For a survey of *Libro* scholarship through 1981, see Seidenspinner-Núñez, 1–8. Less polarized readings have become more abundant recently; see especially Brownlee, *Status*; Gerli, "Recta voluntas"; and Seidenspinner-Núñez. Dagenais's *Ethics of Reading*, which appeared too late to be incorporated fully into my argument, is a major contribution to this effort at rethinking and remedievalizing the *Libro*; see especially his introduction, xiv–xv.

5. I have borrowed this metapedagogical question from Johnson, iii.

6. The sermon appears only in *Libro, S*, where it follows ten stanzas of invocation also unique to that manuscript. The sermon's position in *S* argues against mere accidental accretion, however, and its close thematic ties to the rest of *S* and to the justificatory frames of other obscure and/or contradictory works (e. g., the *De amore*, the *Conde Lucanor* of Juan Manuel, the *Disciplina clericalis* of Petrus Alfonsi, and Chaucer's retraction of the *Canterbury Tales*) make its interpretation a necessary part of any reading of the *Libro* in its manuscript tradition.

7. Peter Lombard, *Sermo* 26 (*PL* 171: 435–36); translation in Dahlberg, 65.

8. The Archpriest later returns to the text's conversionary utility, suggesting that his book will inspire another group of readers—the unhappily married—to turn their hearts to God, though for a somewhat less spiritual reason: "It has a good trait: wherever it may be read, if some man hears it who has an ugly wife, or if a woman hears it whose husband is of no account, each will immediately feel the desire to serve God" (Buena propiedat ha do quiera que se lea, / que si lo oye alguno que tenga muger fea, / o si muger lo oye que su marido vil sea, / fazer a Dios serviçio en punto lo desea) (*Libro, ST* 1627).

9. Cf. *Libro, ST* 1634bcd: "this book was finished, for many evils and wrongs that many men and women do to others with their deceits, and to display to simple people exemplary tales and ingenious verses" (fue conpuesto el rromançe por muchos males e daños, / que fazen muchos e muchas a otras con sus engaños, / e por mostrar a los sinples fablas e versos estraños). The first modern editor of the *Libro*, Tomás Antonio Sánchez, justified his undertaking on similar grounds, presenting the *Libro* as an exemplary collection of medieval poetic forms (Ruiz, *Poesías del Arcipreste de Hita*).

10. Typically for the *Libro*, this flexibility is at once scriptural and erotic. The immediate scriptural resonance is Pauline: "I became all things to all men, that I might save all" (omnibus omnia factus sum ut omnes facerem salvos) (1 Corinthians 9.22). However, the *Libro* will also point such versatility toward a less salvific

seduction: sweet-talking one of the protagonist's love interests, the go-between praises his ability to act wise with the wise and foolish with fools (*SG* 728c, *SG* 729abc).

11. In his edition and translation of the *Libro*, Willis resolves the anacoluthon by emending the line in question to "puede {a} cada uno bien dezir," making the subject of *poder* the *Libro* and not, as *S* has it, the readers themselves. He also renders *amor loco* (mad love) throughout as "mad and heedless love," which I have silently shortened in all my citations from his translation.

12. A winking reapplication of 1 Thessalonians 5.21. The speaker's role as sinner rapidly takes on wildly fictional form in the love adventures to follow, as the *Libro* sets about counterfeiting a confessional autobiography. The most celebrated of these amatory metamorphoses is certainly the one effected in the doña Endrina episode, where the first-person narrator is at once the Archpriest, Pamphilus, and one "Sir Melon of the Garden." At the end of the story, he tells us to understand him well: the tale is exemplary, not autobiographical; nothing of the sort actually happened to him (*Libro*, *SGT* 909ab). The very next line in *S* snaps right back to a most unexemplary autobiography: "After this, while I was living without love and with worrisome care, I saw a charming lady sitting in her parlor; she instantly took my heart away ravished" ({Seyendo} yo, después desto, sin amor e con cuidado, / vi una apuesta dueña ser en su estrado; / mi coraçón en punto levó me lo forçado) (*S* 910abc). For more on the *Libro*'s protean narrator, see A. Castro; Brownlee, *Status*, 59–73; Seidenspinner-Núñez, 40–58; Zahareas, *Art*, 12–15, 39–58; and Spitzer.

13. For studies of the *Libro*'s counterfeited logic, see especially Cantarino and Rico.

14. Joset, 123 n. 10. Clarke provides the most detailed—if not entirely convincing—discussion of correspondences between the *Libro de buen amor* and the *De amore*; see also Gericke; Heugas; and Wise. For the *Libro de buen amor* and the medieval arts of love in general, Lecoy remains essential; for more recent source-hunting see Burkard, "Pseudo *Ars Amatoria*"; for the *Libro* and Guiart's *Art d'amors*, see Kinkade. A list of correspondences between Ovid's *Ars* and the *Libro* may be found in Gybbon-Monypenny's edition of the *Libro* (48n). For Juan Ruiz as reader of Ovid, see especially Burkard, "Dize Pánfilo." The *Libro* participates even more clearly in the medieval Ovid via its translation of the well-known elegiac comedy *Pamphilus* (*Libro*, stanzas 578–891, portions in both *S* and *G*). It is not coincidental that the *Pamphilus* is the text most frequently copied with the *De amore* (for the data, see Roy, "Un Art d'aimer: Pour qui?").

15. Love's pernicious effect on both body and soul is emphasized throughout the Archpriest's section of the dispute with Love (e.g., *Libro*, *S* 184cd, *S* 197c, *S* 207d, *S* 217a, *SG* 399, etc.). For more, see Walker; Gerli, "Don Amor, the Devil."

16. This is not to say that the narrator has not been identified with the author—the fifteenth-century copyist of *S* is the first of many who have taken the Archpriest for the author himself. In the dispute with Amor, though, the conven-

tions of the dream vision are too strong and the Ovidian flavor too pronounced for anyone, medieval or modern, to have taken this particular episode as a documentary transcription of a real-life event.

17. The presence of these "misappropriated exempla" (Brownlee, *Status*, 88–97) in an ostensibly moralizing context may well be related to the contemporary concern for the personal morality of the preacher examined in Leclercq, "Magistère"; and Minnis, "Chaucer's Pardoner." Regalado notes a similar dissonance between exemplum and context in Jean de Meun's part of the *Roman de la Rose* (68).

18. The scriptural reference "virgam virtutis tue" is to Psalm 109.2. A thirteenth-century Flemish Psalter glosses this line with a *bas-de-page* image that makes the same obscene pun: a man lies with his head in his lady's lap; her right hand grips the clearly anatomical "rod of his power" (Oxford, Bodleian MS Douce 6, fol. 80r; reproduced in Robertson, *Preface*, fig. 23).

19. The story of the fox's and wolf's court case occupies stanzas 321–71 of the collated *Libro*, with the following attestations in the manuscripts: *S* 321–29, *SG* 330–71, and *SGT* 367–71.

20. Compare the analogous episode of don Carnal's confession (*Libro*, *SGT* 1130–72), which, like the trial episode, links parody with promises of useful professional instruction and judgments on contemporary issues. Here, two *quaestiones* concern the speaker: whether mere contrition or full auricular confession is necessary for true penance, and whether a simple priest has the power to absolve all comers. As in the don Ximio episode, the *Libro*'s strategy is to exacerbate the problem by multiplying authorities and technical terms, and then to defer a clear solution.

21. Matthew of Vendôme's definition makes especially clear this opposition of the literal and the allegorical: "Allegory is alien discourse, and occurs when the meaning disagrees with the signification of the words" (Allegoria est alienum eloquium quando a verborum significatione dissidet intellectus) (*Ars versificatoria* 3.43). In integumental allegory, meaning is made *in spite of* proper signification, not in addition to it (Dane, 205); see also Paré: "engaged in this moral interpretation, the gloss becomes even the opposite of the natural interpretation of the text" (*Idées*, 21 n. 2). For antitheses and the integument in the *Libro*, see Urbina.

22. Minnis has written widely on the self-authorizing strategies of secular vernacular writing; see his *Medieval Theory of Authorship* and the texts collected in Minnis, Scott, and Wallace, *Medieval Literary Theory*, 373–438. For understanding the practice of commentary and translation in the vernacular and secular *auctores*, Copeland is essential.

23. Bernard Silvester (attr.), *Commentary on the "Aeneid,"* Latin in Paré, *Idées*, 20; my translation. For theoretical implications of the integument, see Dane; Frese, 234–53; Hanning, 104–5; Lerer; Copeland, 81–82, 130–32; Woods.

24. For these allegories of reading, see Brownlee, *Status*, especially chap. 5, "Parables of Interpretation."

25. For a catalogue of these integumental metaphors and an influential discussion of the vocabulary of auto-exegesis in secular letters, see Robertson, "Some Medieval Literary Terminology."

26. For sophistry as a cover-up, see *De amore* 1.6.319; 130.

27. Zahareas, 43. The tale occupies pride of place in most attempts at a global reading of the *Libro* and has offered itself almost epigrammatically to medievalists in other fields; on this last count, see Kendrick, 1–23; and Reiss, "Ambiguous Signs," 113–15.

28. The citation follows *Libro*, S, as usual, and I have emended Willis's translation accordingly. *G* keeps the first person throughout: "So, most assuredly, will *I* speak" (Tal te *diré* çiertamente). Both manuscript readings are witty in their ways, but I prefer the indeterminacy of S's shifting verb persons, in which the most disarming of medieval literary personifications reveals its artifice even as it charms.

29. On *interpretatio* and translation, see especially Copeland, 87–92.

30. Once again, at one of the narrator's more dialectical declarations (*Libro*, 65c), the manuscript tradition equivocates. I have cited and translated S here: "to know how to speak good and ill, cryptically and gracefully" (saber bien e mal dezir encobierto e doñeguil). *G*, on the other hand, makes the poet's activity something quite different: "to know how to speak evil well, cryptically, gracefully" (saber el mal desir bien, encobierto, doñeguil). The *G* copyist also adds a line that, though metrically superfluous, shows that he was taken by the poet's emphasis on subtlety: "for not all [troubadours] do it with very subtle art" (que todos non lo fasen con arte muy sotil) (*G* 65e; my translation).

31. For the book and the bawd, see Seidenspinner-Núñez, 77–93.

32. The term *buen amor* occurs fifteen times in the collated *Libro*: twice with a meaning unambiguously divine (S sermon, 106), five times in a worldly sense (*SG* 18d, *G* 443b, *S* 933b, *S* 1331d, *SGT* 1452b), and eight times ambiguously (*SG* 13c, *SG* 66d, *SG* 68a, *S* 932b, *SGT* 1507c, *ST* 1578b, *ST* 1630a, *ST* 1630d). For a useful survey of *buen amor*'s occurrences in the *Libro*, see Dutton.

33. The Toledo manuscript offers a slightly different reading of the last line of the stanza: "For good love, the boughten kind, has no delight or grace" (ca non ha grado nin graçia buen amor el conprado) (*T* 1630d; my translation).

34. Aelred of Rievaulx, *Speculum charitatis* 1.9 (*PL* 195: 513AB). The title of this chapter of the *Speculum* indicates Aelred's take on the problem: "That our love is divided by contrary appetite against itself in charity and cupidity" (quod amor noster adversum se ex charitate et cupiditate contrario appetitu dividatur) (513A).

35. For more on this sophistical fallacy, see Rivero.

36. On the *Libro*'s parody of Augustinian *caritas*, see Seidenspinner-Núñez, 26–27.

37. "Poetic fictions are ordered to no other end than to signify" (Fictiones poeticae non sunt ad aliud ordinate nisi ad significandum) (Aquinas, *Quaestiones quodlibetales* 6.a16.ad2; 565A).

38. For more, see Brown, "Meretricious Letter"; portions of the present chapter are revised from this article.

39. It is germane to note here that the early uses of "exegete" among the Greeks referred to those priests who read the stars (*Oxford English Dictionary*, 2nd ed , s v. "exegete").

40. Stanzas *SGT* 1533–34, which make life a *mal juego*, a bad gamble, evoke memories of another game, love, described with the same metaphor (*Libro, SG* 469–70). Games are not entirely innocent in the *Libro*: the go-between lures doña Endrina to her house, where the protagonist will rape her, with promises of a ball game (*SG* 861); comparison with *Pamphilus* shows the ball game to be Juan Ruiz's addition. The *libro* itself is also, of course, a ball game (*ST* 1629d).

41. The echoes of the *ordo commendationis animae* in the invocation were first noted by Castro Guisasola (72). Walsh provides examples of other *cuaderna vía* reworkings of the prayer and suggests that Juan Ruiz's relation to them is primarily parodic. For Psalm 31 and the *ordo commendationis*, see Ruiz, *Libro*, ed. Blecua, p. 5 n. 5.

42. In this the *Libro*'s *doctrina* refuses the transcendence mapped out in another medieval model text, Boethius's *Consolatio philosophiae*, which begins with the protagonist imprisoned in the *regio dissimilitudinis* of Fortune, but slowly teaches him (and the reader) out of it. Boethius is an exile in a land not his own (1. prose 5); the Archpriest, however, is trapped in one that *is*. While Boethius learns to reject the worldly consolations of secular verse, the Archpriest never unlearns them: for example, while the clever Muslim girl, in rejecting his advances, "showed good sense" (fizo buen seso), the Archpriest can only say in response, "I made a lot of songs" (yo fiz mucho cantar) (*Libro, SGT* 1508d; my translation).

Conclusion

1. Thanks to Sandra Watts for this one.

Bibliography

Primary Sources

Abelard, Peter. *Carmen ad Astralabium: A Critical Edition*. Ed. José María A. Rubingh-Bosscher. Groningen: José María A. Rubingh-Bosscher, 1987.

———— *Commentariam in epistolam Pauli ad romanos*. In *Petri Abaelardi. Opera theologica*, ed. E. M. Buytaert, 1–340. Corpus Christianorum Continuato Mediaevalis 11. Turnhout: Brepols, 1969.

———— " 'Confessio Fidei ad Heloissam': Abelard's Last Letter to Heloise? A Discussion and Critical Edition of the Latin and Medieval French Versions." Ed. Charles S. F. Burnett. *Mittellateinisches Jahrbuch* 21 (1986): 147–55.

———— *Dialectica*. Ed. L. M. de Rijk. 2nd edition. Assen: Van Gordum, 1970.

———— *Logica ingredientibus*. In *Peter Abaelards Philosophische Schriften*, ed. Bernhard Geyer. Beiträge zur Geschichte der Philosophie des Mittelalters, no. 21, pts. 1–3. Münster: Aschendorff, 1919–27.

———— *Theologia "Summi Boni," Theologia "Scholarium."* Vol. 13, *Petri Abaelardi. Opera theologica*, ed. E. M. Buytaert and C. J. Mews. Corpus Christianorum Continuatio Mediaevalis 13. Turnhout: Brepols, 1987.

Abelard, Peter, and Heloise. *Lettere*. Trans. N. C. Truci. Turin: Einaudi, 1979.

———— "The Letter of Heloise on the Religious Life and Abelard's First Reply." Ed. J. T. Muckle. *Mediaeval Studies* 18 (1956): 241–92.

Accessus ad auctores. Ed. R. B. C. Huygens. Brussels: Latomus, 1954.

Alan of Lille. *Anticlaudianus*. Ed. R. Bossuat. Paris: Vrin, 1955.

———— *Anticlaudianus*. Trans. James J. Sheridan. Toronto: Pontifical Institute of Medieval Studies, 1973.

———— *De planctu Naturae*. Ed. Nikolaus M. Häring. *Studi Medievali* 19 (1978): 797–879.

———— *The Plaint of Nature*. Trans. James J. Sheridan. Toronto: Pontifical Institute of Medieval Studies, 1980.

Andreas Capellanus. *De amore*. Ed. Amadeu Pagès. Castelló de la Plana: Sociedad Castellonense de Cultura, 1930.

———— [*De amore.*] *The Art of Courtly Love.* Trans. John J. Parry. New York: Columbia University Press, 1941.

———— [*De amore.*] *Li livres d'amours de Drouart la Vache.* Ed. Robert Bossuat. Paris: Champion, 1926.

———— [*De amore.*] *Trattato d'amore.* Ed. Salvatore Battaglia. Rome: Perella, 1947.

Aquinas, Thomas. *Quaestiones quodlibetales.* In *Opera omnia*, vol. 9. Parma: Fiaccadori, 1859.

———— "Sermones dominicales." In *Opera omnia*, 29: 194–95. Paris: Vives, 1876.

Aristotle. *Analytica priora.* Trans. A. J. Jenkinson. In *The Works of Aristotle*, ed. W. D. Ross, vol. 1, 24a–70b. Oxford: Oxford University Press, 1928.

———— *Categories.* Trans. E. M. Edgehill. In *The Works of Aristotle*, ed. W. D. Ross, vol. 1, 1a–15b. Oxford: Oxford University Press, 1928.

———— *De interpretatione.* Trans. E. M. Edgehill. In *The Works of Aristotle*, ed. W. D. Ross, vol. 1, 16a–23b. Oxford: Oxford University Press, 1928.

———— *De Sophisticis elenchis.* Trans. W. A. Pickard-Cambridge. In *The Works of Aristotle*, ed. W. D. Ross, vol. 1, 164a–184b. Oxford: Oxford University Press, 1928.

Augustine of Hippo. *De civitate Dei.* 7 vols. Trans. George E. McCracken, W. M. Green, and W. C. Greene. Loeb Classical Texts. Cambridge, Mass.: Harvard University Press, 1957–60.

———— *De magistro.* Trans. Goulven Madec. Bibliothèque Augustinienne. Oeuvres de St. Augustin 6. Paris: Desclée de Brouwer, 1976.

———— *De mendacio.* Ed. Joseph Zycha. In *Sancti Aureli Augustini de fide et symbolo. . . . De mendacio. . . . De patentia*, 413–66. Corpus Scriptorum Ecclesiasticorum Latinorum 41. Vienna: Tempsky, 1900.

———— *De ordine.* Trans. R. Jolivet. Bibliothèque Augustinienne. Oeuvres de St. Augustin 4. Paris: Desclée de Brouwer, 1948.

———— *De Trinitate.* Trans. M. Mellet and T. Camelot. Bibliothèque Augustinienne. Oeuvres de St. Augustin 15–16. Paris: Desclée de Brouwer, 1955.

Babio. In Bate, *Three Latin Comedies*, 35–60.

Bate, Keith, ed. *Three Latin Comedies.* Toronto Medieval Latin Texts. Toronto: Pontifical Institute of Medieval Studies, 1976.

Beatus of Liébana. *Apologeticum ad Elipandum.* Ed. and trans. Alberto del Campo Hernández. In *Obras Completas de Beato de Liébana*, 698–953. Madrid: Biblioteca de Autores Cristianos/Estudio Teológico de San Ildefonso, 1995.

Bernard of Clairvaux. *Epistolae.* Ed. Jean Leclercq and H. Rochais. Vol. 8 of *Opera Sancti Bernardi.* Rome: Editiones Cistercienses, 1957.

Biblia Sacra iuxta vulgatam versionem. 4th edition. Ed. Robert Weber, Roger Gryson, B. Fischer, H. I. Frede, H. F. D. Sparks, and W. Thiele. Stuttgart: Deutsche Bibelgesellschaft, 1994.

Bigazzi, Vanna Lippi. *I volgarizzamenti trecenteschi dell' Ars amandi e dei Remedia amoris.* 2 vols. Florence: L'Accademia della Crusca, 1987.

Boethius, Anicius Manlius Severinus. *De consolatione philosophiae*. Trans. S. J. Tester. Cambridge, Mass.: Harvard University Press, 1973.

———— *In Isagogen Porphyrii commenta*. Ed. George Schepps and Samuel Brandt. Corpus Scriptorum Ecclesiasticorum Latinorum 48. Vienna: Tempsky, 1906.

Canon "B." Letter. Paris, Bibliothèque Nationale NAL 886, fols. 84r–85r.

Chaucer, Geoffrey. *The Riverside Chaucer*. Ed. Larry D. Benson. Boston: Houghton Mifflin, 1987.

Cicero, Marcus Tullius. *De inventione*. Trans. H. M. Hubbell. Cambridge, Mass.: Harvard University Press, 1949.

Clement of Alexandria. "The Instructor." In *The Ante-Nicene Fathers*, vol. 2, ed. Alexander Roberts and James Donaldson, revised by A. Cleveland Coxe, 207–98. Grand Rapids, Mich.: Eerdmans, 1973.

Denifle, Henry, ed. *Chartularium Universitatis Parisiensis*. Vol. 1. Paris, 1889.

Deschamps, Eustache. *Un traictié de Geta et d'Amphitrion*. Ed. Gaston Raynouard. In *Oeuvres complètes*, 8: 211–46. Société des Anciens Textes Français 16. Paris, 1893.

Finoli, Anna Maria, ed. *Artes amandi: Da Maître Elie ad Andrea Cappellano*. Milan: Cisalpino, 1969.

Fulco of Deuil. Epistle 16. In *PL* 178: 371B–376B.

Godfrey of Saint Victor. *Fons philosophiae*. Ed. Pierre Michaud-Quantin. Analecta Mediaevalia Namurcensia 8. Namur: Godenne, 1956.

Gregory the Great. *Homiliae in Hiezechihelem*. Ed. Marc Adriaen. Corpus Christianorum Series Latina 142. Turnhout: Brepols, 1971.

Guiart. *L'art d'amors*. Ed. L. Karl. In *Artes amandi: Da Maître Elie ad Andrea Cappellano*, ed. Anna Maria Finoli. Milan: Cisalpino, 1969.

Guibert of Nogent. [*De vita sua*.] *Self and Society in Medieval France: The Memoirs of Abbot Guibert of Nogent*. Trans. J. F. Benton. New York: Harper and Row, 1970.

Guillaume de Lorris and Jean de Meun. *Roman de la Rose*. Ed. Felix Lecoy. 3 vols. Classiques Français du Moyen-Âge. Paris: Champion, 1965–70.

Henri d'Andeli. *Lai d'Aristote*. In *Twelve Fabliaux from MS. Fr. 19152 of the B.N.*, ed. T. B. W. Reid, 70–82. Manchester: Manchester University Press, 1958.

Holy Bible. Rheims-Douay Version. Los Angeles: C. F. Horan, 1941.

Hugh Primas. *The Oxford Poems of Hugh Primas and the Arundel Lyrics*. Ed. C. J. McDonough. Toronto: Pontifical Institute of Medieval Studies, 1984.

Isidore of Seville. *Etimologías*. Ed. and trans. J. Oroz-Reta and Manuel-A. Marcos Casquero. 2 vols. Biblioteca de Autores Cristianos. Madrid: Editorial Católica, 1982.

———— *Etymologiae: II*. Ed. and trans. Peter K. Marshall. Auteurs Latins du Moyen-Âge. Paris: Les Belles Lettres, 1983.

John of Salisbury. *Entheticus*. Ed. and trans. Jan van Laarhoven. 3 vols. Leiden: Brill, 1987.

———— *Metalogicon*. Ed. J. B. Hall and K. S. B. Keats-Rohan. Corpus Christianorum Continuatio Mediaevalis 98. Turnhout: Brepols, 1991.

———— [*Policraticus*.] *The Statesman's Book*. Trans. John Dickinson. New York, 1927.

Juan Manuel. *El Conde Lucanor*. Ed. José Manuel Blecua. Madrid: Castalia, 1982.

———— *Libro de los Estados*. Ed. Ian Macpherson and Brian Tate. Madrid: Castalia, 1991.

Julian of Toledo. *Antikeimenon, hoc est contrapositorum sive contrariorum in speciem utriusque testamenti locorum*. PL 96: 586–704.

Map, Walter. *De nugis curialium*. Ed. and trans. M. R. James. Oxford: Clarendon, 1983.

Martianus Capella. *De nuptiis Philologiae et Mercurii*. Ed. Adolphus Dick. Leipzig: Teubner, 1925.

———— [*De nuptiis Philologiae et Mercurii*.] *The Marriage of Philology and Mercury*. Vol. 2, *Martianus Capella and the Seven Liberal Arts*, trans. William Harris Stahl and E. L. Burge. New York: Columbia University Press, 1971.

Martínez de Toledo, Alfonso. *Arçipreste de Talavera o Corbacho*. Ed. Michael Gerli. Madrid: Cátedra, 1981.

Matthew of Vendôme. *Ars versificatoria*. In *Matthew of Vendôme, Opera*, ed. Franco Munari, 39–221. Raccolta di Studi e Testi 171. Rome: Storia e Letteratura, 1988.

———— *Ars versificatoria*. Trans. Roger P. Parr. Vol. 22, *Medieval Philosophical Texts in Translation*. Milwaukee: Marquette University Press, 1981.

Nebrija, Antonio de. *Dictionarium Latino-Hispanicum*. Salamanca: Impresor de la Gramática de Nebrija, 1492. In *ADMYTE (1)*, version 1.0 (CD-ROM). Madrid: Micronet, 1993.

Otto of Freising. *Deeds of Frederick Barbarossa*. Trans. Charles C. Mierow. New York: Columbia University Press, 1953.

Ovid. [*Ars amatoria*.] *L'art d'amors: Traduction et commentaire de l' "Ars amatoria" d'Ovide*. Ed. Bruno Roy. Leiden: Brill, 1974.

———— *"Art of Love" and Other Poems*. Trans. Rolphe Humphries. Bloomington: Indiana University Press, 1957.

Panphilus. In Bate, *Three Latin Comedies*, 61–89.

Peter of Spain. *Summulae logicales*. Venice, 1572. Reprint, Hildesheim: Olms, 1981.

Peter the Chanter. *"De tropis loquendi* (Praefatio)." In *Materials for a Study on Twelfth-Century Scholasticism*, by Franco Giusberti, 87–109. History of Logic 2. Naples: Bibliopolis, 1982.

Roscelin of Compeigne. Letter to Abelard. In *Der Nominalismus in der Frühscholastik*, ed. J. Reiners, 62–80. Beiträge zur Geschichte des Philosophie des Mittelalters, no. 8, pt. 5. Münster: Aschendorff, 1910.

Ruiz, Juan. *Libro de buen amor*. Ed. Alberto Blecua. Letras Hispánicas. Madrid: Cátedra, 1992.

——— *Libro del Arcipreste (también llamado "Libro de buen amor"): Edición sinóptica.* Ed. Anthony Zahareas and Thomas McCallum. Madison: Hispanic Seminary of Medieval Studies, 1989.

——— *Poesías del Arcipreste de Hita.* Vol. 4, *Colección de poesías castellanas anteriores al siglo XV ilustradas con notas,* ed. Tomás Antonio Sánchez. Madrid, 1779–90.

Shapiro, Norman, trans. *The Comedy of Eros: Medieval French Guides to the Art of Love.* Urbana: University of Illinois Press, 1971.

Vitalis of Blois. *Geta.* In Bate, *Three Latin Comedies,* 15–34.

Walter of St. Victor. *Contra quatuor labyrinthos Franciae.* Ed. Palémon Glorieux. *Archives d'histoire doctrinale et littéraire du Moyen-Âge* 27 (1952): 187–335.

William of Conches. *Dragmaticon.* Ed. Gul. Gratarolus. Strasbourg, 1567.

William of St. Thierry. *Disputatio adversus Petrum Abaelardum.* In *PL* 180: 249A–282D.

Secondary Sources

Alessio, Franco. "Notizie e questioni sul movimento cornificiano." *Atti dell'Accademia delle scienze di Torino. Classe di scienze morali, storiche, e filolologiche* 88 (1953–4): 125–35.

Allen, Judson. "Exemplum as Autobiography: Abelard's Complaints and Lacan." Paper presented at the Medieval Institute Congress of Medieval Studies, Kalamazoo, Mich., May 1985.

Allen, Peter L. *"Ars amandi, Ars legendi*: Love Poetry and Literary Theory in Ovid, Andreas Capellanus, and Jean de Meun." *Exemplaria* 1 (1989): 181–206.

——— *The Art of Love: Amatory Fiction from Ovid to the "Romance of the Rose."* Philadelphia: University of Pennsylvania Press, 1992.

——— *"Assidua lectio* and the *duplex sententia*: Andreas Capellanus and the Rhetoric of Love." Forthcoming in *The Rhetoric of Transgression,* ed. Katharina Wilson and Sarah Spence.

Alton, D. H., and D. E. W. Wormwell. "Ovid in the Medieval Schoolroom." *Hermathena* 94 (1960): 21–38; 95 (1961): 67–82.

Amsler, M. "Genre and Code in Abelard's *Historia calamitatum.*" *Assays* 1 (1981): 35–50.

Aspelin, Gunnar. "John of Salisbury's *Metalogicon*: A Study in Medieval Humanism." *Arsberättelse: Bulletin de la Société Royale des Lettres de Lund* 1951–52: 19–37.

Astell, Ann. *The Song of Songs in the Middle Ages.* Ithaca, N.Y.: Cornell University Press, 1990.

Austin, J. L. *How to Do Things with Words.* 2nd edition. Ed. J. O. Urmson and Marina Sbisà. Cambridge, Mass.: Harvard University Press, 1962.

Bakhtin, Mikhail. *Rabelais and His World*. Trans. Hélène Iswolsky. Bloomington: Indiana University Press, 1965.

Baldwin, John W. "L'*ars amatoria* au XIIe siècle en France: Ovide, Abélard, et Pierre le Chantre." In *Histoire et société: Mélanges offerts à Georges Duby*, 1: 19–29. Aix: Publications de l'Université de Provence, 1992.

———— *The Language of Sex: Five Voices from Northern France Around 1200*. Chicago: University of Chicago Press, 1994.

———— "Masters at Paris from 1179–1215: A Social Perspective." In *Renaissance and Renewal in the Twelfth Century*, ed. R. Benson and Giles Constable, 138–72. Cambridge, Mass.: Harvard University Press, 1983.

Barney, Steven A. "Visible Allegory: The *Distinctiones Abel* of Peter the Chanter." In *Allegory, Myth, and Symbol*, ed. Morton Bloomfield, 87–107. Cambridge, Mass.: Harvard University Press, 1981.

Barthes, Roland. "L'ancienne rhétorique: Aide-mémoire." *Communications (École pratique des hautes études)* 16 (1970): 172–229.

Benoît, Marie. "Le *De amore*: Dialectique et rhétorique." In Ruhe and Behrens, *Mittelalterbilder aus neuer Perspektive*, 31–42.

Benton, John. "Consciousness of Self and Perceptions of Individuality." In *Renaissance and Renewal in the Twelfth Century*, ed. R. Benson and Giles Constable, 263–95. Cambridge, Mass.: Harvard University Press, 1983.

———— "Fraud, Fiction, and Borrowing in the Correspondence of Abelard and Heloise." In *Pierre Abélard / Pierre le Vénérable: Les courants philosophiques, littéraires, et artistiques au milieu du XIIe siècle*, ed. R. Louis, 469–506. Paris: Editions du Centre National de Recherche Scientifique, 1975.

Beonio-Brocchieri Fumagalli, Maria Teresa. "Conceptes philosophiques dans l'*Historia calamitatum* et dans autres oeuvres abélardiennes." In *Petrus Abaelardus (1079–1142): Person, Werk, und Wirkung*, ed. Rudolph Thomas and Jean Jolivet, 121–24. Trier Theologische Studien 38. Trier: Paulinus, 1980.

———— *The Logic of Abelard*. Dordrecht: Reidel, 1970.

Bertini, Feruccio. "Il *Geta* di Vitale di Blois e la scuola di Abelardo." *Sandalion* 2 (1979): 257–65.

Bertola, Ermenegildo. "Le critiche di Abelardo ad Anselmo di Laon ed a Guglielmo di Champeaux." *Rivista di Filosofia Neo-scolastica* 52 (1960): 495–522.

———— "La 'glossa ordinaria' biblica e i suoi problemi." *Revue de Théologie Ancienne et Médiévale* 45 (1978): 34–78.

———— "I precedenti storici del metodo del 'Sic et non' di Abelardo." *Rivista di Filosofia Neo-scolastica* 53 (1961): 255–80.

Bloch, R. Howard. *Etymologies and Genealogies*. Chicago: University of Chicago Press, 1983.

Blodgett, E. D. "The Well-Wrought Void: Reflections on the *Ars amatoria*." *Classical Journal* 68 (1973): 322–33.

Bochenski, I. M. *A History of Formal Logic*. Trans. Ivo Thomas. South Bend, Ind.: University of Notre Dame Press, 1961.

Boler, J. F. "Abailard and the Problem of Universals." *Journal of the History of Philosophy* 1 (1963): 37–51.

Bonner, Stanley. *Education in Ancient Rome*. Berkeley: University of California Press, 1977.

Bossuat, Robert. *Drouart la Vache traducteur d'André le Chapelain*. Paris: Champion, 1926.

Bowden, Betsy. "The Art of Courtly Copulation." *Mediaevalia et Humanistica* 9 (1978): 67–83.

Boyarin, Daniel. *A Radical Jew: Paul and the Politics of Identity*. Berkeley: University of California Press, 1994.

Brasa Diez, Mariano. "Tres clases de lógica en Juan de Salisbury." In *Sprache und Erkentnniss im Mittelalter: Akten des VI. Internationalen Kongresses für Mittelalterliche Philosophie des Société Internationale pour l'Étude de la Philosophie Médiévale*, ed. Jan Beckmann et al., 1: 357–68. Miscellanea Mediaevalia 13, 1–2. Berlin: Walter de Gruyter, 1981.

Broadie, Alexander. *Introduction to Medieval Logic*. Oxford: Clarendon, 1987.

Brown, Catherine. "The Meretricious Letter of the *Libro de Buen Amor*." *Exemplaria* 9 (1997): 63–90.

——— "*Muliebriter*: Doing Gender in the Letters of Heloise." In *Gender and Text in the Later Middle Ages*, ed. Jane Chance, 25–51. Gainesville: University of Florida Press, 1996.

Brownlee, Marina Scordilis. "Hermeneutics of Reading in the *Corbacho*." In *Medieval Texts and Contemporary Readers*, ed. Laurie A. Fink and Martin B. Schichtman, 201–15. Ithaca: Cornell University Press, 1987.

——— *The Status of the Reading Subject in the "Libro de Buen Amor."* Chapel Hill: North Carolina University Press, 1985.

Burkard, Richard W. " 'Dize Pánfilo e Nasón': The Case for the Archpriest's Direct Knowledge of Greek and Roman Classics." In *Selected Proceedings of the 39th Annual Mountain Interstate Foreign Language Conference*, ed. Sixto Torres and S. Carl King, 9–16. Clemson, S.C.: Clemson University Press, 1991

——— "Pseudo *Ars amatoria*: A Medieval Source for the *Libro de Buen Amor*." *Kentucky Romance Quarterly* (1979): 385–98.

Burke, James F. "Counterfeit and the Curse of Mediacy in the *Libro de Buen Amor* and the *Conde Lucanor*." In *Discourses of Authority in Medieval and Renaissance Literature*, ed. Kevin Brownlee and Walter Stephens, 203–15. Hanover: University Press of New England for Dartmouth College, 1989.

——— *Desire Against the Law: The Juxtaposition of Contraries in Early Medieval Spanish Literature*. Stanford, Calif.: Stanford University Press, 1998.

Burke, Kenneth. *The Rhetoric of Religion*. Berkeley: University of California Press, 1970.

Burnett, Charles S. F. " 'Confessio Fidei ad Heloissam': Abelard's Last Letter to Heloise?" *Mittellateinisches Jahrbuch* 21 (1986): 147–55.

Butler, Judith. *Gender Trouble: Feminism and the Subversion of Identity.* New York: Routledge, 1990.

Camille, Michael. *Image on the Edge: The Margins of Medieval Art.* Cambridge, Mass.: Harvard University Press, 1992.

Cantarino, Vicente. "La lógica falaz de don Juan Ruiz." *Thesaurus* 29 (1974).

Cantin, André. *Les sciences séculières et la Foi: Les deux voies de la science au jugement de St. Pierre Damien.* Spoleto: Centro Italiano sull'alto medioevo, 1975.

Carré, M. H. *Realists and Nominalists.* Oxford: Oxford University Press, 1946.

Carruthers, Mary. *The Book of Memory: A Study of Memory in Medieval Culture.* Cambridge, Eng.: Cambridge University Press, 1990.

Castro, Américo. "El *Libro de buen amor* del Arcipreste de Hita." *Comparative Literature* 4 (1952): 193–213.

Castro Guisasola, Florentino. Review of *Glosario sobre Juan Ruiz*, by José María Aguado. *Revista de Filología Española* 16 (1929): 72.

Châtillon, Jean. "Abélard et les écoles." In *D'Isidore de Séville à Saint Thomas d'Aquin*, by Jean Châtillon, 133–60. London: Variorum, 1985.

Chenu, M.-D. "Antiqui-Moderni." *Revue des Sciences Philosophiques et Théologiques* 17 (1960): 212–47.

——— *La théologie comme science au XIIe siècle.* 2nd edition. Paris, 1943.

Cherchi, Paolo. "Andreas's *De amore*: Its Unity and Polemical Origin." In *Andrea Cappellano, i trovatori, ed altri temi romanzi*, by Paolo Cherchi, 83–111. Rome: Bulzoni, 1979.

——— "New Uses of Andreas's *De amore*." In Ruhe and Behrens, *Mittelalterbilder aus neuer Perspektive*, 22–30.

Clanchy, M. T. "Abelard's Mockery of St. Anselm." *Journal of Ecclesiastical History* 41 (1990): 1–23.

Clarke, Dorothy C. "Juan Ruiz and Andreas Capellanus." *Hispanic Review* 40 (1972): 390–411.

Colish, Marcia. *The Mirror of Language: A Study in the Medieval Theory of Knowledge* [1968]. 2nd edition. Lincoln: University of Nebraska Press, 1983.

——— *Peter Lombard.* 2 vols. Leiden: Brill, 1994.

Cooley, Charles Horton. *Life and the Student: Roadside Notes on Human Nature, Society, and Letters.* New York: Knopf, 1931.

Copeland, Rita. *Rhetoric, Hermeneutics and Translation in the Middle Ages: Academic Traditions and Vernacular Texts.* Cambridge, Eng.: Cambridge University Press, 1991.

Corti, Maria. "Models and Anti-Models in Medieval Culture." *New Literary History* 10 (1979): 343–60.

Cottiaux, J. "La conception de la théologie chez Abélard." *Revue d'Histoire Ecclésiastique* 28 (1932): 247–95, 533–51, 788–828.

Curtius, Ernst Robert. *European Literature in the Latin Middle Ages* [1952]. Trans. Willard R. Trask. Bollingen Series 36. Princeton, N.J.: Princeton University Press, 1973.

Dagenais, John. "'Como pella a las dueñas': Medieval Readings of the *Libro de Buen Amor.*" Paper presented at the Modern Language Association convention, December 29, 1990.

―――― *The Ethics of Reading in Manuscript Culture: Glossing the "Libro de buen amor."* Princeton, N.J.: Princeton University Press, 1994.

Dahlberg, Charles. *The Literature of Unlikeness*. Hanover: University Press of New England, 1988.

Dales, Richard C. "The Origin of the Doctrine of the Double Truth." *Viator* 15 (1984): 169–79.

dal Pra, Mario. *Giovanni di Salisbury*. Storia universale della filosofia 3. Milan: Bocca, 1951.

Dane, Joseph A. "*Integumentum* as Interpretation: Note on William of Conches' Commentary of Macrobius (I, 2, 10–11)." *Classical Folia* 32 (1978): 201–15.

Dawson, David. *Allegorical Readers and Cultural Revision in Ancient Alexandria*. Berkeley: University of California Press, 1992.

Delhaye, Philippe. "L'organisation scolaire au XIe siècle." *Traditio* 5 (1947): 211–68.

Dembowski, Peter F. "Two Old French Recastings/Translations of Andreas Capellanus's *De amore*." In *Medieval Translators and Their Craft*, ed. Jeanette Beer, 185–212. Studies in Medieval Culture 25. Kalamazoo, Mich.: Medieval Institute, 1989.

Denomy, A. J. "The *De amore* of Andreas Capellanus and the Condemnation of 1277." *Mediaeval Studies* 8 (1946): 107–49.

Dinshaw, Carolyn. *Chaucer's Sexual Poetics*. Madison: University of Wisconsin Press, 1989.

Donaldson, E. T. "Patristic Exegesis in the Criticism of Medieval Literature: The Opposition." In *Critical Approaches to Medieval Literature*, ed. Dorothy Bethrum, 1–26. New York: Columbia University Press, 1960.

Dragonetti, Roger. *Le mirage des sources: L'art du faux dans le roman médiéval*. Paris: Seuil, 1987.

Dronke, Peter. *Abelard and Heloise in Medieval Testimonies*. W. P. Ker Lecture No. 26. Glasgow: University of Glasgow Press, 1976.

―――― "Andreas Capellanus." *Journal of Medieval Latin* 4 (1995–96): 51–63.

―――― "Orléans, Bibl. Mun. 284 (228): An Edition of the Poems and Fragments on Pp. 183–4." *Archives d'Histoire Doctrinale et Littéraire du Moyen Âge* 57 (1982): 277–81.

―――― *Women Writers of the Middle Ages*. Cambridge, Eng.: Cambridge University Press, 1984.

Dungey, Kevin R. "Faith in the Darkness: Allegorical Theory and Aldhelm's

Obscurity." In *Allegoresis: The Craft of Allegory in Medieval Literature*, ed. J. Stephen Russell, 3–26. New York: Garland, 1988.

Durling, R. "Ovid as *praeceptor amoris*." *Classical Journal* 53 (1958): 157–67.

Dutton, Brian. "'Con Dios en Buen Amor': A Semantic Analysis of the Title of the *Libro de Buen Amor*." *Bulletin of Hispanic Studies* 43 (1966): 161–76.

Eco, Umberto. *The Aesthetics of Thomas Aquinas* [1970]. Trans. Hugh Bredin. Cambridge, Mass.: Harvard University Press, 1988.

———— "Overinterpreting Texts." In *Interpretation and Over-Interpretation*, ed. Stephan Collini, 45–66. Cambridge, Eng.: Cambridge University Press, 1992.

Elbow, Peter. *Oppositions in Chaucer*. Middletown, Conn.: Wesleyan University Press, 1973.

Evans, Gillian R. *The Language and Logic of the Bible: The Earlier Middle Ages*. Cambridge, Eng.: Cambridge University Press, 1984.

———— "Peter the Chanter's *De tropis loquendi*: The Problem of the Text." *The New Scholasticism* 55 (1981): 95–103.

———— "'Ponendo theologica exempla': Peter the Chanter's *De tropis loquendi*." *History of Universities* 2 (1982): 1–14.

———— "A Work of 'Terminist Theology?': Peter the Chanter's *De tropis loquendi* and Some Fallacie." *Vivarium* 20 (1982): 40–58.

Ferruolo, Stephen C. *The Origins of the University: The Schools of Paris and Their Critics, 1100–1215*. Stanford, Calif.: Stanford University Press, 1985.

Ferster, Judith. *Chaucer on Interpretation*. Cambridge, Eng.: Cambridge University Press, 1985.

Fleming, John V. *Reason and the Lover*. Princeton, N.J.: Princeton University Press, 1984.

———— *The "Roman de la Rose": A Study in Allegory and Iconography*. Princeton, N.J.: Princeton University Press, 1969.

Flint, Valerie. "The 'School of Laon': A Reconsideration." *Revue de Théologie Ancienne et Médiévale* 43 (1976): 89–110.

Frappier, Jean. "Sur un procès fait à l'amour courtois." *Romania* 93 (1972): 145–93.

Fredborg, Karin. "The Commentaries in Cicero's *De inventione* and the *Rhetorica ad Herennium* by William of Champeaux." *Cahiers de l'Institut du Moyen-Âge Grec et Latin* 17 (1976): 1–39.

Frese, Dolores Warwick. *An "Ars Legendi" for Chaucer's "Canterbury Tales": Re-Constructive Reading*. Gainesville: University of Florida Press, 1991.

Freud, Sigmund. "The Antithetical Meaning of Primal Words." In *The Standard Edition of the Complete Psychological Works of Sigmund Freud*, ed. James Strachey, 11: 155–61. London: Hogarth Press, 1957.

———— *The Interpretation of Dreams*. Trans. James Strachey. New York: Avon, 1965.

Fyler, John M. *Chaucer and Ovid*. New Haven, Conn.: Yale University Press, 1979.

Gabriel, Astrik L. "The Cathedral Schools of Notre Dame and the Beginnings of the University of Paris." In *Garlandia: Studies in the History of the Medieval University*, by Astrik Gabriel, 39–64. Notre Dame, Ind.: Mediaeval Institute, University of Notre Dame, 1969.

Gallop, Jane, ed. *Pedagogy: The Question of Impersonation*. Bloomington: Indiana University Press, 1995.

Gehl, Paul F. "Mystical Language Models in Monastic Educational Psychology." *Journal of Medieval and Renaissance Studies* 14 (1984): 219–43.

Gellrich, Jesse. *The Idea of the Book in the Middle Ages*. Ithaca: Cornell University Press, 1985.

Gericke, Philip O. " 'Mucho de bien me fizo con Dios en limpio amor': Doña Garoça, Andreas Capellanus y el amor cortés en el *Libro de buen amor*." *Explicación de Textos Literarios* 6 (1977–78): 89–92.

Gerli, Michael. "Boccaccio and Capellanus: Tradition and Innovation in *Arçipreste de Talavera*." *Revista de Estudios Hispánicos* 12 (1978): 255–74.

———. "Don Amor, the Devil, and the Devil's Brood: Love and the Seven Deadly Sins in the *Libro de Buen Amor*." *Revista de Estudios Hispánicos* 16 (1982): 67–80.

———. " 'Recta voluntas est bonus amor': St. Augustine and the Didactic Structure of the *Libro de Buen Amor*." *Romance Philology* 35 (1982): 500–508

Ghellinck, J. de. "Dialectique et dogme aux Xe–XIIe siècles." In *Studien zur geschichte der philosophie. Festgabe zum 60, geburtstag Clemens Baeumker gewidmet von seinen schülern und freunden*, 79–99. Beiträge zur Geschichte der Philosophie des Mittelalters, supp. vol. Münster: Aschendorff, 1913.

———. *Le mouvement théologique au XIIe siècle*. 2nd edition. Bruges: De Tempel, 1948.

Gibson, Margaret, ed. *Boethius, His Life, Thought, and Influence*. Oxford: Blackwell, 1981.

Gide, André. *The Journals of André Gide*. Trans. Justin O'Brien. Vol. 2. London: Secker and Warburg, 1948.

Giusberti, Franco. *Materials for a Study on Twelfth Century Scholasticism*. History of Logic 2. Naples: Bibliopolis, 1982.

Glorieux, Palémon. "Mauvais action et mauvais travail: Le 'Contra quatuor labyrinthos Franciae.' " *Revue de Théologie Ancienne et Médiévale* 21 (1954): 179–93.

Grabmann, Martin. *Die Geschichte der scholastischen Methode*. 2 vols. Darmstadt: Wissenschaftliche Buchgesellschaft, 1957.

Green, Otis. *Spain and the Western Tradition*. Vol. 1. Madison: University of Wisconsin Press, 1963.

Guyer, Foster E. "The Dwarf on Giant's Shoulders." *Modern Language Notes* 45 (1930): 398–402.

Hadot, Ilsetraut. *Arts libéraux et philosophie dans la pensée antique*. Paris: Études Augustiniennes, 1984.

Hadot, Pierre. "La préhistoire des genres littéraires philosophiques médiévaux dans l'antiquité." In *Les genres littéraires dans les sources théologiques et philoso-phiques médiévales: Définitions, critique, exploitation. Actes du Colloque Inter-national de Louvain-la-Neuve, 25–27 mai 1981,* ed. R. Bultot, 1–10. Publications de L'Institut d'Études Médiévales, 2ᵉ série 5. Louvain: Université Catholique de Louvain, 1982.

Hanning, Robert. " 'Ut Enim Faber . . . Sic Creator': Divine Creation as Context for Human Creativity in the Twelfth Century." In *Word, Picture, and Spectacle,* ed. Clifford Davidson, 95–149. Kalamazoo, Mich.: Medieval Institute Publications, 1984.

Häring, Nikolaus M. "Commentary and Hermeneutics." In *Renaissance and Renewal in the Twelfth Century,* ed. Robert Benson and Giles Constable, 173–99. Cambridge, Mass.: Harvard University Press, 1983.

——— "The *Sententiae Magistri A.* and the School of Laon." *Mediaeval Studies* 17 (1955): 1–45.

——— "Thierry of Chartres and Dominicus Gundissalinus." *Mediaeval Studies* 26 (1964): 271–86.

Harpham, Geoffrey Galt. *The Ascetic Imperative in Culture and Criticism.* Chicago: University of Chicago Press, 1987.

Hartman, Geoffrey. "The Interpreter: A Self-Analysis." *New Literary History* 4 (1973): 213–27.

Heer, Friedrich. *Mittelalter von 1100 bis 1350.* Zurich: Kindler, 1961.

Hernández, Francisco. "The Venerable Juan Ruiz, Archpriest of Hita." *La Corónica* 13 (1984–85): 10–22.

Heugas, P. "La tradition et sa ré-interprétation dans le *Libro de buen amor*: Juan Ruiz et l'art d'aimer." In *Le Moyen Âge en Espagne,* 41–53. Saint-Etienne: Université de Saint-Etienne, 1975.

Hexter, Ralph. *Ovid and Medieval Schooling.* Munich: Arbeo, 1986.

Hissette, Roland. "André le Chapelain et la double vérité." *Bulletin de Philosophie Médiévale* 21 (1979): 63–67.

——— "Une 'duplex sententia' dans le *De amore* d'André le Chapelain?" *Revue de Théologie Ancienne et Médiévale* 50 (1983): 246–51.

——— *Enquête sur les 219 articles condamnés à Paris le 7 mars 1277.* Louvain: Publications Universitaires, 1977.

——— "Étienne Tempier et ses condamnations." *Revue de Théologie Ancienne et Médiévale* 47 (1980): 230–70.

Huizinga, Johan. *The Waning of the Middle Ages* [1924]. New York: Doubleday-Anchor, 1954.

Hult, David. "Closed Quotations: The Speaking Voice in the *Roman de la Rose.*" *Yale French Studies* 67 (1984): 248–69.

——— *Self-Fulfilling Prophecies: Readership and Authority in the First "Roman de la Rose."* Cambridge, Eng.: Cambridge University Press, 1986.

——— "1277, 7 March: The Bishop of Paris Condemns as Errors 219 Propositions Taught at the University of Paris." In *A New History of French Literature*, ed. Denis Hollier, 97–103. Cambridge, Mass.: Harvard University Press, 1989.

Hunt, R. W. "The Introduction to the *Artes* in the Twelfth Century." In *Collected Papers on the History of Grammar in the Middle Ages*, ed. G. L. Bursill-Hall, 85–112. Amsterdam: John Benjamins B.V., 1980.

Hunt, Tony. "Aristotle, Dialectic, and Courtly Literature." *Viator* 10 (1979): 95–129.

Huygens, R. B. C. "Guillaume de Tyr étudiant: Un chapitre (XIX,2) de son *Histoire* retrouvé." *Latomus* 21 (1962): 811–29.

Illich, Ivan. *In the Vineyard of the Text: A Commentary to Hugh's "Didascalicon."* Chicago: University of Chicago Press, 1993.

Irvine, Martin. "Abelard and (Re)Writing the Male Body: Castration, Identity and Remasculinization." In *Becoming Male in the Middle Ages*, ed. Jeffrey Jerome Cohen and Bonnie Wheeler, 87–106. New York: Garland, 1997.

——— *The Making of Textual Culture: "Grammatica" and Literary Theory, 350–1100*. Cambridge, Eng.: Cambridge University Press, 1994.

Iser, Wolfgang. "The Reality of Fiction: A Functionalist Approach to Literature." *New Literary History* 7 (1975): 7–38.

Iwakuma, Yukio, and Sten Ebbesen. "Logico-Theological Schools from the Second Half of the Twelfth Century: A List of Sources." *Vivarium* 30 (1992): 173–210.

Jackson, William T. H. "The *De amore* of Andreas Capellanus and the Practice of Love at Court." In *The Challenge of the Medieval Text*, 3–13. New York: Columbia University Press, 1985. Originally published in *Romanic Review* 49 (1958): 243–51.

Jacobi, Klaus. "Logic (ii): The Later Twelfth Century." In *A History of Twelfth-Century Western Philosophy*, ed. Peter Dronke, 227–51. Cambridge, Eng.: Cambridge University Press, 1988.

Jaeger, C. Stephen. *The Envy of Angels: Cathedral Schools and Social Ideas in Medieval Europe, 950–1200*. Philadelphia: University of Pennsylvania Press, 1994.

Jager, Eric. *The Tempter's Voice: Language and the Fall in Medieval Literature*. Ithaca, N.Y.: Cornell University Press, 1993.

Jeauneau, Edouard. "Deux rédactions des gloses de Guillaume de Conches sur Priscien." *Revue de Théologie Ancienne et Médiévale* 27 (1960): 212–47.

——— "Nani gigantum humeris insidentes." *Vivarium* 5 (1967): 79–99.

——— "L'usage de la notion d'integumentum à travers les gloses de Guillaume de Conches." *Archives d'Histoire Doctrinale et Littéraire du Moyen Âge* 24 (1957): 35–100.

Jeudy, Colette. "Un nouveau manuscrit de la correspondance d'Abélard et Héloïse." *Latomus* 50 (1991): 872–81.

Johnson, Barbara. "Teaching as a Literary Genre." *Yale French Studies* 63 (1982): iii–vii.

Jolivet, Jean. *Arts de langage et théologie chez Abélard* [1969]. 2nd edition. Paris: Vrin, 1982.

——— "Données sur Guillaume de Champeaux, dialecticien et théologien." In *L'abbaye parisienne de Saint-Victor au Moyen-Âge*, ed. Jean Longère, 235–51. Paris: Brepols, 1991.

——— "Le traitement des autorités contraires selon le *Sic et Non* d'Abélard." In *Aspects de la pensée médiévale: Abélard. Doctrines du langage*, 79–92. Paris: Vrin, 1987.

Joset, Jacques. *Nuevas investigaciones sobre el "Libro de buen amor."* Madrid: Cátedra, 1988.

Jung, Marc-René. "Jean de Meun et l'allégorie." *Cahiers de l'Association Internationale des Études Françaises* 28 (1976): 21–36.

Kamuf, Peggy. *Fictions of Feminine Desire*. Lincoln: University of Nebraska Press, 1982.

Karnein, Alfred. "*Amor Est Passio*: A Definition of Courtly Love?" In *Court and Poet: Selected Proceedings of the Third Congress of the International Courtly Literature Society*, ed. Glyn S. Burgess et al., 215–21. Liverpool: Cairns, 1981.

——— "Le *De amore* et l'enseignement de l'amour dans la littérature française médiévale." *Romania* 102 (1981): 501–42.

——— *"De amore" in volkssprachlicher Literatur: Untersuchungen zur Andreas-Cappellanus-Rezeption in Mittelalter und Renaissance*. Heidelberg: Winter, 1985.

——— "La réception du *De amore* d'André le Chapelain au XIIIe siècle." *Romania* 102 (1981): 324–51.

Kaske, R. E. "The Defense." In *Critical Approaches to Medieval Literature*, ed. Dorothy Bethrum, 27–60. New York: Columbia University Press, 1960.

Kauffman, Linda S. *Discourses of Desire: Gender, Genre, and Epistolary Fictions*. Ithaca, N.Y.: Cornell University Press, 1986.

Kearney, Eileen Frances. "Master Peter Abelard, Expositor of Sacred Scripture: An Analysis of Abelard's Approach to Biblical Exposition in Selected Writings on Scripture." Ph.D. diss., Marquette University, 1980.

——— "*Scientia* and *Sapientia*: Reading Sacred Scripture at the Paraclete." In *From Cloister to Classroom: Monastic and Scholastic Approaches to Truth*, ed. E. Rozanne Elder, 111–29. Cistercian Studies 90. Kalamazoo, Mich.: Cistercian Publications, 1986.

Keats-Rohan, K. S. B. "The Chronology of John of Salisbury's Studies in France: A Reading of *Metalogicon* 2.10." *Studi Medievali* 28 (1987): 193–207.

——— "John of Salisbury and Education in Twelfth-Century Paris from the Account of His *Metalogicon*." *History of Universities* 6 (1986–87): 1–45.

Kelly, Douglas. "Courtly Love in Perspective: The Hierarchy of Love in Andreas Capellanus." *Traditio* 24 (1968): 119–47.

———— *Internal Difference and Meanings in the "Roman de la Rose."* Madison: University of Wisconsin Press, 1995.

Kendrick, Laura. *The Game of Love: Troubadour Wordplay.* Berkeley: University of California Press, 1988.

Kenny, Anthony, and Jan Pinborg. "Medieval Philosophical Literature." In *Cambridge History of Later Medieval Philosophy*, ed. Norman Kretzmann, 9–42. Cambridge, Eng.: Cambridge University Press, 1982.

Ker, W. P. *The Dark Ages.* Edinburgh: William Blackwood, 1904.

Kermode, Frank. *The Genesis of Secrecy.* Cambridge, Mass.: Harvard University Press, 1979.

Kinkade, Richard. "A Thirteenth-Century Precursor of the *Libro de Buen Amor*: The *Art d'Amors.*" *La Corónica* 24, no. 2 (1996): 123–39.

Kluge, Eike-Henner W. "Roscelin and the Medieval Problem of Universals." *Journal of the History of Philosophy* 14 (1976): 405–14.

Lacan, Jacques. "The Agency of the Letter in the Unconscious or Reason Since Freud." Trans. Alan Sheridan. In *Écrits: A Selection*, 146–78. New York: Norton, 1977.

LaCapra, Dominick. *Rethinking Intellectual History.* Ithaca, N.Y.: Cornell University Press, 1983.

Lafleur, Claude. "Logique et théorie de l'argument dans le *Guide de l'étudiant* (c. 1230–40) du ms. Ripoll 109." *Dialogue* 29, no. 3 (1990): 335–55.

Lalande, André, ed. *Vocabulaire technique et critique de la philosophie* [1926]. Paris: PUF, 1967.

Landgraf, Artur Michael. *Introduction à l'histoire de la littérature théologique de la scolastique naissante.* Trans. Louis-B. Geiger. Montreal: Institut d'Études Médiévales, 1973.

Lange, Hanne. "Traités du XIIe siècle sur la symbolique des nombres: Geoffroy d'Auxerre et Thibaut de Langres." *Cahiers de l'Institut du Moyen-Âge Grec et Latin* 29 (1978): 1–108.

Leclercq, Jean. "Aspects spirituels de la symbolique du livre au XIIe siècle." In *L'homme devant Dieu. Mélanges offerts au Père Henri de Lubac*, 2: 62–72. Paris: Aubier, 1964.

———— "Les caractères traditionnels de la *lectio divina*." In *La Liturgie et les paradoxes chrétiens*, 243–57. Lex Orandi 36. Paris: Éditions du Cerf, 1963.

———— *The Love of Learning and the Desire for God: A Study of Learning in Monastic Culture.* Trans. Catherine Misrahi. New York: Fordham University Press, 1961.

———— "Le magistère du prédicateur au XIIIe siècle." *Archives d'Histoire Doctrinale et Littéraire du Moyen Âge* 21 (1946): 105–47.

———— "Modern Psychology and the Interpretation of Medieval Texts." *Speculum* 48 (1973): 476–90.

Lecoy, Félix. *Recherches sur le "Libro de buen amor" de Juan Ruiz, Archiprêtre de Hita*. Paris: Droz, 1938. Reprint with prologue, supplementary bibliography and index by Alan Deyermond, Westmead: Gregg International, 1974.

Lefèvre, G. *Les variations de Guillaume de Champeaux et la question des universaux*. Lille, 1898.

Le Goff, Jacques. *Les intellectuels au Moyen-Âge*. Paris: Seuil, 1957.

——— "Quelle conscience l'université médiévale a-t-elle d'elle-même?" *Miscellanea Mediaevalia* 3 (1964): 15–29.

Leo XIII. "On the Study of Holy Scripture." In *Holy Bible*, Rheims-Douay Version, ix–xxvi. Los Angeles: C.F. Horan, 1941.

Lerer, Seth. "John of Salisbury's Virgil." *Vivarium* 20 (1982): 24–39.

Lewis, Carlton, and Charles A. Short. *A Latin Dictionary*. Oxford: Clarendon, 1879.

Liebeschütz, Hans. *Mediaeval Humanism in the Life and Writings of John of Salisbury*. London: Warburg Institute, 1950.

Lloyd, G. E. R. *Polarity and Analogy: Two Types of Argumentation in Early Greek Thought*. Cambridge, Eng.: Cambridge University Press, 1966.

Lochrie, Karma. *Margery Kempe and the Translations of the Flesh*. Philadelphia: University of Pennsylvania Press, 1991.

Lohr, J. "Peter Abelard und die Scholastischen Exegese." *Freiburg Zeitschrift für Philosophie und Theologie* 28 (1981): 95–110.

Lubac, Henri de. "À propos de la formule 'Diversi, sed non adversi.'" *Recherches de Science Religieuse* 40 (1952): 27–40.

Luscombe, David. "Masters and Their Books in the Schools of the Twelfth Century." *Proceedings of the PMR [Patristic Mediaeval Renaissance] Conference* 9 (1984): 17–34.

——— "Peter Abelard." In *A History of Twelfth-Century Western Philosophy*, ed. Peter Dronke, 279–307. Cambridge, Eng.: Cambridge University Press, 1988.

——— "Philosophy and Philosophers in the Schools of the Twelfth Century." In Weijers, ed., *Vocabulaire des écoles*, 73–85.

——— *The School of Peter Abelard: The Influence of Abelard's Thought in the Early Scholastic Period*. Cambridge, Eng.: Cambridge University Press, 1969.

——— "The School of Peter Abelard Revisited." *Vivarium* 30, no. 1 (1992): 127–38.

MacDonald, A. J. *Authority and Reason in the Middle Ages*. London: Oxford University Press, 1933.

Mackey, Louis. "Eros into Logos: The Rhetoric of Courtly Love." In *The Philosophy of (Erotic) Love*, ed. Robert C. Solomon and Kathleen M. Higgins, 336–51. Lawrence: University Press of Kansas, 1991.

Maierù, Alfonso. "La terminologie de l'Université de Bologne de médecine et des arts: 'Facultas' et 'verificare.'" In Weijers, ed., *Vocabulaire des écoles*, 140–56.

Marenbon, John. *Early Medieval Philosophy (480–1150): An Introduction*. London: Routledge and Kegan Paul, 1983.

———— *The Philosophy of Peter Abelard*. Cambridge, Eng.: Cambridge University Press, 1997.

Margerie, Bertrand de. *Introduction à l'histoire de l'exegèse*. 4 vols. Paris: Cerf, 1980.

Marrou, Henri-Irénée. " 'Doctrina' et 'disciplina' dans la langue des Pères de l'Église." *Bulletin du Cange (Archivum Latinitatis Medii Aevi)* 9 (1934): 5–25.

———— *Histoire de l'éducation dans l'antiquité*. 6th edition. Paris: Seuil, 1965.

———— *St. Augustin et la fin de la culture antique*. Paris, 1958.

McCallum, J. Ramsay. *Abelard's Christian Theology*. 1948. Reprint, Merrick, N.Y.: Richwood, 1976.

McGarry, Daniel. "Educational Theory in the *Metalogicon* of John of Salisbury." *Speculum* 23 (1948): 659–75.

McGregor, J. "Ovid at School: From the Ninth to the Fifteenth Century." *Classical Folia* 32 (1978): 29–51.

McLaughlin, Mary Martin. "Abelard as Autobiographer." *Speculum* 42 (1967): 463–88.

McNally, Robert E. *The Bible in the Early Middle Ages*. Woodstock Papers 4. Westminster, Md.: Newman Press, 1959.

Meadows, D. *A Saint and a Half: A New Interpretation of Abelard and St. Bernard*. New York: Devin Adair, 1963.

Merlet, Lucien. "Lettres d'Ives de Chartres et d'autres personnages de son temps." *Bibliothèque de l'Ecole des Chartes*, 4th series, no. 1 (1855): 443–71.

Mews, Constant. "Nominalism and Theology Before Abelard: New Light on Roscelin." *Vivarium* 30 (1992): 4–33.

———— "St. Anselm and Roscelin: Some New Texts and Their Implications: 'De incarnatione verbi' and the 'Disputatio inter christianum et gentilem.'" *Archives d'Histoire Doctrinale et Littéraire du Moyen-Âge* 66 (1991): 55–98.

Michaud, E. *Guillaume de Champeaux et les écoles de Paris au XIIe siècle*. Paris, 1867.

Minio-Paluello, Lorenzo. *Twelfth Century Logic: Texts and Studies*. Vol 1, *Adam Balsamiensis Parvipontani "Ars disserendi."* Rome: Storia e Letteratura, 1956.

Minnis, Alastair J. "Chaucer's Pardoner and the 'Office of Preacher.'" In *Intellectuals and Writers in Twelfth Century Europe*, ed. Piero Boitani and Anna Torti, 88–119. Tübingen: Narr, 1986.

———— *Medieval Theory of Authorship: Scholastic Literary Attitudes in the Later Middle Ages*. London: Scolar Press, 1984.

Minnis, Alastair J.; A. B. Scott; and David Wallace, eds. *Medieval Literary Theory and Criticism, c. 1100–c. 1375: The Commentary Tradition*. Oxford: Clarendon, 1991.

Monson, Donald. "Andreas Capellanus and the Problem of Irony." *Speculum* 63 (1988): 539–72.

——— "*Auctoritas* and Intertextuality in Andreas Capellanus' *De amore.*" In *Poetics of Love in the Middle Ages*, ed. Moshe Lazar and Norris J. Lacy, 69–80. Fairfax, Va.: George Mason University Press, 1989.

Morin, Germain. "Les monuments de la prédication de St. Jérome." *Études, textes, découvertes: Contributions à la littérature et à l'histoire des douze premiers siècles*, 1: 220–93. Anecdota Maredsolana, 2ᵉ série. Paris: Picard, 1913.

Muscatine, Charles. *Chaucer and the French Tradition*. Berkeley: University of California Press, 1960.

Nederman, Cary. "Knowledge, Virtue, and the Path to Wisdom: The Unexamined Aristotelianism of John of Salisbury's *Metalogicon.*" *Mediaeval Studies* 51 (1989): 268–86.

Nepaulsingh, Colbert. *Towards a History of Literary Composition in Medieval Spain*. Toronto: University Toronto Press, 1986.

Newman, Barbara. "Authority, Authenticity, and the Repression of Heloise." *Journal of Medieval and Renaissance Studies* 22 (1992): 121–57.

Nichols, Stephen G. "Periodization and the Politics of Perception: A Romanesque Example." *Poetics Today* 10 (1989): 127–54.

Nicolau d'Olwer, L. "Sur la date de la *Dialectica* d'Abélard." *Revue du Moyen Âge Latin* 1 (1945): 375–90.

Nouvet, Claire. "La castration d'Abélard: Impasse et substitution." *Poétique* 21 (1990): 259–80.

Nye, Andrea. "A Woman's Thought or a Man's Discipline? The Letters of Abelard and Heloise." *Hypatia* 7, no. 3 (1992): 1–22.

Omont, H. *Notice sur le manuscrit latin 886 des nouvelles acquisitions de la Bibliothèque Nationale*. Paris: Imprimerie Nationale, 1906.

Orduna, Germán. "El *Libro de buen amor* y el *textus receptus.*" In *Studia Hispanica Medievalia*, ed. L. Teresa Valdivieso and Jorge H. Valdivieso, 81–88. Buenos Aires: Ergon, 1988.

Owen, G. E. L., ed. *Aristotle on Dialectic*. Oxford: Clarendon, 1968.

Pagès, Amadeu. "La version catalane du *De amore.*" *Annales du Midi* 39 (1928): 362–74.

Paré, Gérard Marie. *Les idées et les lettres au XIIIᵉ siècle: Le "Roman de la Rose."* Publications de l'Institut d'Études Médiévales Albert-le-Grand. Montreal: Centre de Psychologie et de Pedagogie, 1947.

Paré, Gérard Marie; A. Brunet; P. Tremblay; and G. Robert. *La Renaissance du XIIᵉ siècle: Les écoles et l'enseignement*. Publications de l'Institut d'Études Médiévales d'Ottowa 3. Paris: Vrin, 1933.

Paris, Gaston. "Études sur les romans de la Table Ronde. Lancelot du Lac." *Romania* 12 (1883): 459–534.

Patterson, Lee. *Negotiating the Past: The Historical Understanding of Medieval Literature*. Madison: University of Wisconsin Press, 1987.

Payen, Jean Charles. "Un *ensenhamen* trop précoce: L'art d'aimer d'André le

Chapelain." In Ruhe and Behrens, *Mittelalterbilder aus neuer Perspektive*, 43–58.

Pelen, Marc M. *Latin Poetic Irony in the "Roman de la Rose."* Vinaver Studies in French 4. Liverpool: Francis Cairns, 1987.

Pellegrin, Elisabeth. "Les *Remedia* d'Ovide, texte scolaire médiévale." *Bibliothèque de l'École des Chartes* 115 (1957): 172–79.

Pépin, Jean. "À propos de l'histoire de l'exégèse allégorique: L'absurdité signe de l'allégorie." In *Studia Patristica*, ed. Kurt Aland and F. L. Cross, 395–413. Berlin: Akademie Verlag, 1957.

——— *St. Augustin et la dialectique.* Villanova, Pa.: Augustinian Institute, 1976.

Picavet, F. *Roscelin philosophe et théologien.* 2nd edition. Paris: Alcan, 1911.

Pontet, Maurice. *L'exégèse de St. Augustin prédicateur.* Paris: Aubier, 1945.

Poole, Reginald L. "The Masters of the Schools of Paris and Chartres in John of Salisbury's Time." In *Studies in Chronology and History*, 223–47. Oxford: Clarendon, 1934. Originally published in *English History Review* 35 (1920): 321–42.

Rajna, Pio. "Tre studi per la storia del libro di Andrea Capellano." *Studi di Filologia Romanza* 5 (1891): 193–276.

Rashdall, Hastings. *The Universities of Europe in the Middle Ages.* Ed. F. M. Powicke and A. B. Emden. Vol. 1. Oxford: Clarendon, 1936.

Reed, Thomas. *Middle English Debate Poetry and the Aesthetics of Irresolution.* Columbia: University of Missouri Press, 1990.

Regalado, Nancy Freeman. "'Des contraires choses': La fonction poétique de la citation et des *exempla* dans le *Roman de la Rose* de Jean de Meun." *Littérature* 41 (1981): 62–81.

Reiners, J. *Der Nominalismus in der Frühscholastik.* Beiträge zur Geschichte des Philosophie und Theologie des Mittelalters, no. 8, pt. 5. Münster: Aschendorff, 1910.

Reiss, Edmund. "Ambiguous Signs and Authorial Deceptions in Fourteenth-Century Fictions." In *Sign, Sentence, Discourse: Language in Medieval Thought and Literature*, ed. Julian Wasserman and Lois Roney, 113–137. Syracuse: Syracuse University Press, 1989.

——— "Conflict and Resolution in Medieval Dialogues." In *Arts libéraux et philosophie au moyen-âge: Actes du Quatrième Congrès Internationale de Philosophie Médiévale, Montréal 1967*, 863–72. Paris: Vrin, 1969.

Riché, Pierre. *Les écoles et l'enseignement dans l'occident chrétien.* Paris: Aubier, 1979.

——— "Jean de Salisbury et le monde scolaire du XIIe siècle." In Wilks, *The World of John of Salisbury*, 39–61.

Richter, D. "Die Allegorie der Pergamentbearbeitung." In *Fachliteratur Des Mittelalters. Festschift Für Gerhardt Eis*, ed. G. Keil, R. Rudolf, W. Schmidt, and N. J. Nermeer, 83–92. Stuttgart, 1968.

Rico, Francisco. "'Por aver mantenencia . . .': El aristotelismo heterodoxo del *Libro de buen amor.*" *Crotalón* 2 (1985): 169–98.

Ridder-Symoens, Hilde de, ed. *Universities in the Middle Ages.* Vol. 1, *A History of the University in Europe.* Cambridge, Eng.: Cambridge University Press, 1992.

Rijk, Lambert Marie de. *Logica Modernorum: A Contribution to the History of Early Terminist Logic.* 3 vols. Wijsgerige Teksten en Studies 6, 16. Assen: Van Gorcum, 1962–67.

——— "The Semantical Impact of Abailard's Solution of the Problem of Universals." In *Petrus Abaelardus (1079–1142): Person, Werk, und Wirkung,* ed. Rudolph Thomas and Jean Jolivet, 139–52. Trier Theologische Studien 38. Trier: Paulinus, 1980.

——— "Some Notes on the Medieval Tract *De insolubiliis* with the Edition of a Tract Dating from the Twelfth Century." *Vivarium* 4 (1966): 83–115.

——— "Specific Tools Concerning Logical Education." *Méthodes et instruments de travail,* ed. Olga Weijers, 62–81. Études sur le vocabulaire intellectuel au Moyen-Âge 3. Turnhout: Brepols, 1990.

Rivero, María Luisa. "Early Scholastic Views on Ambiguity: Composition and Division." *Historiographica Linguistica* 2 (1975): 25–47.

Robertson, Durant Waite, Jr. *Abelard and Heloise.* New York: Dial, 1972.

——— "The Doctrine of Charity in Medieval Literary Gardens: A Topical Approach Through Symbolism and Allegory." In *Essays in Medieval Culture,* 21–50. Princeton, N.J.: Princeton University Press, 1980.

——— *A Preface to Chaucer: Studies in Medieval Perspectives.* Princeton, N.J.: Princeton University Press, 1962.

——— "Some Medieval Literary Terminology, with Special Reference to Chrétien de Troyes." In *Essays in Medieval Culture,* 51–72. Princeton, N.J.: Princeton University Press, 1980.

——— "The Subject of the *De amore* of Andreas Capellanus." *Modern Philology* 50 (1952–3): 145–61.

Ross, Jill. "Corporeality and Textuality in Selected Medieval Hispanic Texts, ca. 400–1350." Ph.D. diss., University of Toronto, 1991.

Rowe, Donald W. *O Love, O Charite! Contraries Harmonized in Chaucer's "Troilus."* Carbondale: Southern Illinois University Press, 1976.

Roy, Bruno. "Un art d'aimer: Pour qui?" In *Une culture de l'équivoque,* 47–74. Études Médiévales. Montreal: Université de Montréal, 1992.

——— "L'obscénité rendue courtoise." In *Une culture de l'équivoque,* 75–88. Études Médiévales. Montreal: Université de Montréal, 1992.

Roy, Bruno, and George Ferzoco. "La redécouverte d'un manuscrit du *De Amore* d'André le Chapelain." *Journal of Medieval Latin* 3 (1993): 135–48.

Roy, Bruno, and Hugues Shooner. "Querelles de maîtres au XIIe siècle: Arnoul d'Orléans et son milieu." *Sandalion* 8–9 (1985–86): 315–41.

Ruhe, Ernstpeter, and Rudolf Behrens, eds. *Mittelalterbilder aus neuer Perspektive.* Kolloquium Würtzburg 1984. Munich: Fink, 1985.

Sargent, Barbara Nelson. "A Medieval Commentary on Andreas Capellanus." *Romania* 94 (1973): 528–41.

Segre, Cesare. "*Ars amandi* classica e medievale." In *La litterature didactique, allegorique et satirique,* ed. Hans Robert Jauss, 1: 109–16. Grundriss der romanischen Literaturen des Mittelalters 6. Heidelberg: C. Winter, 1968.

Seidenspinner-Núñez, Dayle. *The Allegory of Good Love: Parodic Perspectivism in the "Libro de Buen Amor."* University of California Publications in Modern Philology 112. Berkeley: University of California Press, 1981.

Shulman, Jeff. " 'Te quoque falle tamen': Ovid's Anti-Lucretian Didactics." *Classical Journal* 76 (1981): 242–53.

Silvestre, H. "Diversi, sed non adversi." *Revue de Théologie Ancienne et Médiévale* 31 (1964): 124–32.

——— "Du nouveau sur André le Chapelain." *Revue du Moyen Âge Latin* 36 (1980): 99–106.

——— " 'Quanto iuniores, tanto perspicatiores.' " In *Receuil commemoratif du Xe anniversaire de la Faculté de Philosophie et Lettres,* 231–55. Louvain: Editions Nauwelaerts, 1968.

Singer, Irving. "Andreas Capellanus: A Reading of the *Tractatus.*" *Modern Language Notes* 88 (1973): 1288–1315.

Smalley, Beryl. "The Bible and Eternity: John Wyclif's Dilemma." *Journal of the Warburg and Courtald Institutes* 27 (1964): 73–89.

——— " 'Prima clavis sapientiae': Augustine and Abelard." In *Studies in Medieval Thought and Learning from Abelard to Wyclif,* 1–8. London: Hambledon, 1981. Originally published in *Fritz Saxl, 1890–1948,* ed. D. J. Gordon, 93–100. London: Nelson, 1957.

——— *The Study of the Bible in the Middle Ages.* 2nd edition. South Bend: University of Notre Dame Press, 1964.

Solterer, Helen. *The Master and Minerva: Disputing Women in French Medieval Culture.* Berkeley: University of California Press, 1995.

Southern, R. W. *Medieval Humanism and Other Studies.* Oxford: Blackwell, 1970.

——— *Scholastic Humanism and the Unification of Europe.* Vol. 1, *Foundations.* Oxford: Blackwell, 1995.

——— "The Schools of Paris and the School of Chartres." In *Renaissance and Renewal in the Twelfth Century,* ed. R. Benson and Giles Constable, 113–37. Cambridge, Mass.: Harvard University Press, 1983.

Spade, Paul Vincent. *Lies, Language and Logic in the Late Middle Ages.* London: Variorum, 1988.

——— *The Medieval Liar: A Catalogue of the "Insolubilia"-Literature.* Subsidia Mediaevalia 5. Toronto: Pontifical Institute of Medieval Studies, 1975.

Spitzer, Leo. "Note on the Poetic and Empirical 'I' in Medieval Authors." *Traditio* 4 (1946): 414–22.

Stahl, William Harris; Richard Johnson; and E. L. Burge. *The Quadrivium of Martianus Capella*. New York: Columbia University Press, 1971.

Stock, Brian. *Augustine the Reader*. Cambridge, Mass.: Harvard University Press, 1996.

——— *The Implications of Literacy*. Princeton, N.J.: Princeton University Press, 1983.

Stump, Eleonore. "Dialectic." In *The Seven Liberal Arts in the Middle Ages*, ed. David Wagner, 125–46. Bloomington: Indiana University Press, 1983.

——— *Dialectic and Its Place in the Development of Medieval Logic*. Ithaca, N.Y.: Cornell University Press, 1989.

Sturges, Robert S. *Medieval Interpretation: Modes of Reading in Literary Narrative, 1100–1500*. Carbondale: Southern Illinois University Press, 1991.

Tacchella, E. "Giovanni di Salisbury e i Cornificiani." *Sandalion* 3 (1980): 272–313.

Thorndike, Lynn. *University Records and Life in the Middle Ages*. Records of Civilization: Sources and Studies 38. New York: Columbia University Press, 1944.

Tong, Andrew. *Countering Contradictions*. [http://www.ugcs.caltech.edu/cgi-bin/webnews/read/contradictions/0]. 1996.

Tweedale, Martin M. *Abailard on Universals*. Amsterdam: North-Holland, 1976.

——— "Abelard and the Culmination of the Old Logic." In *Cambridge History of Later Medieval Philosophy*, ed. Norman Kretzmann, 143–57. Cambridge, Eng.: Cambridge University Press, 1982.

——— "Logic (i): From the Late Eleventh Century to the Time of Abelard." In *A History of Twelfth-Century Western Philosophy*, ed. Peter Dronke, 196–226. Cambridge, Eng.: Cambridge University Press, 1988.

Urbina, E. "Now You See It, Now You Don't: The Antithesis *Corteza-Meollo* in the *Libro de Buen Amor*." In *Florilegium Hispanicum: Medieval and Renaissance Studies Presented to Dorothy C. Clarke*, ed. J. Geary, 139–50. Madison: Hispanic Seminary of Medieval Studies, 1983.

Vance, Eugene. *From Topic to Tale: Logic and Narrativity in the Middle Ages*. Minneapolis: University of Minnesota Press, 1987.

——— *Mervelous Signals*. Lincoln: University of Nebraska Press, 1986.

van der Lecq, Ria. "The 'Sententie secundum Magister Petrum.'" In *Gilbert de Poitiers et ses contemporains: Aux origines de la "logica modernorum." Actes du 7e Symposium européen d'histoire de la logique et de la sémantique médiévales*, ed. Jean Jolivet and Alain de Libéra, 43–56. History of Logic 5. Naples: Bibliopolis, 1987.

van Steenberghen, Fernand. "'Averroïsme' et 'double vérité' au siècle de Saint Louis." In *Septième centenaire de la mort de Saint Louis: Actes des colloques de Royaumont et de Paris (21–27 mai 1970)*, 351–60. Paris: Belles Lettres, 1976.

———— "Une légende tenace: La théorie de la double vérité." In *Introduction à l'étude de la philosophie médiévale*, 555–70. Philosophes médiévaux 18. Louvain: Editions Universitaires, 1974.

Verger, Jacques. "Abélard et les milieux sociaux de son temps." In *Abélard en son temps*, ed. Jean Jolivet, 107–32. Paris: Les Belles Lettres, 1981.

Viola, Coloman. "Manières personnelles et impersonnelles d'aborder un problème: St. Augustin et le XIIᵉ siècle. Contribution à l'histoire de la *quaestio.*" In *Les genres littéraires dans les sources théologiques et philosophiques médiévales: Définitions, critique, exploitation. Actes du Colloque International de Louvain-la-Neuve, 25–27 mai 1981*, ed. R. Bultot, 11–30. Publications de l'Institut d'Études Médiévales, 2ᵉ série 5. Louvain: Université Catholique de Louvain, 1982.

Visser, Derk. "Reality and Rhetoric in Abelard's 'Story of My Calamities.'" *Proceedings of the PMR [Patristic Mediaeval Renaissance] Conference* 3 (1978): 143–56.

Walker, Roger M. "'Con miedo de la muerte la miel non es sabrosa': Love, Sin, and Death in the *Libro de Buen Amor.*" In *"Libro de Buen Amor" Studies*, ed. G. B. Gybbon-Monypenny, 231–52. London: Tamesis, 1970.

Walsh, John K. "Juan Ruiz and the *mester de clerecía*: Lost Context and Lost Parody in the *Libro de Buen Amor.*" *Romance Philology* 33 (1979): 62–86.

Ward, J. O. "The Date of the Commentary on Cicero's *De inventione* by Thierry of Chartres (ca. 1095–1160?) and the Cornifician Attack on the Liberal Arts." *Viator* 3 (1972): 219–73.

Weijers, Olga. "The Chronology of John of Salisbury's Studies in France (*Metalogicon* ii.10)." In Wilks, *The World of John of Salisbury*, 109–16.

———— ed. *Vocabulaire des écoles et des methodes de l'enseignement au Moyen-Âge*. Etudes sur le vocabulaire intellectuel au Moyen-Âge 5. Turnhout: Brepols, 1991.

Weingart, Richard E. *The Logic of Divine Love: A Critical Study of the Soteriology of Peter Abelard*. Oxford: Clarendon, 1970.

Wenin, C. "La signification des universaux chez Abélard." *Revue Philosophique de Louvain* 80 (1982): 414–48.

Wheeler, Bonnie. "Originary Fantasies: Abelard's Castration and Confession." In *Becoming Male in the Middle Ages*, ed. Jeffrey Jerome Cohen and Bonnie Wheeler, 107–28. New York: Garland, 1997.

Whitman, Jon. *Allegory: The Dynamics of an Ancient and Medieval Technique*. Oxford: Clarendon, 1987.

Whittaker, John. "Catachresis and Negative Theology: Philo of Alexandria and Basilides." In *Platonism in Late Antiquity*, ed. Stephen Gersh and Charles Kannengiesser, 61–82. Christianity and Judaism in Antiquity 8. Notre Dame, Ind.: University of Notre Dame Press, 1992.

Wilks, Michael. "John of Salisbury and the Tyranny of Nonsense." In Wilks, *The World of John of Salisbury*, 263–86.

———— ed. *The World of John of Salisbury*. Studies in Church History, Subsidia 3. Oxford: Blackwell, 1984.

Wise, David O. "Reflections of Andreas Capellanus' *De reprobatione Amoris* in Juan Ruiz, Alfonso Martínez, and Fernando de Rojas." *Hispania* 63 (1980): 506–14.

Wood, Chauncey. "Speech, the Principle of Contraries, and Chaucer's Tales of the Manciple and the Parson." *Mediaevalia* 6 (1980): 209–29.

Woods, Marjorie Curry. "In a Nutshell: 'Verba' and 'Sententia' and Matter and Form in Medieval Composition Theory." In *The Uses of Manuscripts in Literary Studies*, ed. Charlotte Cook Morse, Penelope Reed Doob, and Marjorie Curry Woods, 19–40. Kalamazoo: Western Michigan University / Medieval Institute Publications, 1992.

Wright, Ellen F. " 'Profanum sunt genus': The Poets of the *Ars amatoria*." *Philological Quarterly* 63 (1984): 1–15.

Zahareas, Anthony. *The Art of Juan Ruiz, Archpriest of Hita*. Madrid: Estudios de Literatura Española, 1965.

Ziolkowski, Jan M. "The Humour of Logic and the Logic of Humour in the Twelfth-Century Renaissance." *Journal of Medieval Latin* 3 (1993): 1–26.

Zumthor, Paul. *Toward a Medieval Poetics* [1972]. Trans. Philip Bennett. Minneapolis: University of Minnesota Press, 1991.

Index

This index of proper names, key words, and conceptual building blocks is offered as a starting point for the operations of the reader's own understanding, will, memory, and powers of invention.

Montero, Ana, 154n9
Muscatine, Charles, 101

opposition (defined), 12–14
Origen, 17, 25–26, 116
overinterpretation, 33–34, 49–50, 85, 133–35
Ovid: *Ars amatoria*, 8, 91–95, 104–5, 111;
    Remedia amoris, 91, 93; *Tristia*, 108

Pamphilus, 136
Paris, Gaston, 93, 96
Parry, John J., 96
Patterson, Lee, 25, 29, 32–33
Payen, Jean Charles, 101
pedagogy, *see* teaching
Peter Damian, 18, 40, 61, 73, 141
Peter Helias, 40
Peter Lombard, 120
Peter of Spain, 60
Peter the Chanter, 16, 23
Peter the Eater, 28, 33
Plato, 154n7
poetics, 9–10, 28–35
postmedieval readings of medieval cultures
    and texts, 4–9, 95–98, 118–19, 144–49
    passim

quaestio (defined), 64

Rajna, Pio, 97
reading: defined, 11; texts as teachers of,
    20–21, 84–88, 93–95, 112–15, 127–40,
    147–48
Richard of St. Victor, 15, 28
Rider, Jeff, 160n52
Robert of Melun, 46
Robertson, Durant Waite, Jr., 6, 22, 97–98
Roman de la poire, 135
Roman de la Rose, 2–3, 10
Roscelin of Compeigne, 76–79
Roy, Bruno, 44, 97–98
Ruiz, Juan: and the *De amore*, 116–17,
    122–29 *passim*; and dialectic, 117, 119–

21, 135–40; and exegesis, 117, 119–123,
    127–35, 140–44; *Libro de buen amor*,
    116–44

Scripture: apparently contrary significa-
    tion in, 29–31, 117, 120; compared with
    secular texts, 49–50, 140; metaphors for,
    26–28, 130–31; multiplicity of meaning
    in, 24–35, 83–90; as teaching text, 7–9,
    17–24. *See also* Bible
sententia, 31, 118, 126–32 *passim*; defined, 95
Shooner, Hugues, 44
Silvestre, H., 97, 98
Singer, Irving, 95
Smalley, Beryl, 28, 31
Solterer, Helen, 12
sophistry, 61–64 *passim*, 108–12, 123, 131
Southern, R. W., 7
Stephen of Tournai, 36
Sturges, Robert, 6

teaching: introduced, 8–14; represented
    in texts, 44–52, 66–75, 91–95. *See also*
    de arte/per artem; didacticism; *doctrina*;
    reading, texts as teachers of
Tempier, Stephen, 108–9
Thibaut of Langres, 32
Thierry of Chartres, 40, 48

unteaching, 42–54 *passim*, 84

Vance, Eugene, 8
Vitalis of Blois, 63–64, 66, 79

Walter of Châtillon, 79, 174n23
Walter of St. Victor, 63, 64
Watts, Sandra, 182
William of Champeaux, 51, 66–68, 74–75
William of Conches, 31, 40
William of St. Thierry, 88
Wolbero of Cologne, 34

Zumthor, Paul, 145–46

Library of Congress Cataloging-in-Publication Data

Brown, Catherine.
Contrary things : exegesis, dialectic, and the poetics of
didacticism / Catherine Brown.
p. cm. — (Figurae)
Includes bibliographical references and index.
ISBN 0-8047-3009-1
1. Literature, Medieval — History and criticism.   2. Teaching.
3. Logic.   I. Title.   II. Series: Figurae (Stanford, Calif.)
PN671.B76   1998
809'.02 — DC21   98-17381
CIP   REV.

♾ This book is printed on acid-free, recycled paper.

Original printing 1998
Last figure below indicates year of this printing:
07 06 05 04 03 02 01 00 99 98